David Carliner practices law in Washington, D.C., specializing in immigration and nationality matters. He is the author of the original edition of the *Rights of Aliens*, published in February 1977. He is a former General Counsel of the American Civil Liberties Union and was Chairman of the Immigration and Nationality Committee of the Administrative Law Section of the American Bar Association. He currently serves on the ABA Coordinating Committee on Immigration Law.

Lucas Guttentag is Director of the National Immigration Rights Project of the American Civil Liberties Union. He teaches immigration law at Columbia Law School and has litigated numerous cases in the area of immigrants' rights, employment discrimination, and criminal justice reform. He is a cum laude graduate of Harvard Law School and served as law clerk to Federal Judge William Wayne Justice.

Arthur C. Helton is Director of the Refugee Project of the Lawyers Committee for Human Rights, and Chair of the Advisory Committee to the New York State Inter-Agency Task Force on Immigration Affairs. He teaches immigration and refugee law at the New York University School of Law, and he has authored numerous articles, testified in Congress and federal court, and litigated several cases concerning immigration and refugee issues.

Wade J. Henderson is the Associate Director of the Washington National Office of the American Civil Liberties Union. For the last six years, he has worked as a lobbyist primarily in the areas of immigration and refugee policy and human rights. He is the author of numerous articles on immigration policy and civil rights issues.

Also in this series

THE RIGHTS OF AUTHORS AND ARTISTS
THE RIGHTS OF CRIME VICTIMS
THE RIGHTS OF EMPLOYEES
THE RIGHTS OF GAY PEOPLE
THE RIGHTS OF OLDER PERSONS
THE RIGHTS OF PATIENTS
THE RIGHTS OF PRISONERS
THE RIGHTS OF SINGLE PEOPLE
THE RIGHTS OF STUDENTS
THE RIGHTS OF TEACHERS
THE RIGHTS OF WOMEN
THE RIGHTS OF YOUNG PEOPLE
YOUR RIGHT TO GOVERNMENT INFORMATION
YOUR RIGHT TO PRIVACY

AN AMERICAN CIVIL LIBERTIES UNION HANDBOOK

THE RIGHTS OF ALIENS AND REFUGEES

THE BASIC ACLU GUIDE TO ALIEN AND REFUGEE RIGHTS

SECOND EDITION
Completely Revised and Up-to-Date

David Carliner
Lucas Guttentag
Arthur C. Helton
Wade J. Henderson

General Editor of the Handbook Series:
Norman Dorsen, President, ACLU

SOUTHERN ILLINOIS UNIVERSITY PRESS
CARBONDALE AND EDWARDSVILLE

Printed in the United States of America
Edited by Teresa White
Production supervised by Linda Jorgensen-Buhman

93 92 91 90 4 3 2 1

Library of Congress Cataloging-in-Publication Data

The rights of aliens and refugees : the basic ACLU guide to alien and refugee rights / David Carliner . . . [et al.].—2d ed., completely rev. and up-to-date.
p. cm.—(An American Civil Liberties Union handbook)
Rev. ed. of: The rights of aliens and refugees / David Carliner. 1977.
Bibliography: p.
1. Aliens—United States. I. Carliner, David. II. Carliner, David. Rights of aliens and refugees. III. American Civil Liberties Union. IV. Series.
KF4800.R54 1990
342.73′083—dc20
[347.30283] 89-11570
ISBN 0-8093-1598-X CIP

The paper used in this publication meets the minimum requirements of American Standard for Information Sciences—Permanence of Paper for Printed Library Materials, ANSI Z39.48-1984. ∞

Contents

Preface

This guide sets forth your rights under the present law and offers suggestions on how they can be protected. It is one of a continuing series of handbooks published in cooperation with the American Civil Liberties Union (ACLU).

Surrounding these publications is the hope that Americans, informed of their rights, will be encouraged to exercise them. Through their exercise, rights are given life. If they are rarely used, they may be forgotten and violations may become routine.

This guide offers no assurances that your rights will be respected. The laws may change, and in some of the subjects covered in these pages they change quite rapidly. An effort has been made to note those parts of the law where movement is taking place, but it is not always possible to predict accurately when the law *will* change.

Even if the laws remain the same, their interpretations by courts and administrative officials often vary. In a federal system such as ours, there is a built-in problem, since state and federal law differ, not to speak of the confusion between states. In addition, there are wide variations in the ways in which particular courts and administrative officials will interpret the same law at any given moment.

If you encounter what you consider to be a specific abuse of your rights, you should seek legal assistance. There are a number of agencies that may help you, among them ACLU affiliate offices, but bear in mind that the ACLU is a limited-purpose organization. In many communities, there are federally funded legal service offices that provide assistance to persons who cannot afford the costs of legal representation. In general, the rights that the ACLU defends are freedom of inquiry and expression; due process of law; equal protection of the laws; and privacy. The authors in this series have discussed other rights (even though they sometimes fall outside the ACLU's usual concern) in order to provide as much guidance as possible.

These books have been planned as guides for the people directly affected; thus the question-and-answer format. (In some areas there are more detailed works available for experts.) These guides seek to raise the major issues and inform the nonspecialist of the basic law on the subject. The authors of these books are themselves specialists who understand the need for information at "street level."

If you encounter a specific legal problem in an area discussed in one of these handbooks, show the book to your attorney. Of course, he or she will not be able to rely exclusively on the handbook to provide you with adequate representation. But if your attorney hasn't had a great deal of experience in the specific area, the handbook can provide helpful suggestions on how to proceed.

Norman Dorsen, President
American Civil Liberties Union

The principal purpose of this handbook, as well as others in this series, is to inform individuals of their legal rights. The authors from time to time suggest what the law should be, but their personal views are not necessarily those of the ACLU. For the ACLU's position on the issues discussed in this handbook the reader should write to Public Education Department, ACLU, 132 West 43d Street, New York, N.Y. 10036.

Acknowledgments

An endeavor such as this book takes a lot of work by many people. The co-authors would like to express appreciation to the following persons whose assistance was invaluable:

Regla Arenas, Eva Barukh, Maurice Belanger, Deborah Carliner, Miriam Carliner, Melissa Crow, Charles Gordon, James Graham, Peter Gruman, Susan Hansen, Trudy Hayden, Marie Jeannot, Beth Lief, Marshall Madow, Makau Matua, Judy Rabinovitz, Rhonda Roberts, Lynda Sun, Ronald Tabak, and Suzanne Unger.

Introduction

> And if a stranger sojourn with thee in your land, ye shall not do him wrong. The stranger that dwelleth with you shall be unto you as one born among you, and thou shalt love him as thyself.
>
> —Leviticus 19–33

> Aliens as a class are a . . . "discrete and insular" minority . . . for whom . . . heightened judicial solicitude is appropriate.
>
> —United States Supreme Court Justice Harry A. Blackmun, *Graham v. Richardson*, 403 U.S. 365, 372 (1971)

The biblical injunction has had a mixed reception during the course of American history. It needs no retelling here how the continuous flow of migrants to America brought in its wake an undertow of hostility to each new ethnic and racial wave. Yet more than fifty-five million immigrants from every continent have settled our land since its beginning, and if aliens were not loved when they came, and they were transformed from "immigrant to ethnic,"[1] the land became theirs, with the right, if not always the reality, of equal access to its resources.

The legal institutions[2] have reflected the ambivalence of the larger society. It is perhaps not without significance that virtually all the protections written into the Constitution are stated in universal terms applicable to all persons, aliens as well as citizens: the freedom of religion, speech, press, and the right of assembly; the bars against unreasonable searches and seizures, charges for infamous crimes without an indictment, double jeopardy, and self-incrimination; the assurance of due process of law in preserving life, liberty, and property; the requirement of equal protection of laws; the right in criminal cases to a speedy and public trial, an impartial jury, with notice of charges, confrontation of adverse witnesses, the compulsory attendance of supporting witnesses, and the assistance of counsel, and to a trial by jury in civil cases; the prohibition against excessive bail and fines, cruel and unusual punishment, a bill of attainder (a statute that inflicts a punishment upon a person without a judicial trial) and *ex post facto* law (a statute that imposes a punishment retroactively); the outlawry of slavery and involuntary servitude; and the guarantee of habeas corpus.[3]

The disparate treatment given to aliens has emerged largely from the legislative acts of the state and federal governments during periods of hostility toward immigrants of differing racial and ethnic origins and against persons regarded as disloyal in times of war and ferment.[4]

The judicial decisions dealing with aliens have developed from two approaches. One is based upon a landmark case, rendered in 1886 during a decade of intense anti-Chinese agitation, which held that a San Francisco ordinance discriminated against laundries owned by aliens. The provisions of the fourteenth amendment that forbid a state to deny to any person the equal protection of the laws, the Supreme Court said, "are universal in their application to all persons within the territorial jurisdiction, without regard to any differences of race, of color, or of nationality; and the equal protection of the laws is a pledge of the protection of equal laws."[5]

The equal treatment of aliens required by the Supreme Court's decision in *Yick Wo* has now been substantially reinforced by a series of recent rulings. One group of cases "rejected the concept that constitutional rights turn upon whether a governmental benefit is characterized as a 'right' or as a 'privilege.' "[6] The other held that classifications based on alienage are "inherently suspect" and can be justified only if the distinction is required to meet a substantial need.[7]

These cases overcame a distinction made between citizens and aliens that allowed legislatures "broad discretion" to deny aliens benefits that they accord to citizens upon the ground that the Constitution itself twice refers to the "privileges and immunities of citizens."[8]

Although there have been Supreme Court rulings that have veered from the principle first enunciated in 1886, the trend of decisions has been to assure the right of resident aliens to receive equal treatment from the states in which they live.

An opposite line of decisions has followed in the wake of two parallel cases dealing with the power of Congress to exclude aliens from the United States and to determine the conditions under which they may continue to live in this country. In the first, the *Chinese Exclusion Case*, decided in 1889, the Supreme Court unanimously upheld a statute that barred Chinese laborers, including those who had prior residence in this country, from entering the United States, asserting a power by Congress to exclude "foreigners of a different race who will not assimilate with us."[9]

In the second case, *Fong Yue Ting v. United States*, decided in 1893, the Supreme Court in a 6–3 decision sustained a statute that required the deportation of Chinese aliens who could not prove their right to reside in the United States, unless they produced a certificate of residence or the testimony of "at least one credible white witness." Deportation, a majority of the Court found, is not a "punishment for a crime . . . in the sense in which that word is often applied to the expulsion of a citizen from his country. . . . It is but a method of enforcing the return to his own country of an alien who has not complied with the conditions" upon which his continuing residence depends.[10]

Each of these decisions was based upon what has been described as the "inherent power of sovereignty," to be exercised exclusively by the political branches of government, not within any limitations imposed by the Constitution, but "in accord with ancient principles of the international law of nation-states."[11]

Since these two rulings, the Supreme Court has continuously held that Congress has the absolute power to exclude and to expel from the United States any aliens it chooses. Repeated efforts to challenge the constitutionality of exclusion and deportation orders and the laws upon which they are based have usually been rejected.[12]

But not always. A major exception, made almost contemporaneously with the earlier cases, is the *Japanese Immigrant Case*,[13] which held that any procedure to deport aliens who are in the United States must conform to the requirements of due process. And the intertwining of "procedural" with what is described as "substantive" due process has resulted in an occasional victory for the alien.[14] More often, however, it has produced only the hint that the Supreme Court may not be comfortable with the doctrine that the power of Congress over aliens is absolute.[15]

There are indications, however slight, that the Court may be rethinking its views regarding the constitutional rights of aliens. The suggestion by Justice Blackmun in *Graham v. Richardson* in 1971[16] that "heightened judicial solicitude is appropriate" for aliens because they are a "prime example of a 'discrete and insular' minority"[17] is a 180-degree turn, perhaps not unintentional, from the language in the *Chinese Exclusion Case* justifying the power of Congress to exclude Chinese laborers because they do not "assimilate with us."[18]

In a 1972 case involving the exclusion of a Belgian Marxist who had been invited to the United States to give a series of lectures at American universities, Justice Blackmun recalled a suggestion by Justice Frankfurter that if the Supreme Court were "writing on a clean slate, 'much could be said for the view' that due process places some limitations on congressional power" in regulating the entry and deportation of aliens.[19] But, speaking for a 6–3 majority, Justice Blackmun stated that the Court was not "inclined in the present context" to reconsider its earlier decisions.

Although a case with a different "context" has not yet reached the Supreme Court, in its 1977 decision in *Fiallo v. Bell,* the Court observed that there is "limited judicial review" of all immigration legislation, while upholding as "largely immune from judicial control" an immigration statute that discriminates against children of American citizen fathers born outside of the United States and outside of wedlock.[20] In 1982, *Landon v. Plasencia,*[21] held that although returning resident aliens may be subjected to exclusion, rather than deportation, proceedings, such proceedings must meet the constitutional requirements of due process, not merely what Congress says is due. Also see *Abourezk v. Reagan,* which upheld by an equally divided Court (therefore without precedential authority) a decision by the District of Columbia Circuit that the first amendment denies the government the power "to deny entry (to an alien visitor) solely on account of speech."[22]

While there have been modest fissures in the Supreme Court's deference to Congress in the field of immigration legislation, the laws themselves have undergone major changes.

1. The Refugee Act of 1980 established for the first time the statutory right of asylum and, in addition provided for a "permanent and systematic procedure" for admitting refugees to the United States.[23] In the decade since the enactment of

the Refugee Act, approximately 900,000 refugees who are of "special humanitarian concern to the United States" have been admitted to the United States.[24]

2. The Immigration Reform and Control Act, enacted in 1986, has permitted nearly three million aliens who were residing in the United States unlawfully since January 1, 1982, to obtain legal status.[25] A rider to the Foreign Relations Authorization Act in 1988 has suspended until March 1, 1991, statutory provisions that exclude nonimmigrants from admission to the United States "because of any past, current, or expected beliefs, statements or associations."[26]

There remains the question of whether the Supreme Court will accord the permanent resident aliens living in the United States—eight million in 1987—the full protections that the Constitution affords citizens. Millions of aliens who are in this country unlawfully, many of whom have fled from war, repression, and crushing poverty, cannot feasibly or conscionably be uprooted and deported. A civilized society must also treat these strangers with solicitude.

This book attempts to define the rights of aliens in the United States under existing laws. It is hoped that it will help aliens and those who assist them to know, to understand, to exercise, and to extend further their opportunities to become full members of the American community.

NOTES

1. The phrase is from Rudolph J. Vecoli, *European Americans: From Immigrants to Ethnics*, 6 Int. Migration Rev. 403 (Winter 1972), a review of the writings on the history of the immigration of European peoples to the United States.
2. The legal institutions, state and federal, involved are the legislative bodies that enact the statutes affecting the rights of aliens, the administrative agencies and executive departments that apply the laws, and the courts that in varying ways interpret and enforce the laws. An extended discussion of the interrelation among the three branches of government is beyond the scope of this work. However, the step-by-step impact that each branch has on a specific problem is set forth in the chapters that follow.
3. U.S. Const., art. I, § 9(2), (3); amend. I, IV, V, VI, VII, VIII, XIII,

XIV. The Constitution also refers to the "privileges and immunities of citizens," art. IV, § 2 (1), and amend. IV, § 1; and the "right of citizens of the United States to vote," amend. XV, XIX, and XXIV; and requires that the President, senators, and representatives be citizens of the United States, art. I, § 2(2), (3), and art. II (4). In addition, federal courts, in the article providing for the judiciary, are given jurisdiction over cases between "citizens of different states" and between citizens of a state and the "citizens or subjects of a foreign state." The latter phrase includes citizens or subjects of foreign states who are residing in the United States as aliens. *Mathews v. Diaz*, 426 U.S. 67 (1975).

4. J. Highma, *Strangers in the Land* (2d ed., 1965); Oscar Handlin, *The Uprooted* (1951). For materials on European immigrants, *see* note 1; on Asians, *see* Milton Konvitz, *The Aliens and Asiatic in American Law* (1946); and Carey McWilliams, *Prejudice: Japanese-Americans, Symbols of Racial Intolerance* (1944).
5. *Yick Wo v. Hopkins*, 118 U.S. 356, 369 (1886).
6. *Sherbert v. Verner*, 374 U.S. 398, 404 (1963), applied to aliens in *Graham v. Richardson*, 403 U.S. 365, 373 (1971).
7. *In re Griffiths*, 413 U.S. 717, 722 (1973); *Takahashi v. Fish and Game Commission*, 334 U.S. 419 (1948).
8. *Cf.Terrace v. Thompson*, 263 U.S. 197, 219–20 (1923).
9. *Chinese Exclusion Case*, 130 U.S. 581, 606 (1889).
10. *Fong Yue Ting v. United States*, 149 U.S. 698, 730 (1892).
11. *Kleindienst v. Mandel*, 408 U.S. 753 (1972), restating and reaffirming the basis of the earlier decisions.
12. *Galvan v. Press*, 347 U.S. 522 (1952); *Harisiades v. Shaughnessy*, 342 U.S. 580 (1952); *Bugajewitz v. Adams*, 228 U.S. 585 (1913); *Zakonaite v. Wolf*, 226 U.S. 272 (1912). For two excellent discussions of the constitutionality issues and an analysis of the Supreme Court's decisions in this field, *see* S. Hesse, *The Constitutional Status of the Lawfully Admitted Permanent Resident Alien*, 68 and 69 Yale L.J. 1578 (1959); and L. Boudin, *The Settler Within Our Gates*, 26 N.Y.U. L. Rev. 266–90, 451–74, 635–62 (1951).
13. *Japanese Immigrant Case*, 189 U.S. 86, 100–101 (1903).
14. *Gastelum-Quinones v. Kennedy*, 347 U.S. 469 (1963); *Rewoldt v. Perfetto*, 355 U.S. 115 (1957). For a recent decision refusing to deport an alien because of a marijuana conviction, see *Lieggi v. INS*, 389 F. Supp. 512 (N.D. Ill.), a temporary victory, summarily reversed without opinion in 529 F.2d 53 (1976).
15. *Harisiades v. Shaughnessy*, *supra* note 12; *Galvan v. Press*, *supra* note 12; *Kleindienst v. Mandel*, *supra* note 11.
16. *Graham v. Richardson*, *supra* note 6, at 377. *See also* Justice Blackmun's reference in *Kleindienst v. Mandel* to *Graham v. Richardson*

as standing in contrast with the "legion" of cases that hold that the congressional power to make rules for the admission of aliens is "plenary," that is, beyond the review of the judiciary. *But see Hampton v. Wong*, 426 U.S. 88 (1975) in which four dissenters, including Justice Blackmun, urged that barring aliens from federal employment is a "political judgment" beyond the power of the courts to set aside.

17. The quotation is from a celebrated footnote by Chief Justice Stone in the *United States v. Crolene Products Co.*, 304 U.S. 144, 153 (1937), which distinguished the approach to the constitutionality of legislation involving "ordinary commercial transactions" and laws affecting first amendment and other rights of national, political, racial, religious, and other minorities. The court posed the question "whether prejudice against discrete and insular minorities may be a special condition, which tends seriously to curtail the operation of those political processes ordinarily relied upon to protect minorities, and which may call for correspondingly more searching judicial inquiry."
18. *Chinese Exclusion Case, supra* note 9.
19. *Kleindienst v. Mandel, supra* note 11, citing *Galvan v. Press, supra* note 12.
20. 430 U.S. 787 (1977). On the same day, the Supreme Court held that the Equal Protection Clause of the fourteenth amendment denied a state legislature the power to bar interstate inheritances by illegitimate children from their fathers, underscoring the difference between the "plenary power" of Congress over immigration and the constitutional limitations imposed upon state legislatures.
21. 459 U.S. 21 (1982).
22. 785 F.2d 1043, *aff'd*, 484 U.S. 1 (1987). *See also* a promising decision in *American-Arab Anti-Discrimination Committee v. Meese*, CIV. No. 87-02107 (C.D. Cal. ____) decided December 22, 1988, holding that the deportation of aliens because of their beliefs or advocacy of the "doctrines of world communism, totalitarian dictatorship, or unlawful destruction of property" violates the first amendment, and that the statutes barring admission to nonimmigrant aliens, including P.L.O. members, and the deportation of permanent residents of the United States on these grounds are unconstitutional.
23. Pub. L. No. 96-212, 94 Stat. 103, Immigration and Nationality Act §§ 207 and 208, *as amended*, 8 U.S.C. §§ 1157–1158.
24. Rep., Refugee Task Force, 1988.
25. Pub. L. No. 99-603, 100 Stat. 3359, Immigration Nationality Act, *as amended*, 8 U.S.C. § 1255 (A).
26. Pub. L. No. 100-461, 102 Stat. 2268.

THE RIGHTS OF ALIENS AND REFUGEES

I
Aliens, Citizens, and Nationals

People who think they are aliens sometimes turn out to be citizens. This can happen because United States citizenship is conferred not only on persons born in this country but also on some persons born abroad. In determining the rights of an alien, the first question is whether a person may in fact be a citizen.

Who are aliens?

An "alien" is defined in the Immigration and Nationality Act as "any person not a citizen or national of the United States."[1] A person born in a foreign country is usually an alien under American law but may be a United States *citizen* or *national* under certain circumstances.

Who are citizens of the United States?

1. Persons born in the United States or in certain territories or possessions of the United States are, under almost all circumstances, American citizens. Such persons' status is recognized by the fourteenth amendment to the Constitution, which states that all persons born in the United States and subject to its jurisdiction are citizens.[2]

2. Persons born outside the United States if one or both parents are American citizens and the child and/or parent meets certain residency requirements.

3. Persons born as aliens in foreign countries who are naturalized as citizens of the United States. Their status is also recognized by the fourteenth amendment, which states that all persons naturalized in the United States are citizens.[3]

4. Persons born in possessions of the United States or in foreign countries who acquire citizenship under laws enacted by Congress. Their status depends upon the specific provisions of the statutes.

Are any persons born in the United States *not* citizens?

Children born to accredited foreign diplomats and to heads of foreign states who are on official visits to this country. These persons and their parents are not "subject to the jurisdiction" of the United States and therefore do not fall within the definition of citizenship in the fourteenth amendment.[4]

Are persons born in United States' territories or possessions citizens at birth?

Their citizenship depends upon their place of birth. Persons born in Puerto Rico, the Virgin Islands, Guam, and the Northern Mariana Islands (including Saipan and Tinian)[5] are citizens of the United States.[6] Persons born in American Samoa and Swains Island, which are defined under the nationality law as "outlying possessions," are nationals, but not citizens, of the United States. Persons born in other possessions of the United States are treated as persons born outside the United States and are aliens unless, as discussed below, they qualify as citizens under other provisions of the nationality laws. A person born in the Panama Canal Zone, over which the United States exercised sovereignty until 1978, is also a citizen of the United States if born prior to 1978, and if at birth, one parent was a citizen.[7]

In 1978 the United States transferred sovereignty of the Canal Zone back to Panama. The treaty and implementing legislation[8] did not refer to nationality status and did not specifically modify the statutory provisions relating to the nationality status of children born to American parents. Therefore those who acquired American citizenship prior to the transfer are unaffected. Since 1978, the transmission of American citizenship to persons born in Panama has been governed by the rules applicable to children born outside the United States, including the provision relating to children whose father and/or mother is a U.S. citizen employed by the U.S. government or by the Panama Railroad Company.[9]

Which persons born in U.S. territories are aliens?

Persons born in islands in the Pacific Ocean that are possessions of the United States but that are not included in the Immigration and Nationality Act for the purpose of conferring citizenship or nationality. These unenumerated territories of the United States are treated as equivalent to foreign countries, with American citizenship acquired at birth under the same conditions as birth in a foreign country.[10] These possessions include Wake and Midway.[11]

Why are persons born in certain U.S. territories treated differently from persons born in other U.S. territories?

The Supreme Court has held in a series of decisions[12] that rights under the Constitution are assured only to persons who live in a territory "incorporated" into the United States. The rights of persons residing in "unincorporated territories" are only those rights that have been granted in treaties or laws adopted by Congress. As a result, the rights provided to the inhabitants vary depending upon political and other factors.

Are any persons born outside the United States citizens at birth?

Under present law, a person born outside of the United States is a citizen at birth:

1. If both parents are citizens, and one parent has resided in the United States or one of its outlying possessions, prior to the birth of such person.[13]

2. If one parent is a citizen and the other is a national of the United States, provided that the citizen parent has previously been physically present in the United States or one of its outlying possessions continuously for one year.[14]

3. If one parent is a citizen and the other is an alien, provided that the citizen parent has previously been physically present in the United States or an (outlying possession) for a period of five years, of which at least two must have been after the age of fourteen.[15]

4. If born in an outlying possession, and one parent is a citizen of the United States and the citizen parent has previously been physically present in the United States or an outlying possession for one year.[16]

5. If the parents are unknown and the child is "found" in the United States before he or she is five years old, unless, before the child reaches the age of twenty-one, he or she is shown to have been born outside the United States.[17]

Other persons, though not qualifying as citizens at birth, may be eligible to become U.S. citizens through the acts of their parents. For example, a child born outside the United States to one citizen and one alien parent is eligible for citizenship if at the time of birth, the citizen had never ceased to be a United States citizen, and the alien parent becomes naturalized. For the child to acquire citizenship, the alien parent must be naturalized while the child is unmarried and under the age of eighteen. In addition, the child must have entered the United States as a lawful permanent resident and must have started to reside permanently in the United States while under the age of eighteen.[18]

Can persons born as U.S. citizens outside the United States lose their citizenship?

Since 1978 there have been no requirements for retention of U.S. citizenship by persons born outside the United States.[19]

Prior to 1978, a person born of one citizen parent and one alien was required to be continuously physically present in the United States for five years between the ages of fourteen and twenty-eight in order to retain U.S. citizenship.[20]

Didn't requirements for maintaining citizenship that distinguished among different categories of United States citizens violate the Constitution?

Persons born or naturalized in the United States are citizens under the fourteenth amendment and may not be deprived of their citizenship by an Act of Congress.[21] However, persons born outside the United States acquire citizenship under Acts of Congress rather than from any language in the Constitution. Since Congress has the power to establish specific requirements for obtaining citizenship, the Supreme Court has held that Congress also has the power to impose conditions for maintaining citizenship—provided that the conditions are not "irrational, arbitrary, or unfair."[22]

Who are naturalized citizens?

They are persons, born as aliens, who acquire citizenship after birth under laws enacted by Congress. The present naturalization statute requires a period of residence in the United States, generally three years for spouses of American citizens and five years for other persons, proof of good moral character, attachment to the principles of the Constitution and the ability to read, write, and speak the English language. Naturalization procedures are more fully discussed in chapter XIV.

Who are nationals?

The term "national" has a number of meanings. Often, it is used interchangeably with the term "citizen," but there is a legal distinction between the two terms. A national owes allegiance to a country and is entitled to its protection.[23] A citizen is entitled not only to protection but also to all the rights of citizenship.

As used in the Immigration and Nationality Act, the term "national" refers to persons who owe permanent allegiance to a country.[24] A national of the United States is a citizen or a person who owes allegiance to this country.[25] Persons who are born in United States territories and certain possessions may be nationals, though not citizens, of the United States.[26]

The power of Congress over nationals and citizens is also different. For example, Congress has no power to take citizenship away from persons who are protected by the fourteenth amendment.[27] However, nationality can be granted and withdrawn as the political status of territories and possessions changes.

Under present law, persons born in specially defined "outlying possessions" of the United States (American Samoa and Swains Island), are nationals but not citizens[28] (unless they qualify as citizens through their parents).[29] Under earlier nationality laws, natives of other possessions, including Puerto Rico, the Virgin Islands, Guam, and the Philippines also had the status of noncitizen nationals. When the Philippines became independent in 1946, its natives lost their status as American nationals and became aliens under American law.[30] Natives of each of the other possessions are now citizens.

NOTES

1. 8 U.S.C. § 1101(a)(3).
2. U.S. Const. amend. XIV, § 1 provides:

> All persons born or naturalized in the United States, and subject to the jurisdiction thereof, are citizens of the United States and of the State wherein they reside. No State shall make or enforce any law which shall abridge the privileges or immunities of citizens of the United States; nor shall any State deprive any person of life, liberty or property, without due process of law;

nor deny to any person within its jurisdiction the equal protection of the laws.

3. *Id.*
4. *Id.* Accredited diplomats include both those who are accredited to the United States and those who are accredited to the United Nations. The term does not include consular officers or employees of foreign embassies who are not entitled to diplomatic immunity. The Department of State publishes a "Diplomatic List," known as the "Blue List," every three months. The "Blue List" contains the names of all regularly accredited diplomatic officers of embassies and legations in Washington, D.C., and the names of family members. The United States Mission to the United Nations publishes a UN "Privileges and Immunities List" containing the names of UN officials entitled to diplomatic privileges and immunities. The Department of State also publishes an "Employees of Diplomatic Missions Not Printed in the Diplomatic List," known as the "White List," every three months and also a "Foreign Consular Officers in the United States" list. Those included in the "Employees" list enjoy some diplomatic immunities, but their children born in the United States are subject to the jurisdiction of the United States. Those included in the "Foreign Consular Officers" list enjoy little or no diplomatic immunity and are subject to the jurisdiction of the United States.
5. The Northern Mariana Islands elected to become a self-governing commonwealth of the United States, and the Covenant of Political Union of Feb. 15, 1975, confers American citizenship on the indigenous inhabitants of the Marianas. 1 C. Gordon & H. Rosenfield, *Immigration Law and Procedure* § 2.4d (1988). The Act of March 24, 1976, Pub. L. No. 94–241, 90 Stat. 263 (1976), approved the Covenant. The text of the Covenant of Feb. 15, 1975 is at 48 U.S.C. § 1681 note.
6. *See* 8 U.S.C. §§ 1402, 1406, 1407b.
7. 8 U.S.C. § 1403.
8. The treaty was implemented by the Panama Canal Act of Sept. 27, 1979, Pub. L. No. 96–70, 93 Stat. 452. Until 1978, the Isthman Canal Convention, 2 Malloy, *Treaties* 1349, 33 Stat. 2234, was the basis for U.S. occupation of the Canal Zone.
9. 8 U.S.C. § 1403(b).
10. *See* text *supra* at notes 5–6.
11. *U.S. v. Paquet*, 131 F. Supp. 32 (D. Haw. 1955); *Application of Reyes*, 140 F. Supp. 130 (D. Haw. 1956); *Aradanas v. Hogan*, 155 F. Supp. 546 (D. Haw. 1957).
12. *Balzac v. Porto Rico*, 258 U.S. 298 (1922); *Hawaii v. Mankichi*, 190 U.S. 197 (1903); *Downes v. Bidwell*, 182 U.S. 244 (1901).
13. 8 U.S.C. § 1401(c).

14. 8 U.S.C. § 1401(d).
15. 8 U.S.C. § 1401(g).
16. 8 U.S.C. § 1401(a).
17. 8 U.S.C. § 1401(f). The provision relating to a child "found" in the United States refers to foundlings whose parents are not known and whose identity or origin is not established.
18. 8 U.S.C. § 1431(a).
19. *See* Act of October 10, 1978, Pub. L. No. 95–432, 92 Stat. 1046, repealing certain sections of 8 U.S.C. §§ 1401 and 1481 governing loss of citizenship.
20. 8 U.S.C. § 1401(b) (1970) (repealed).
21. *Afroyim v. Rusk*, 387 U.S. 253 (1967). *See also Schneider v. Rusk*, 377 U.S. 163 (1964).
22. *Rogers v. Bellei*, 401 U.S. 815, 833 (1971).
23. Moore, Nationality Digest Int. L. 315–18; 8 U.S.C. § 1101(a)(22). Under the Immigration and Nationality Act, a national may enter the United States without restrictions, and if otherwise qualified, be naturalized as a citizen. 8 U.S.C. § 1436.
24. 8 U.S.C. § 1101(a)(21).
25. 8 U.S.C. § 1101(a)(22).
26. 8 U.S.C. § 1408.
27. *Afroyim v. Rusk*, 387 U.S. 253 (1967).
28. 8 U.S.C. § 1408.
29. *See* 8 U.S.C. §§ 1401, 1408.
30. *Rabang v. Boyd*, 353 U.S. (1957).

II

The Immigration Reform and Control Act of 1986

After more than five years of difficult and often bitter debate, the Immigration Reform and Control Act, also known as IRCA or Simpson-Rodino, was signed into law on November 6, 1986.

IRCA was designed to address two primary concerns: unregulated immigration into the U.S. and the plight of America's undocumented immigrants who live in fear on the margins of American society.

The Act contained two major provisions aimed at the workplace. The first of these imposes sanctions on employees who *knowingly* employ undocumented workers. The second significantly expands federal prohibitions against employment discrimination on the basis of national origin or citizenship status.

What is the Immigration Reform and Control Act of 1986? Why was it passed? What does it provide?

The Immigration Reform and Control Act (IRCA)[1] is a series of amendments to the existing Immigration and Nationality Act. The new law is intended to serve two basic purposes: to control and discourage unregulated, unauthorized immigration into the U.S. and to grant legal status to some of the many undocumented aliens already living in this country.[2] One of the law's chief provisions establishes that anyone who has resided in the U.S. unlawfully and continuously since before January 1, 1982, and who has no significant criminal record,[3] can apply for "legalization" (or "amnesty") and obtain permanent resident status.[4] Special legalization provisions apply to certain Cubans and Haitians[5] and agricultural workers.[6]

On the flip side, there are measures, including increased border control,[7] aimed at stemming unauthorized immigration into the U.S.

Finally, there are two key provisions aimed at the workplace, one intended to stop employers from hiring undocumented aliens,[8] the other to ensure that citizens and authorized aliens do not become the victims of employment discrimination.[9]

EMPLOYMENT

What are the specific provisions that affect the workplace?

The first is an "employer sanctions" provision, which is designated as Section 274A of the Immigration and Nationality Act.[10] This provision imposes penalties on employers who knowingly hire or employ aliens not authorized to work in the United States or who fail to document properly the legal status of all new employees.[11] This part of the law does *not* apply to workers already hired as of November 6, 1986, the day the bill was signed.[12] The second provision, designated as Section 274B,[13] is an antidiscrimination provision added to the bill because of concern that employers would refuse to hire aliens, or any "foreign"-looking or "foreign"-sounding workers, even though they are authorized to be engaged in employment, for fear of violating the sanctions provision. Section 274B prohibits employment discrimination on the basis of national origin (if employers are not already covered by existing federal antidiscrimination laws) and on the basis of citizenship status. Specifically, the law applies to hiring, firing, or referral or recruitment for a fee.[14]

The Employer Sanctions Provisions

What is the employer sanctions provision?

The employer sanctions provision has two separate elements. First, the law prohibits employers from *knowingly* hiring any person who is not authorized to work.[15] Second, the law requires employers to review documentation from *every* new employee and to fill out a government form (I-9) verifying that documents have been checked and that the employee is authorized to work.[16] Neither requirement applies to employees who were hired before November 7, 1986.[17]

The law imposes sanctions—ranging from warnings to citations to administrative fines to criminal penalties[18]—on employers who knowingly employ any unauthorized worker, unless the employee was hired as of November 6, 1986. The law also imposes administrative fines of up to $1,000 per violation for failure to comply with the I-9 verification requirement for all new employees.[19]

When did this provision go into effect?

Employer sanctions were phased in periods from November 6, 1986, the day the bill became law, through June 1, 1988, when sanctions became fully enforceable against all nonagricultural employers[20] and December 1, 1988, when sanctions started applying to all persons.[21]

The first six months (November 6, 1986, to June 1, 1987) were designated for public education, and employers were not subject to penalties for violating the provision during that time.[22] On June 1, 1987, the sanctions became enforceable, but for the first three months (until September 1, 1987) any worker or applicant who asserted he or she was eligible for legalization was authorized to work without documentation.[23] Until June 1, 1988, employers who were first-time violators were subject only to a citation.[24]

Do employer sanctions apply to everyone? Are there exceptions for individual employers or small businesses? Are part-time workers and household employees covered?

Employer sanctions apply to every "person or entity" who hires even a single employee.[25] There is no exception for small businesses, and part-time and domestic workers are subject to the same documentation requirements as other workers.

However, an employer need not verify independent contractors or individuals who provide "sporadic, irregular or intermittent" domestic service in a private home.[26]

Does an employer have to verify or fire workers who were hired before IRCA was enacted?

No. Under the law, an employer is *not* required to verify or document any worker who was hired before November 6, 1986. Congress specifically included a "grandfather clause" in the law that exempts employees hired before November 7, 1986, from the sanctions provision. An employer *cannot* be penalized for continuing to employ these workers or for not filling out an I-9 form, no matter what the worker's legal status is.[27]

Immigration Service regulations provide that an employee continues to qualify as a "grandfathered" worker even if he or she temporarily interrupted his or her employment because of a layoff, strike, wrongful discharge, or an approved paid or unpaid leave for such reasons as pregnancy, maternity, paternity, illness, vacation, or union business.[28]

May an employer nonetheless discharge "grandfathered" employees without violating IRCA or other federal laws?

As noted, discharging undocumented "grandfathered" employees is neither required nor prohibited by IRCA. However, such conduct may subject an employer to liability under other antidiscrimination laws. Since IRCA's enactment, a number of courts have held, as the Supreme Court had previously, that immigration status is irrelevant to an employee's right to invoke the protections of federal labor laws.[29] So, for example, Title VII's prohibitions against an employment practice or procedure that has a "disparate impact" on the basis of race or national origin can be invoked by undocumented or "unauthorized" workers who would not be able to state a discrimination claim under IRCA.[30] Thus, if the discharge of "grandfathered" employees has a disparate impact, Title VII will be triggered and the employer will not be able to invoke IRCA as a defense (under the "business necessity" doctrine), since IRCA does not *require* the discharge of grandfathered workers.[31] The same theory of liability would apply to any employment practice that is not required by IRCA if it causes an unlawful disparate impact, even if the victims are undocumented workers.

Who is an authorized worker?

Citizens, nationals, and any aliens whose visa status entitles them to work or those who have been granted work authorization by the Immigration Service. Aliens authorized to work include legal permanent residents, temporary agricultural workers, students with part-time or full-time work permission, applicants for legalization or political asylum with work authorization, and many others. An alien need *not* have a "green card" to be authorized to work.[32]

Undocumented aliens who certified that they were eligible for legalization were authorized to work without showing any documentation until September 1, 1987.[33]

What is considered valid proof of work authorization? Employees may prove their work authorization either by producing a single document that shows both identity and permission to work[34] or by producing a combination of two documents that together show identification and work authorization.[35] For example, a United States passport or "green card" by itself is sufficient. Alternatively, a combination of both a driver's license and a Social Security card (unless specifically stamped "not valid for employment") is also sufficient. An employee may show any document or combination of documents that satisfy the law, and the employer may not require more or different documentation.

Category A: *Identity and Employment Authorization*[36]
Any one of the following documents is equally valid and *by itself* shows identity *and* work authorization:

- U.S. passport
- Citizenship or naturalization certificate
- Unexpired foreign passport with valid work authorization or with a "processed for I-551" stamp in the passport or on an I-94 Arrival/Departure Record document
- Legal resident or alien registration receipt card ("green card") (I-551 or I-151)
- Temporary resident or employment authorization card (I-688 or I-688A)
- Certification from a state employment agency that it has verified an employee's status
- Any other document that may be provided for in future regulations, such as a proposed "citizen identification card"

Alternatively, work authorization may be evidenced by a combination of two documents—one from each of the following categories:

Category B: *Identity*[37]

- State driver's license
- State identification card
- School identification card with photograph
- Voter registration card
- Federal, state, or local identification card
- Canadian driver's license

- For children under sixteen: school or hospital record or parental verification

Category C: Work Authorization[38]

- Social Security card (unless endorsed with "not valid for employment")
- U.S. birth certificate
- INS reentry permit
- INS employment authorization document such as I-94 with work authorization stamp
- INS citizen identification card
- Refugee travel document

An employer must review the documents and execute the I-9 form within three business days of hiring the new employee.[39] Persons who are unable to produce the required documents may present a receipt showing they have applied for the documents and then produce the necessary documents within twenty-one days of hire.[40]

Is an employee or job applicant required to show documents even if they reveal information that the individual wishes to keep private, such as age or date of birth?

Documentation may be used solely to meet requirements of the I-9 form and not for any other personnel decisions. If an employer considers information such as age in deciding whom to hire, the employer may be in violation of other federal or state laws.[41] To ensure that information contained on identity and employment documents is not used for improper purposes, an employer is best served by requiring a job applicant to produce documentation only after a conditional job offer has been extended.

What specific steps does an employer have to take to comply with the verification requirement?

First, the employer must view the required documentation within three business days of hiring a new employee. If the employee has evidence that the necessary documentation is not available but has been requested, a three-week grace period is provided.[42]

Then the employer and the new employee must fill out the official INS form I-9 attesting, under penalty of perjury, that the employee is authorized to work and that the employer has checked the required documents and that the documents appear to be valid.[43] Employers are permitted to make copies of the documents, but that is *not* required or necessary.[44]

The I-9 forms must be kept on file for three years after the date of hire or one year after termination, whichever is later.[45] During that time period, these records are subject to review *upon three days notice* by an officer of the INS or the Department of Labor.[46] Failure to comply with a proper request can be treated as a violation of the I-9 retention requirement.[47] To compel production of the I-9 itself, the INS must obtain a judicial subpoena.[48]

Do employers have to ask for documentation from people they are certain are American citizens?

Yes. Employers must document every new employee. Failure to do so would violate both the sanctions requirements and the antidiscrimination prohibitions.

Do employers have to obtain any documentation from "grandfathered" employees—those hired before November 7, 1986?

No. Employers have no obligation to document the legality of anyone who was hired as of November 6, 1986. The grandfather clause exempts these employees from all provisions of the employer sanctions section, including the verification requirement. As noted previously, a "grandfathered" employee is not subject to the law even if he or she was temporarily away from work due to a strike, layoff, leave, or other permissible reason.[49] In addition, an employer is not required to verify any worker (even if hired after November 6) who was no longer employed on May 31, 1987.[50]

Does an employer have an obligation to verify the authenticity of the documents offered by an employee?

No. If an employer in good faith believes that a document "reasonably appears on its face to be genuine," the employer cannot be found to have violated the law.[51] However, an individual who uses counterfeit or fraudulent documents is subject to criminal prosecution.[52]

Is an employer entitled to a hearing if the INS alleges that a violation of employer sanctions has occurred?

Yes. If the INS believes that an employer has violated the employer sanctions requirements and seeks to impose a penalty, the INS must issue a Notice of Intent to Fine.[53] (Until June 1, 1988, the INS could issue only a citation to first-time offenders.) The notice must contain factual allegations setting forth the practices alleged to be unlawful and the penalty to be imposed.[54] The employer may contest the allegation and request an administrative hearing. At such a hearing the burden is on the government to show that the employer *knowingly* violated the law. The employer is entitled to be represented by an attorney.

An administrative law judge (ALJ) conducts the hearing and determines whether a violation has occurred.[55] The decision may be appealed to the Attorney General within thirty days.[56] Judicial review of an administratively final order may be sought within forty-five days from the federal court of appeals in the circuit where the violation occurred.[57]

An employer who shows that he or she has complied in good faith with the I-9 verification process has "established an affirmative defense" to a charge that the employer knowingly hired unauthorized aliens.[58]

What are the penalties for violating the employer sanctions provision?

There are separate penalties for failing to comply with the I-9 paperwork verification requirement and for knowingly employing unauthorized workers.

Employers who violate the I-9 paperwork verification requirement—who do not review workers' documents, fill out attestation forms, and keep the forms on file for the required period of time—are subject to a maximum civil fine of $100 to $1,000 per violation.[59]

Employers who are found to have knowingly hired, referred, or recruited for a fee, or continued to employ an unauthorized alien (unless hired before November 7, 1986), are subject to a civil penalty of $250 to $2,000 per unauthorized alien for the first offense; $2,000 to $5,000 for the second offense; and $3,000 to $10,000 for subsequent offenses.[60]

If an employer is found to have engaged in a "pattern or

practice" of knowingly employing unauthorized workers, a criminal prosecution in federal court can be initiated, which can result in imposition of criminal penalties of up to $3,000 per unauthorized alien and six months in jail.[61]

What can employers do to protect themselves from being charged under the sanctions provision?

The best defense—the only defense needed—is to follow the I-9 paperwork verification requirements and to recognize that employees who qualify under the grandfather clause are not subject to the sanctions requirements.

The Antidiscrimination Provision

What kind of discrimination is prohibited?

Section 274B of the IRCA (often referred to as the Frank Amendment)[62] prohibits discrimination in employment on the basis of "national origin" or "citizenship status." Specifically, the law prohibits discrimination in hiring, firing, recruiting, or referring for a fee.[63]

What is national origin discrimination?

National origin discrimination encompasses any differing treatment of an individual because of the person's ancestry or country of birth or because the person has the physical, cultural, or linguistic characteristics of a national origin group.[64]

What is citizenship status discrimination?

Citizenship status or alienage discrimination occurs when a person is treated any differently or less favorably because he or she is not a United States citizen.

Does IRCA's prohibition against discrimination apply equally to all employers?

The antidiscrimination provision applies to all employers, public or private, who have more than three workers. That includes all governmental entities as well as private individuals who employ domestic help.[65] The law also applies to employment agencies, "headhunters," contractors, and anyone else who refers or recruits workers for a fee.[66]

However, the protection afforded by IRCA depends on

whether a charge of discrimination is based on *citizenship status* or *national origin.*

The *citizenship status* (alienage) prohibition applies to all employers with more than three workers, but it protects only those persons who are U.S. citizens or "intending citizens."[67] Unless specifically permitted by the law,[68] an employer may not treat an alien who meets the legal definition of "intending citizen" less favorably than a citizen.[69]

The *national origin* prohibition applies only to those employers (with more than three workers) who are not already covered by Title VII of the 1964 Civil Rights Act. Generally speaking, that means Section 274B applies to employers with four to fourteen employees.[70] An employer bound by Section 274B is prohibited from engaging in national origin discrimination against any authorized workers. Aliens do *not* need to qualify as citizens or "intending citizens" to invoke the protection against national origin discrimination.

Who qualifies as an "intending citizen"?

An intending citizen is any alien who is a legal permanent resident, a temporary resident under IRCA's legalization provision, an asylee, or a refugee,[71] and who also does the following:

Files a Declaration of Intending Citizen form (I-772) with the INS.[72]

Files an application for naturalization (INS form N-400) within six months of becoming eligible to do so. (Resident aliens who were eligible for naturalization on November 6, 1986, when the law was enacted, were supposed to apply for naturalization by May 6, 1987.)[73]

After filing an application for naturalization, becomes naturalized within two years of applying (not counting the processing time) or shows that naturalization is being pursued actively.[74]

Must the Declaration of Intending Citizen form be filed *before* the discriminatory act occurs?

No. The regulations enforcing Section 274B provide that the declaration may be filed at any time before the discrimination charge form is submitted and need not have been executed when the discrimination occurred.[75] A declaration is not required at all if the discrimination is based on national origin.

When did the antidiscrimination provision go into effect?

It went into effect the day IRCA became law, November 6, 1986.

What kind of conduct by an employer could constitute national origin or citizenship status discrimination?

Any practice that is not specifically required by IRCA, and that subjects ethnic minorities or noncitizens to greater scrutiny or less favorable treatment could constitute illegal discrimination.[76] Specific discriminatory practices include:

- Firing or refusing to hire someone because he or she looks foreign
- Hiring only citizens or imposing across-the-board citizenship preference requirements
- Hiring only aliens who have "green cards"
- Imposing different or stricter documentation requirements on job applicants who look or sound "foreign"
- Asking only persons with accents to prove work authorization
- Refusing to accept documents that satisfy the employer sanctions requirements
- Preferring one kind of acceptable documentation over another (a United States passport is not preferable to a foreign passport with work authorization; a passport is not preferable to a Social Security card and state identification card or driver's license)
- Changing recruitment methods in a manner that reduces minority applicants
- Refusing to hire persons solely because they have an accent
- Requiring employees to speak English at all times
- Requiring English fluency where it is not legitimately job-related
- Discharging a newly legalized alien because he or she had been working under a false Social Security card[77]

How do persons who believe they have been illegally discriminated against on the basis of national origin or citizenship status, enforce their rights?

They can file a discrimination charge with the special Justice

Department office established to enforce the antidiscrimination provisions of IRCA, the Office of Special Counsel for Immigration-Related Unfair Employment Practices.[78]

A special form is available on which a charge may be filed, but use of the form is not required. Further information may be obtained from:

Office of Special Counsel for Immigration-Related Unfair Employment Practices
P.O. Box 65490
Washington, D.C. 20035-5490
1-800-255-7688 (toll free) or (202) 653-8121

Is there a time limit for the filing of charges with the Office of Special Counsel?

The law states that a discrimination charge must be filed within 180 days of the date on which the discrimination occurred.[79] Failure to comply with this requirement may result in a charge being rejected. However, under certain limited circumstances the 180-day period can be subject to "equitable tolling."[80] This means that a charge may be filed late if there is a legally sufficient reason for doing so. Valid reasons could include a victim's ignorance of the law, good faith efforts to file, misinformation from federal agencies, or incorrect filing with federal, state, or local entities.[81]

Can anyone other than the discrimination victim file a charge with the Special Counsel?

Under the law, a person can file a charge "on behalf of" the individual who was "adversely affected directly" by an act of discrimination.[82] That includes friends, relatives, union representatives, attorneys—anyone. The INS, which is not involved with enforcing the antidiscrimination provision, can also file charges of discrimination.

In addition, the Special Counsel may choose to initiate his or her own investigations independent of outside charges.

Once a case goes before an administrative law judge (ALJ), interested parties not directly involved may intervene (with the ALJ's permission) to participate in the proceedings.[83]

How does the Office of Special Counsel handle a discrimination complaint?

Upon receiving a charge of discrimination, the Office of Special Counsel conducts an investigation that could include interviews with the charging party, the employer, and other witnesses, as well as a review of relevant documents.[84] The Special Counsel has 120 days to decide whether there is "reasonable cause to believe" that the charge is true and, if so, to file a formal complaint before an ALJ.[85]

If the Office of Special Counsel does not file an ALJ complaint within the 120-day period, and if the initial charge alleged that the discrimination was "intentional" or constituted a "pattern or practice," the charging party may file an ALJ complaint on its own.[86] An individual ALJ complaint must be filed within 90 days of the Special Counsel's decision not to prosecute or within 90 days of the expiration of the 120-day investigation period, whichever is sooner.[87]

Under either procedure, a hearing will be held before an ALJ, who will determine whether discrimination occurred and the type of penalty that should be imposed. At the hearing and throughout the process, the charging party is entitled to be represented by an attorney.

How do you prove discrimination?

Most commentators, including Representative Barney Frank (D-Mass.) (one of the provision's primary authors), the ACLU, and other groups, assumed that the criteria would be the same as in employment discrimination cases brought under Title VII, where any job requirement or test is illegal if it has a discriminatory *effect* (even if unintended) unless the test is proven to be "job-related."[88]

However, when President Reagan signed IRCA into law, he issued a statement saying that he understood the provision to require proof of an employer's "discriminatory intent." This interpretation seems clearly flawed and would narrow the provision's scope considerably.[89]

Representative Frank called President Reagan's claim "intellectually dishonest, mean-spirited," and incorrect. The regulations issued by the Department of Justice require a discrimination victim to prove intent but appear to give a somewhat broader definition to the term.[90] Litigation will ultimately resolve this conflict. Until then, a discrimination victim should allege intent whenever there is a basis for doing so.

Are there circumstances in which citizens can be preferred over noncitizens?

IRCA specifically states that Section 274B does not prohibit preferring a citizen under certain, specified circumstances. Other federal and state laws remain in effect and could nonetheless render any citizen preference illegal.

IRCA's antidiscrimination provision does not apply to cases where laws, regulations, or contracts with governmental entities *require* employers to *hire* only U.S. citizens.[91] In some states, for example, police officers have to be citizens, and such a requirement would not be a violation of Section 274B.

In addition, the law permits an employer to prefer to hire (but not fire) a citizen instead of a noncitizen "if the two individuals are equally qualified,"[92] and if such decisions are made on a careful, case-by-case basis.

Neither of these exceptions is a defense to existing constitutional or statutory provisions (including Title VII and local laws or ordinances) that prohibit employment discrimination.[93]

When an employer is found to have discriminated, what are the penalties?

First, of course, the employer will be ordered to stop the discriminatory practice.[94] In addition, the ALJ can order any or all of the following:

- Reinstatement of a discharged employee, with or without back pay, depending on the circumstances
- Civil penalties of up to $1,000 per individual for the first offense and up to $2,000 per individual for each subsequent offense
- Maintaining a record of all job applicants for a period of up to three years[95]

Can the employer also be required to pay the charging party's attorneys' fees?

Yes, if the charging party wins and shows that the employer's arguments were "without reasonable foundation in law and fact."[96] That standard is taken from other federal law and may be difficult to satisfy. Employers too are entitled to seek reimbursement for their attorneys' fees if they win a case, although they will have to meet the same high standard or (as under other discrimination laws) an even tougher one.[97]

What if either side—charging party or employer—is dissatisfied with the decision of the ALJ? Can it be appealed?

Yes. The ALJ's final decision may be appealed within sixty days of issuance to the appropriate United States Court of Appeals.[98]

Isn't national origin and citizenship status discrimination already outlawed under other civil rights laws?

To some extent, yes. There are existing federal provisions that outlaw various forms of discrimination, and some states and localities also have relevant laws. But taken together, these provisions still leave loopholes. Section 274B is intended to plug as many of them as possible.

Title VII of the 1964 Civil Rights Act prohibits employment discrimination on the basis of race and national origin (and several other grounds).[99] Discrimination on the basis of citizenship status is not explicitly covered but is prohibited if it causes—intentionally or unintentionally—national origin discrimination.[100] But Title VII applies only to employers that have fifteen or more employees who work twenty or more weeks a year.[101] In contrast, Section 274B covers all employers with more than three employees without regard to the amount of time the employees work.

Section 1981, one of several post–Civil War civil rights statutes, prohibits private employers of any size from treating any person less favorably than a "white citizen."[102] This law clearly prohibits alienage discrimination by governmental entities.[103] The law's applicability to private employers who discriminate on the basis of alienage is less clear.[104] Under Section 1981, discriminatory intent has to be proved.[105]

The Equal Protection Clause of the U.S. Constitution limits the power of state and local governments to discriminate on the basis of alienage[106] but imposes few limits on the power of the federal government to refuse to hire noncitizens.[107]

In some areas, there are also state and local statutes prohibiting discrimination on the basis of national origin, alienage, or citizenship status. Similarly, collective bargaining agreements and general state laws limiting an employer's right to discharge workers unilaterally may also afford employees protection against discrimination.

In many instances a discrimination victim may be able to file claims under a combination of state and federal laws or several federal laws. The only overlap that is precluded is pursuing a national origin claim under both Title VII and Section 274B.[108]

Can a discrimination victim file charges against an employer under Section 274B and under another antidiscrimination statute, such as Title VII, at the same time?

A discrimination victim can simultaneously pursue numerous legal remedies. These may include state and local as well as federal laws. For example, a person who is illegally fired may be able to file a citizenship status charge under Section 274B, a national origin charge under Title VII, an alienage discrimination complaint under Section 1981, and a combination of those same charges under state or local discrimination and human rights laws. The only parallel filings that are prohibited are *national origin* discrimination claims under Section 274B and Title VII.[109]

What steps can employers take to protect themselves from charges of discrimination?

The simple answer, of course, is not to discriminate against any worker or job applicant on the basis of national origin or citizenship status.

The best advice for employers is: Don't fire or refuse to hire anyone simply because of their ethnic origin, their appearance, or their speech; don't treat any employment-authorized aliens less favorably than citizens; and don't impose any different or stricter documentation requirements than *required* by IRCA's employer sanctions provision.

Which government agencies will be enforcing the law?

The INS is responsible for enforcing employer sanctions.[110] The antidiscrimination provision falls under the jurisdiction of the Justice Department Office of Special Counsel for Immigration-Related Unfair Employment Practices.[111]

Are the antidiscrimination and sanctions provisions temporary, or are they going to be the law from now on?

There is no built-in expiration date for the law. The U.S. General Accounting Office (GAO) is required to issue annual reports in 1987, 1988, and 1989 evaluating the effect of both the sanctions and antidiscrimination provisions.[112] The sanctions provision will be revoked if the third and final GAO report finds a "widespread pattern of discrimination" against citizens, nationals, or eligible workers resulting "solely from the implementation" of sanctions, and if Congress votes to accept that report within thirty days.[113]

The antidiscrimination provision will be terminated if the final GAO report finds either that no significant discrimination has resulted or that the provision puts an unreasonable burden on employers, and if Congress ratifies that report within thirty days.[114] Also, the antidiscrimination provision will automatically be terminated if the sanctions provision is revoked.[115]

The first GAO report, issued in November 1987, reported that sixty-seven charges alleging immigration-related employment discrimination claims had been filed with federal agencies and thirty-four charges with state and local government agencies. The report recognized that it was too early to draw any conclusions.[116] The second GAO report found that a significant number of employers had adopted unlawful employment practices since the enactment of IRCA. These practices included asking only "foreign"-looking or "foreign"-sounding job applicants for documentation and adopting policies of hiring only citizens. The report declined to conclude that these practices constituted discrimination from the implementation of employer sanctions.[117]

Legalization Provisions

What are the specific provisions that affect immigration status?

Although IRCA was primarily an attempt to control unlawful immigration to this country by making it illegal for employers to hire undocumented persons, it allowed millions of resident, undocumented persons to become legal residents of the United States. Nearly three million undocumented persons applied for legal status under the general amnesty provisions and the special agricultural provisions of IRCA. By enacting these provisions of IRCA, Congress recognized at once the need for these individuals to be in our country and the impossibility of expelling them from our borders, and so rewarded them with the opportunity to live here legally. Stories of immigrants who had long lived in the shadows of our society and who now had the opportunity to become legal residents of this country were extensively covered in the press.

The Select Commission on Immigration and Refugee Policy, on March 1, 1981, recommended to Congress that persons who came to the United States prior to January 1, 1980, be given temporary legal status. In part, it was a recognition that the massive deportation of millions of persons here illegally would be impossible, and that any attempt to do so would likely result in the violation of the civil rights and liberties of a large number of U.S. citizens and permanent resident aliens. Legalizing the status of undocumented persons would likely result in the rise in wages and working conditions of aliens and U.S. citizens, as the pool of easily exploitable workers acquired the rights of legal residents.[118]

A date by which undocumented aliens had to have been here was chosen to be not so far in the past that it would leave a large number of aliens in illegal status. At the same time, the 1980 date, in the Commission's opinion, was far enough in the past so as not to encourage illegal immigration resulting from the public discussion in the United States of an amnesty program.[119]

By the time IRCA was passed in 1986, the original proposal was modified to require that in order to qualify for amnesty, an alien must have lived in the United States unlawfully since January 1, 1982. The caution of the Select Commission was ignored in this case. In the five years between the cutoff eligibility date for legalization and the passage of IRCA, a large number of undocumented persons had arrived. Perhaps twice as many people will be left in illegal status as will be legalized by IRCA.[120] Though generous in theory, the amnesty concept became, in practice, only a partial amnesty.

Apart from the 1982 cutoff date, however, there were other barriers to taking advantage of the amnesty program. A combination of factors combined to prevent a significant portion of the number of potential applicants from applying for legalization.[121]

These factors include the historical, adversarial relationship between INS and undocumented persons; the restrictive requirements of the law itself; problems with the implementation of the law; and regulations that restricted eligibility for the program beyond the restrictions imposed by Congress in the statute.

Historically, undocumented aliens have feared INS; to be discovered by INS meant possible deportation. With the passage of IRCA, the Service and those aiding in the implementation of the law had to convince eligible aliens that approaching INS would not lead to deportation—that the IRCA specifically provided that amnesty applications were "confidential" and could not be used as a basis for deportation. Nontheless, fear remained a factor in preventing otherwise qualified persons from applying.[122] But aliens feared more than deportation for themselves. Some members of families were eligible for amnesty and some were not. The fear of splitting up the family was a factor in keeping some people from applying.[123] In November of 1987, INS announced a "family fairness" policy. By that policy, unmarried minor children of legalized temporary residents who arrived in the U.S. prior to November 6, 1986 were granted "indefinite voluntary departure." Spouses or other children of legalized temporary residents could qualify, based on compelling or humanitarian reasons; but applications for "family fairness" are not covered by IRCA's confidentiality provisions. Persons who applied for "family fairness" and were denied that relief could be placed in deportation proceedings as a result of the disclosure of their undocumented status.[124]

The law itself placed a number of obstacles in the path of aliens trying to apply for amnesty. Among these was the requirement that aliens show continuous, illegal residence in the U.S. since 1982. Some persons never could gather sufficient documentation to prove this element.[125]

IRCA presented INS and private groups assisting in implementation of legalization with enormous practical problems. A system had to be established to inform the public and to handle millions of applications. Among the most serious problems that developed in the implementation of legalization was the inadequacy of the public education effort. That effort required that the alien population not only had to be alerted to the opportunities made available to them by IRCA but also had to be assured that approaching INS would not lead to their deportation. An all-out effort by INS to publicize amnesty was begun only a few months before the application period ended.[126]

Certain provisions of the regulations that were promulgated to implement IRCA were overly restrictive and prevented many persons from applying. In some instances, INS liberalized their regulations in the middle of the legalization program.[127] In other instances, regulations were changed or invalidated as the result of litigation.[128] In either case, there were many persons who had been denied or who had given up on the idea of applying for legalization because they thought themselves ineligible owing to restrictive regulations. There was little or no follow-up educational effort to get these people to come back and apply after the regulations were changed.[129]

Litigation challenging certain INS interpretations of the law is ongoing. Some litigation has already expanded the class of persons eligible for legalization. In the future, it is possible that some of those persons who now qualify for amnesty will be given another opportunity to apply.

In addition to the amnesty program, IRCA provided additional legalization programs for other classes of people. To accommodate agricultural growers who feared their interest in maintaining a sufficiently stable agricultural work force would be jeopardized by employer sanctions, provisions were included in IRCA to ensure that there would be an ample supply of labor for agricultural work. The Special Agricultural Workers program (SAW) provided an opportunity for aliens who had performed at least ninety man-days of agricultural work in the twelve months prior to May 1, 1986, to legalize their status. The requirements were much simpler for this program than for general amnesty, and agricultural workers were given an eighteen-month application period that ended on November 30, 1988. Although the less rigorous documentation requirements for this program made it easier for applicants to apply, many still had trouble proving their work in U.S. agriculture during the specified time period. Many persons found it difficult to obtain work documents from employers. On the other hand, the easier documentation requirements in some instances may have encouraged fraud. In reacting to a perceived prevalence of fraud in the SAW program, INS adopted policies that denied legalization to legitimate applicants or discouraged some from applying. Advocate groups brought suit against INS to get the Service to stop denying legalization to those who were eligible.[130]

If, in the future, there is found to be a shortage of workers in agriculture, more alien farm workers will be legalized. But unlike SAW applicants, who are free to leave agricultural work once they are legalized, these "Replenishment Agricultural Workers" (RAWs) will be bound to agricultural work for a period of three consecutive years after a grant of temporary residence.

Other groups of aliens with long-standing ties to this country were affected by IRCA. Cubans and Haitians who were designated as "Cuban/Haitian Entrants" or other Cubans or Haitians who were not admitted to the U.S. as nonimmigrants and who have continuously resided in this country since January 1, 1982, are eligible for a special adjustment program. These persons, if they applied within two years of the enactment of IRCA, may adjust to permanent resident status.[131]

Also in IRCA, the registry date was updated from June 30, 1948, to January 1, 1972.[132] Aliens who have resided in this country since that date may qualify for permanent resident status.

Is it too late to apply for amnesty?

Generally yes. However several lawsuits have challenged INS regulations that denied legalization to certain classes of undocumented aliens. In instances, federal courts have decided that these regulations did not comply with the intent of Congress when it enacted IRCA. But some of these decisions were not made until near the end or after the end of the May 4, 1988, amnesty application period. To give the adversely affected groups of individuals a fair chance to apply, the amnesty deadline may be extended.

What classes of persons may still qualify for amnesty?

There are at least three groups of individuals who may still qualify for amnesty.

One such group is persons who are otherwise eligible for legalization, but who left the United States after May 1, 1987, for any length of time without advance permission from INS. INS regulations disqualified such persons from amnesty. A lawsuit was brought in California challenging these regulations.[133] The court decided that the eligibility of such persons should be decided on a case-by-case basis, depending on whether the absence was "brief, casual, and innocent." Persons who had already been denied legalization on this basis had their cases reopened.

But the court reached its decision on May 3, the day before the deadline for amnesty applications. Many persons who should have been eligible could not be reached in time to apply. The court granted additional time for these persons. INS is appealing this extension, but in the interim, persons who were otherwise eligible for amnesty, but who left the country after May 1, 1987, for a "brief, casual and innocent" departure, may not be deported by INS and must be granted work authorization. If the lower court's decision is upheld on appeal, these persons will have an extra 120 days to apply for legalization beginning on the date of the appeals court's decision.

A second group originally excluded from eligibility for legalization were persons otherwise eligible but who had left the U.S. and reentered on a fraudulently obtained visa after January 1, 1982, to resume their unlawful residence. INS argued that if such persons obtained status by obtaining a visa or other document, the continuity of their unlawful status was broken. A lawsuit was filed challenging this contention;[134] such persons fully intended to resume unlawful residence here and therefore should not be considered to have broken their illegal status.

In November 1987, INS changed its regulation, but by this time, many persons had been discouraged from applying, thinking they were ineligible. These persons have been granted extra time to apply. INS has appealed the extension of time; but while the appeal is pending, persons who are eligible for legalization, i.e., left the United States and returned on a fraudulently obtained visa or other document prior to January 1, 1982, and who did not apply for legalization before May 4, 1988, may file "skeletal" legalization applications with the INS. A skeletal application contains basic information with the $185 application fee, but without supporting documents. If such a person has been apprehended, he or she must apply for legalization within thirty days of being apprehended.

The third category of potentially eligible persons involves whether the individual's undocumented status was "known to the government." IRCA provided that persons who came to the U.S. in a legal status but subsequently violated that status, whose illegal status was "known to the Government" prior to January 1, 1982, could apply for legalization. INS, in its regulations, interpreted "known to the Government" to mean "known to INS." A lawsuit challenged that interpretation,[135] and a federal district court decided that "known to the Government," as phrased in IRCA, meant known to any federal agency. Persons denied legalization based on this regulation were eligible to have their cases reopened. INS has been approving applications in which, for example, employment not authorized by INS was reported to the Social Security Administration or Internal Revenue Service, and the records of those agencies reflect earnings prior to 1982, even if SSA or IRS learned of the earnings after January 1, 1982, and even if SSA or IRS had no way of knowing whether or not the earnings were authorized by INS. Those persons who never applied for legalization, because they were told they were ineligible, were given extra time to apply for some as yet undetermined relief from the court. However, the court of appeals vacated the decision on the ground of lack of jurisdiction under the statutory scheme, creating general uncertainty as to the availability of judicial review under IRCA.

There are several lawsuits that have recently been filed that hold out the possibility that certain classes of individuals may yet be granted additional time to apply for IRCA legalization.[136]

In California, a class action covering the jurisdiction of the Ninth Circuit Court of Appeals[137] may give extra time to those persons who failed to apply by May 4, 1988, because they thought they were ineligible due to past receipt of financial assistance. A court has invalidated INS requirements that applicants prove financial responsibility in order not to be considered a "public charge."

There is the possibility that persons who are otherwise eligible for legalization but had left the U.S. after January 1, 1982, for a single absence of more than 45 days or several absences totaling more than 180 days, and who did not apply for legalization or appeal a denial, may someday get another chance to apply. A pending lawsuit[138] challenges the lack of procedures or standards for obtaining a waiver of this rule. The court may decide to grant such persons an additional period to apply for legalization.

A nationwide class action lawsuit has been filed in Illinois[139] on behalf of undocumented persons who were apprehended after November 6, 1986; who were never issued an Order to Show Cause (OSC) after being apprehended; who were eligible for legalization; and who did not apply by June 3, 1987. The law says that persons apprehended after November 6, 1986, and issued Orders to Show Cause must apply for legalization within thirty days of the beginning of the application period (June 3, 1987). INS regulations additionally required persons apprehended but not issued an OSC to apply by June 3. The lawsuit seeks to invalidate the INS rule, and it seeks additional application time for those who thought themselves ineligible because of this rule.

In the future, other provisions of INS regulations implementing IRCA may be found to have unfairly excluded certain groups of individuals from the benefits of IRCA legalization. Lawsuits may yet be filed in the hope that courts will remedy the unfair treatment these groups have experienced.

When can a lawful temporary resident apply for permanent residence?

Within the one-year period that begins after the alien has been a temporary resident for eighteen months.[140] The date of temporary residence begins on the date shown on the temporary resident fee receipt, that is, when the application and fee were first submitted. Some caution should be exercised in judging the beginning date of temporary residence. It is *not* the date on which INS approves the temporary resident application which could be many months after the date shown on the fee receipt. It also may not be the date that appears on the applicant's temporary residence card (I-688). The date on that card may be the interview date.[141]

There is another item of possible confusion. The temporary resident card is valid for thirty-one months. Applicants must apply before the end of the thirtieth month of temporary residence, at the latest.

Applications may be sent to the appropriate INS Regional Processing Facilities at any time during the thirty-month period. These applications will be held by INS and will be adjudicated after the applicant has completed the mandatory eighteen-month waiting period.[142]

Is an alien allowed to leave the United States while the application for permanent residence is pending?

Aliens applying for permanent residence may continue to travel outside of the United States, but no single absence may be greater than thirty days, nor can the aggregate of all absences exceed 90 days since the original application for temporary residence was filed, unless the alien can show that "emergent reasons" prevented him or her from returning to the United States within the specified time.[143]

What would disqualify an alien from obtaining permanent resident status?

An alien will not be adjusted to permanent residence under IRCA if he or she fails to apply within one year after the beginning of his or her application period; breaks continuous residence in the U.S. with absences longer than thirty days at a time or more than ninety days total during the period of temporary residence; is inadmissable as an immigrant; has been convicted of a felony or three or more misdemeanors; either fails to show a minimal understanding of ordinary English and the history and government of the U.S.; or does not "satisfactorily pursue" a course of study in these areas.[144]

What makes an alien inadmissible as an immigrant?

Certain classes of persons are not eligible to apply for permanent residence under IRCA. For example, aliens are not eligible if they have committed certain crimes (defined in Section 212(a)(9) and (10) of the Immigration and Nationality Act (INA)); if they are likely to become a "public charge"; if they have been convicted of crimes relating to possession of or trafficking in illegal drugs, except if they have been convicted of simple possession of thirty grams or less of marijuana; if it is determined that they may engage in activities that would be prejudicial to the public interest (defined in INA Section 212(a)(27)); if they are a member of or affiliated with certain organizations (defined in INA Section 212(a)(28)); if they would engage in subversive activity (paragraph (29) of Section 212(a)); or if they participated in Nazi persecutions. (*See* ch. IV.)

Will an alien be considered "likely to become a public charge" if he or she has ever received cash assistance from the government?

Possibly. In determining who is likely to become a public charge, IRCA requires that an alien's history of employment in the U.S. be examined. If an alien establishes proof of self-support, without receipt of public cash assistance, then the alien will not be considered ineligible as "likely to become a public charge."

In the first phase of IRCA, INS regulations defining who is "likely to become a public charge" were challenged in lawsuits as more restrictive than required by the law.[145]

Regulations for the second stage of legalization detail the information INS will consider when making a determination on the likelihood of becoming a public charge. This information includes, first, inadmissibility under Section 212(a)(15) of the INA; an employment history showing the alien's ability to support himself or herself and his or her family; past acceptance of public cash assistance; and the length of time such assistance was received.[146]

What public benefits are available to newly legalized aliens?

Newly legalized aliens are eligible for a range of public benefits such as certain emergency medical care and certain educational and vocational programs.

To satisfy concerns in Congress that the newly legalized aliens may become a burden on the government, these persons are prohibited from receiving certain federal cash assistance, such as food stamps or Aid to Families with Dependent Children, for a period of five years after the grant of temporary resident status.[147] A newly legalized alien wishing to apply for any federal benefit should consult first with social service or alien rights organizations regarding the programs that may have restrictions barring assistance to various categories of aliens.

How can an alien show an understanding of ordinary English and of the history and government of the U.S.?

An alien can demonstrate an understanding of ordinary English and of the history and government of the U.S. either by showing "satisfactory pursuit" of a course of study in the subject areas or by taking a test with an INS examiner during the permanent residence interview.[148] The questions will come from a prepared list of one hundred questions on U.S. history and government.

If an alien fails to pass the English/civics test with the INS examiner, will the alien be denied permanent residence?

No. The individual will be given another chance to pass the test after a period of six months. The alien will be given the six-month period for retesting even if his or her one-year application period has expired.[149] At the time either of the first interview or of a reinterview, a "certificate of satisfactory pursuit" may be submitted in lieu of taking the INS test.

How might an alien show "satisfactory pursuit" of knowledge of the English language and of the history and government of the U.S.?

"Satisfactory pursuit" of knowledge of English and civics may be demonstrated in a number of ways. The alien may present a Certificate of Satisfactory Pursuit from an English/civics program approved by an INS district director.[150] To obtain such a certificate, he or she must have attended such a course for at least forty hours.[151] The alien may instead present an American high school diploma or general equivalency diploma. The alien may also present certification from a state-recognized-and-accredited learning institution that he or she attended such an institution for a period of one academic year and studied English, American history, and government. Finally, the alien may present evidence of having passed a proficiency test that is equivalent to having completed forty hours of an approved English/civics course.[152] This evidence may be presented either with the filed application, or at the interview.

Must all aliens demonstrate knowledge of English and civics in applying for permanent residence under IRCA?

No. Persons sixty-five years or older need not meet this

requirement.[153] INS has also exempted persons younger than sixteen and those over fifty years of age who can demonstrate they have been in the United States for at least twenty years. Persons physically unable to comply are also exempt.[154]

What if an alien legalized under IRCA fails to apply for permanent resident status before the alien's application period expires?

At the end of thirty-one months of temporary residence, he or she will revert to illegal status and be subject to deportation.[155]

If an alien's application for permanent residence is denied, is there a right to appeal?

Yes. Appeals may be made to the Legalization Appeals unit of INS. Any appeal must be filed with a Regional Processing Facility within thirty days of a Notice of Denial. An additional thirty days will be allowed for the review of the record of proceeding, if the record is requested for review.[156] If an alien has appealed and lost but feels that the grounds for denial have been overcome, he or she may submit another application for adjustment of status, provided that the alien's one-year application period has not expired.

Will an alien's authorization to work end if a decision on an application or an appeal has not been reached by the time the alien's one-year application period has expired?

An alien's period of temporary residence and authorization to work cannot be terminated if a decision has not been reached on an application for permanent residence (unless the alien commits a felony or three or more misdemeanors in the United States, or commits an act making the alien inadmissible).[157] An alien's work authorization will be extended during the period in which an appeal is being considered, or until the period for filing an appeal has expired.[158]

If the alien fails to apply for permanent residence, or if the application for permanent residence is denied, will INS use information in the temporary resident or permanent resident application to try to deport the alien?

No, generally IRCA prohibits the use of information filed

with a legalization application to be used for any purpose other than to make a determination on the application.[159] Congress adopted these confidentiality provisions because it recognized that in order for the legalization program to be successful, potential applicants had to be free from the fear that making an application to INS would result in their deportation. Fines and imprisonment are provided for violations of the confidentiality provisions.

There is an exception. An applicant for legalization may be prosecuted if he or she makes false statements or "knowingly and willfully falsifies, misrepresents, conceals or covers up material facts" or uses fraudulent documents.[160] In addition, petitions for naturalization and other benefits by legalized aliens may be decided by relying upon information contained in the alien legalization file.[161]

When can an alien who is a Special Agricultural Worker (SAW) granted temporary residence apply for permanent residence?

IRCA provides that SAWs shall be adjusted to permanent residence in two phases. The first 350,000 of those who can demonstrate at the time of their application for temporary residence that they worked at least ninety man-days in agriculture in each of the three years ending on May 1, 1984, 1985, and 1986, will be adjusted to permanent residence on November 30, 1989, or one year after they are granted temporary residence, whichever comes later. Any number over 350,000, or those SAWs who can demonstrate that they worked ninety man-days in agriculture only in the year ending 1986, will be adjusted to permanent residence on November 30, 1990, or two years after they were granted temporary residence, whichever comes later.[162]

While in temporary resident status, can special agricultural workers travel outside of the U.S.?

IRCA provides that a temporary resident Special Agricultural Worker has the right to travel abroad.[163]

Must an alien granted temporary residence in the SAW program continue to work in agriculture?

A grant of temporary residence under the SAW program

entitles the alien to work authorization.[164] There is no provision that the alien must remain in agriculture. However, aliens who are given temporary residence in the future under the so-called Replenishment Agricultural Worker (RAW) program will be required to work at least ninety man-days in agriculture for three consecutive years after being granted temporary resident status in order to avoid deportation.[165] RAWs will be required to work at least ninety man-days in agriculture for another two years before being eligible for naturalization.[166]

NOTES

1. Pub. L. No. 99-603, 100 Stat. 3359 (1986) (codified throughout 8 U.S.C. § 1101 *et seq.*).
2. *See* 8 U.S.C. §§ 1324a (employer sanctions), 1255a (legalization). *See also* 8 U.S.C. § 1259 (registration date amended to Jan. 1, 1972); IRCA § 202 (uncodified provision establishing Cuban/Haitian adjustment procedure).
3. An applicant is not eligible for legalization if he or she has any felony or three (or more) misdemeanor convictions. 8 U.S.C. § 1255a(a)(4)(B).
4. 8 U.S.C. § 1255a. An alien who qualifies for legalization will eventually be eligible to apply for citizenship.
5. Pub. L. No. 99-603, § 202, 100 Stat. 3359, 3404 (1986).
6. 8 U.S.C. § 1160.
7. Pub. L. No. 99-603, § 111, 100 Stat. 3359, 3381 (1986).
8. 8 U.S.C. § 1324a.
9. 8 U.S.C. § 1324b.
10. *See supra* note 8.
11. 8 U.S.C. §§ 1324a(a)(1)&(b).
12. Pub. L. No. 99-603, § 101(a)(3), 100 Stat. 3359, 3372 (1986) (uncodified) provides:

    (3) Grandfather for Current Employees.
    (A) Section 274A(a)(1) of the Immigration and Nationality Act shall not apply to the hiring, or recruiting or referring of an individual for employment which has occurred before the date of the enactment of this Act.
    (B) Section 274A(a)(2) of the Immigration and Nationality Act shall not apply to continuing employment of an alien who was hired before the date of the enactment of this Act.

13. 8 U.S.C. § 1324b.

14. 8 U.S.C. § 1324b(a)(1)&(2)(b).
15. 8 U.S.C. § 1324a(a)(1)(A) provides: "It is unlawful for a person or other entity to hire, or to recruit or refer for a fee, for employment in the United States an alien *knowing* the alien is an unauthorized alien" (emphasis added).
16. *Id.* at § 1324a(a)(l)(B). The specifics of the documentation requirement are set forth in § 1324a(b). The contents of the I-9 form are established by regulation. *See* 8 C.F.R. § 274a.2.
17. *See supra* note 12.
18. 8 U.S.C. §§ 1324a(e)(4)(A) & 1324a(f)(1).
19. *Id.* at § 1324a(e)(5).
20. *Id.* at § 1324a(i)(1)&(2).
21. *Id.* at § 1324a(i)(3). *See* 8 U.S.C. § 1160(a)(1).
22. *Id.* at § 1324a(i)(1).
23. 8 C.F.R. § 274a.11.
24. 8 U.S.C. § 1324a(i)(2).
25. *Id.* at § 1324a(a)(1); 8 C.F.R. § 274a.1(f)&(g).
26. 8 C.F.R. § 274a.1(j) (independent contractor) and (h) (domestic service).
27. *See supra* note 12. *See also* 8 C.F.R. § 274a.7.
28. 8 C.F.R. § 274a.2(b)(1)(viii)(A)–(G).
29. *See Sure-Tan v. NLRB*, 467 U.S. 883 (1984). *See also Local 512, Warehouse & Office Workers' Union v. NLRB (Felbro)*, 795 F.2d 705 (9th Cir. 1986). Since IRCA's passage in 1986, the courts have continued to enforce the same principle. *See, e.g., NLRB v. Ashkenazy Property Management Corp.*, 817 F.2d 75 (9th Cir. 1987); *Patel v. Quality Inn South*, 846 F.2d 700 (11th Cir. 1988); *Rios v. Steam Fitters Local 638*, 860 F.2d 1168 (2d Cir. 1988). *See also* Memorandum of NLRB General Counsel 88-9 (GC 88-9)(Sept. 1, 1988).
30. IRCA § 274B provides that its prohibitions apply to any individual "other than an unauthorized alien." As noted in *supra* note 29, no such limitation applies to Title VII.
31. *See infra* text at note 96. Title VII of the 1964 Civil Rights Act, 42 U.S.C. § 2000e *et seq.*, prohibits any employment practices or procedures that have a disparate impact on the basis of race or national origin, unless justified by "business necessity." *See, e.g., Griggs v. Duke Power Co.*, 401 U.S. 424 (1971); *Dothard v. Rawlinson*, 433 U.S. 321 (1977). An immigration-related employment practice will not qualify as a business necessity if it is not *required* by IRCA.
32. 8 C.F.R. § 274a.12 sets forth all the classes of aliens authorized to work either by virtue of their visa status or pursuant to work authorization granted by the Immigration Service.
33. 8 C.F.R. § 274a.11.

34. *Id.* at § 274a.2(b)(1)(v)(A).
35. *Id.* at § 274a.2(b)(1)(v)(B)&(C).
36. *See supra* note 34.
37. 8 C.F.R. § 274.2(b)(1)(v)(B).
38. *Id.* at § 274a.2(b)(1)(v)(C).
39. *Id.* at § 274a.2(b)(1)(vi). If the employee works for fewer than three days, the documentation requirement must be complied with by the end of the first day of work. *Id.* at § 274a.2(b)(1)(iii).
40. *Id.*
41. *See, e.g.*, Age Discrimination in Employment Act, 29 U.S.C. § 621 *et seq.*; Title VII of 1964 Civil Rights Act, 42 U.S.C. § 2000e *et seq.*
42. The job applicant or employee must "present a receipt for the application of the document or documents within three days of the hire and present the required document or documents within 21 days of the hire." 8 C.F.R. § 274a.2(b)(1)(vi).
43. *See infra* text at note 51.
44. 8 U.S.C. § 1324a(b)(4).
45. *Id.* at § 1324a(b)(3).
46. *Id.* at § 1324a(b)(3); 8 C.F.R. § 274a.2(ii).
47. *Id.*
48. *Id.*
49. *See supra* note 28.
50. 8 C.F.R. § 274a.2A.
51. 8 U.S.C. § 1324a(b)(1)(A).
52. *See, e.g.*, 18 U.S.C. § 1546.
53. 8 U.S.C. § 1324a(e)(3)(A). *See also* 8 C.F.R. § 274a.9(c)(1).
54. 8 C.F.R. § 274a.9(c)(1)(ii).
55. 8 U.S.C. § 1324a(e)(3)(B).
56. *Id.* at § 1324a(e)(6). The regulations provide for review of the ALJ's decision by the Chief Administrative Hearing Judge if a written request and brief are filed within five days. Such review is *not* a prerequisite for judicial review. *See* 28 C.F.R. §168.52(a)&(a)(2).
57. 8 U.S.C. § 1324a(e)(7).
58. *Id.* at § 1324a(a)(3).
59. *Id.* at § 1324a(e)(5).
60. *Id.* at § 1324a(e)(4)(A)(i)–(iii).
61. *Id.* at § 1324a(f)(1).
62. Codified at 8 U.S.C. § 1324b.
63. 8 U.S.C. § 1324b(a).
64. The term "national origin" is not defined by IRCA. A significant body of case law and administrative practice has defined the term in the context of Title VII, where the statute is also silent. In *Espinoza v. Farah Mfg. Co.*, 414 U.S. 86 (1973), the Supreme Court concluded

that the term refers both to "the country where a person was born" as well as to "the country from which his or her ancestors come." The Equal Employment Opportunity Commission (EEOC), the administrative agency charged with enforcing Title VII, defines national origin discrimination as encompassing differing treatment of an individual because he or she "has the physical, cultural or linguistic characteristics of a national origin group." 29 C.F.R. § 1606.1.

65. The term employee is not defined in § 1324b, the regulations implementing it, or elsewhere in the Immigration and Nationality Act. However, the term also appears in the employer sanctions section of IRCA and is defined in those regulations as "an individual who provides services or labor for an employer for wages or other renumeration" excluding independent contractors and certain qualifying domestic employees. 8 C.F.R. § 274a.1(f).
66. 8 U.S.C. § 1324b(a)(1). The "recruiting and referral for a fee" terminology parallels the language in the employer sanctions portion of IRCA. The regulations promulgated pursuant to the sanctions provision specifically provide that union hiring halls do not engage in "referral for a fee." 8 C.F.R. § 274a(1)(e). The discrimination regulations are silent on this issue.
67. 8 U.S.C. § 1324b(a)(1)(B).
68. *Id.* at § 1324b(a)(2)(C). *See infra* text at notes 92 & 93.
69. *Id.* at § 1324b(a)(3).
70. Title VII applies only to employers who employ fifteen or more workers for at least twenty weeks in the current or previous calendar year. The national origin prohibition of IRCA thus applies to all employers with fewer than fifteen (and more than three) employees, i.e., with four to fourteen employees, to employers with a seasonal work force, and to employers who do not come under the jurisdiction of Title VII for any other reason.
71. 8 U.S.C. § 1324b(a)(3)(B)(i).
72. *Id.* at § 1324b(a)(3)(B)(ii); *see also* Notice by Office of Special Counsel *re* Declaration of Intending Citizen, 53 Fed. Reg. 40,498 (1988).
73. *Id.* at § 1324b(a)(3)(B)(ii).
74. *Id.*
75. 8 C.F.R. § 44.101(c)(2)(ii) as *amended by* 53 Fed. Reg. 48, 248 (Nov. 30, 1988). *See also* 53 Fed. Reg. 9715 (1988).
76. The preamble to the regulations implementing IRCA states that Section 274B does not prohibit discrimination in compensation, promotion or any other terms or conditions of employment other than hiring, firing or recruiting. However, the issue is not free from controversy since the legislative history explicitly asserts that a pay disparity between citizen and alien employees would constitute unlawful discrimi-

nation. *See Joint House-Senate Hearings on Anti-Discrimination Provision of H.R. 3080*, 99th Cong., 1st Sess. (Oct. 9, 1985), at 95 & 101. In addition, practices not explicitly required by IRCA may constitute violations of other laws, such as Title VII.

77. *See United Latin Amer. Cit. v. Pasadena Ind. Sch. Dist.*, 662 F. Supp. 443 (S.D. Tex. 1987). *See generally* EEOC Policy Statement, Feb. 26, 1987.
78. Regulations governing the operation of the Office of Special Counsel are set forth at 28 C.F.R. pt. 44.
79. 8 U.S.C. § 1324b(d)(3); 28 C.F.R. § 44.300(b).
80. The Office of Special Counsel has stated in a letter to the ACLU Immigration Task Force that the principle of equitable tolling governing Title VII charges is also applicable to charges filed under Section 274B. *See generally Zipes v. Trans World Airlines Inc.*, 455 U.S. 385 (1982).
81. *See generally Miller v. Marsh*, 766 F.2d 490 (11th Cir. 1985); *Jennings v. American Postal Workers Union*, 672 F.2d 712 (8th Cir. 1982); *Antonopulos v. Aerojet-General Corp.*, 295 F. Supp. 1390 (E.D. Cal. 1968); *Georgia Power Co. v. EEOC*, 295 F. Supp. 950 (N.D. Ga. 1968).
82. 8 U.S.C. § 1324b(b)(1).
83. 8 U.S.C. § 1324b(e)(3).
84. 8 C.F.R. § 44.302(a)&(b).
85. 8 U.S.C. § 1324b(d)(1); 28 C.F.R. §§ 44.303(a), 44.101(d).
86. 8 U.S.C. § 1324b(d)(2); 28 C.F.R. § 44.303(c)(1).
87. The ninety-day limitations period for filing the ALJ complaint is contained only in the regulations. 28 C.F.R. § 44.303(c)(1)&(2). This period too may be subject to equitable tolling, though the standard may be stricter than for the filing of an administrative charge. *See, e.g., Zipes v. Trans World Airlines Inc.*, 455 U.S. 385, 398 (1982) (ninety-day period for filing Title VII complaint in district court may be tolled); *Baldwin County Welcome Center v. Brown*, 466 U.S. 147 (1984) (same).
88. *See, e.g., Griggs v. Duke Power Co.*, 401 U.S. 424 (1971).
89. Statement by President Ronald Reagan upon signing S. 1200, 22 Weekly Comp. Pres. Doc. 1534 (Nov. 10, 1986) *reprinted in* 1986 U.S. Code Cong. & Admin. News 5649, 5856–1. The statement asserted that Section 274B incorporated only the intentional "disparate treatment" standard of Title VII and not the more potent "disparate impact" basis for liability. The President claimed that the two standards of Title VII were derived from two separate statutory provisions and that the language of Section 274B resembled only the statutory basis for outlawing intentional discrimination. *Compare* 42 U.S.C. §12000e-2(a)(1) *with* § 2000e-2(a)(2).

However, both the premise and the conclusion of the President's statement appear mistaken. First, the only two cases that have explicitly considered the President's assertion, that the disparate impact and disparate treatment standards of Title VII are derived from discrete statutory language, have rejected that view. *See Colby v. J.C. Penney Co. Inc.*, 811 F.2d 1119 (7th Cir. 1987); *Wambheim v. J.C. Penney Co. Inc.*, 705 F.2d 1492 (9th Cir. 1983). Second, the language and structure of Section 274B supports the view that Congress intended to outlaw more than just intentional discrimination. In setting forth prohibited conduct, the statute never mentions intent. The only reference to intentional discrimination in IRCA is in relation to bringing a *private* administrative complaint when the Special Counsel chooses not to act. Thus unintended discriminatory effects give rise to liability in cases where a pattern or practice is proven or where the Special Counsel prosecutes the action. *See United Latin Amer. Cit. v. Pasadena Ind. Sch. Dist.*, 662 F. Supp. 443, 449 n.6 (S.D. Tex. 1987).

90. 52 Fed. Reg. 37,403-5 (Oct. 6, 1987).
91. *See* 8 U.S.C. § 1324b(a)(2)(c); 28 C.F.R. §144.200(b)(iii).
92. 8 U.S.C. § 1324b(a)(4).
93. For example, the Constitution prohibits state laws that impose across-the-board "citizen only" requirements on state or private employment. *See infra* note 106.
94. 8 U.S.C. § 1324b(g)(2)(A).
95. *Id.* at § 1324b(g)(2)(B).
96. *Id.* at § 1324b(h)&(j)(4).
97. *See Christiansburg Garment Co., v. EEOC*, 434 U.S. 412 (1978).
98. 8 U.S.C. § 1324b(i).
99. 2 U.S.C. § 2000e–2(a)(1).
100. *Espinoza v. Farah Manufacturing Co.*, 414 U.S. 86 (1973).
101. 2 U.S.C. § 2000e(b).
102. 2 U.S.C. § 1981 provides:

> All persons within the jurisdiction of the United States shall have the same right in every State and Territory to make and enforce contracts, to sue, be parties, give evidence, and to the full and equal benefit of all laws and proceedings for the security of persons and property as is enjoyed by white citizens, and shall be subject to like punishment, pains, penalties, taxes, licenses, and exactions of every kind, and to no other.

103. *See, e.g., Takahashi v. Fish and Game Commission*, 334 U.S. 410 (1948).
104. *Compare Bhandari v. First National Bank of Commerce*, 829 F.2d

1343 (5th Cir. 1987) *pet. for cert. filed*, No. 87–1293 (Feb. 2, 1988). *See generally Runyon v. McCrary.*, 427 U.S. 160 (1976); *Patterson v. McLean Credit Union*, 805 F.2d 1143 (4th Cir. 1986) *cert. granted* (No. 87–107), *reargument heard on* Oct. 12, 1988.

105. *General Building Contractors Assoc. v. Pennsylvania*, 458 U.S. 375 (1982).
106. *See Truax v. Raich*, 239 U.S. 33 (1915); *Sugarman v. Dougall*, 413 U.S. 634 (1973); *In re Griffiths*, 413 U.S. 717 (1973). *See also Bernal v. Fainter*, 467 U.S. 216 (1984). *But see Cabell v. Chavez-Salido*, 454 U.S. 432 (1982); *Ambach v. Norwick*, 441 U.S. 68 (1979); *Foley v. Connelie*, 435 U.S. 291 (1978).
107. *See Hampton v. Mow Sun Wong*, 426 U.S. 88 (1976).
108. 8 U.S.C. § 1324b(a)(2)(B).
109. *Id. See also* 8 U.S.C. § 1324b(b)(2).
110. *Id.* at § 1324a(e)(1)(D).
111. *Id.* at § 1324b(c)(1).
112. *Id.* at § 1324a(j)&(*l*).
113. *Id.* at § 1324a(*l*)(1)(A)&(B).
114. *Id.* at § 1324b(k)(2)(A)&(B).
115. *Id.* at § 1324b(k)(1).
116. GAO Report (1987). Immigration Reform: *Status of Implementing Employer Sanctions After One Year*, (GAO/GGD–88–14) (Nov. 1987).
117. GAO Report (1988). Immigration Reform: *Status of Implementing Employer Sanctions After Second Year*, (GAO/GGD–892D16) (Nov. 1988).
118. *U.S. Immigration Policy and the National Interest; the Final Report and Recommendations of the Select Commission on Immigration and Refugee Policy* (Mar. 1981), at 72–74.
119. Report of the Select Commission, at 77.
120. Doris Meissner and Demetrious Papademetriou, *The Legalization Countdown: A Third Quarter Assessment* (Feb. 1988), at 111.
121. For a discussion of the numbers who may not have applied, *see* David North and Anna Mary Portz, *Through the Maze: An Interim Report on the Alien Legalization Program*, Mar. 28, 1988, at 46–54.
122. This factor was mentioned in numerous press reports as the May 4, 1988, application deadline approached. See, *e.g.*, stories in the New York Times, Apr. 24, 1988, and the Miami Herald, Apr. 27, 1988.
123. Meissner and Papademetriou, *op. cit.*, at 34–36.
124. Memo from Crystal Williams, American Immigration Lawyers Association, Nov. 17, 1988.

125. Again, this factor was named in press accounts that appeared near the May application deadline.
126. Meissner and Papademetriou, *op. cit.*, at 20–21.
127. Meissner and Papademetriou, at 25–39. Also North and Portz, at 14–20.
128. A memo from Crystal Williams, American Immigration Lawyers Committee, dated Oct. 7, 1988, provides a summary of IRCA Legalization and SAW Litigation.
129. Certain classes of people, defined in various lawsuits, have been given extra time to apply after the May 4, 1988, deadline for application to the amnesty program. *See* memo from Williams on legalization litigation, *op. cit.*
130. *Haitian Refugees v. Meese*, No. 88–1066 (S.D. Fla. 1988). *See supra* memo from Crystal Williams, Oct. 7, 1988, for a summary of this and other litigation dealing with SAWs issues.
131. IRCA § 202(a)&(b).
132. IRCA § 203.
133. *Catholic Social Services v. Meese*, No. S-86-1343-LKK (E.D. Calif., 9th Cir. 1987, 1988).
134. *LULAC v. INS*, No. 87-4757-WDK (C.D. Cal. 1988).
135. *Ayuda v. Meese*, 687 F. Supp. 650 (D.D.C. 1988), *vacated for lack of jurisdiciton*, No. 88-5226 (D.C.C., July 18, 1989); *id.* note.
136. For example, a lawsuit has been filed in Washington State that deals with "known to the Government" issues similar to those mentioned above. This lawsuit applies only to INS' Northern and Western Region. *Legalization Assistance Project v. INS*, No. C88-379 (W.D. Wash. 1988).
137. *Zambrano v. INS*, No. S-88-455 EJG-M (E.D. Cal. 1988).
138. *Hernandez v. Meese*, No. S-88-385LKK (E.D. Cal. 1988).
139. *Doe & Roe v. Nelson*, No. 88-C-6987 (N.D. Ill. 1988).
140. IRCA § 201(b)(1)(A).
141. Letter to Raymond Penn, INS Assistant Commissioner for Legalization, from the Ad Hoc Coalition for IRCA Implementation (draft) dated Nov. 18, 1988.
142. 54 Fed. Reg. 13, 360 (codified at 8 C.F.R. § 2458).
143. IRCA § 201(b)(3)(A); 53 Fed. Reg. 43, 9993 (codified at 8 C.F.R. § 2458).
144. IRCA § 201(b)(1); 8 C.F.R. § 245a.3(b)(1)–(4).
145. The most important of these, *Zambrano v. INS*, is now in the Ninth Circuit Court of Appeals.
146. 8 C.F.R. § 245a.3(f)(4).
147. IRCA § 201(h).
148. 8 C.F.R. § 245a.3(b)(iii)(A).

149. 8 C.F.R. § 245a.3(b)(4)(iii)(B).
150. 8 C.F.R. § 245a.3(b)(4)(iv).
151. 8 C.F.R. § 245a.1(s).
152. 8 C.F.R. § 245a.3(b)(4)(iv).
153. IRCA § 201(b)(1)(D)(ii).
154. 8 C.F.R. § 245a.3(b)(4)(ii).
155. IRCA § 201(b)(2)(C).
156. 8 C.F.R. § 245a.3(i).
157. IRCA § 201(b)(2).
158. 8 C.F.R. § 245a.3(h).
159. IRCA § 201(c)(5)(A).
160. IRCA § 201(c)(6).
161. 8 C.F.R. § 245a.3(m)(1).
162. IRCA § 302(a)(2).
163. IRCA § 302(a)(4).
164. IRCA § 302(a)(4).
165. IRCA § 303(d)(5)(A).
166. IRCA § 303(d)(5)(B).

III

The Right to Refugee Protection

The United States has a tradition of providing protection to those fleeing persecution. Hundreds of thousands of refugees have been admitted into the United States since World War II. In 1980, legislation was enacted that, for the first time, defines the term "refugee" and provides comprehensive procedures for granting protection to individuals seeking refuge in the United States.

Who is a "refugee"?

The Refugee Act of 1980 defines the term "refugee." Under the Act, a refugee is a person who is outside of his or her country of nationality (or last habitual residence for a stateless person), who has been persecuted in the past, or who has a well-founded fear of future persecution on account of race, religion, nationality, membership in a particular social group, or political opinion.[1] The refugee definition comes from international law in the form of a treaty to which the United States is a party.[2] If an individual cannot meet the refugee definition, then he or she is not entitled to protection in the United States.

What is "persecution"?

Persecution is ordinarily a threat to an individual's life or freedom. Under certain circumstances, discrimination or deprivation of basic rights can constitute persecution.[3] For example, depriving one of the ability to earn a living, to receive education, or to have a normal family life can constitute persecution, even if the deprivation does not rise to the level of a threat to life or freedom. However, more than harassment is required to constitute persecution.

Ordinarily, persecution must come from a government source. Under certain circumstances, those forces that a government either cannot or will not control can be "agents" of persecution for purposes of granting refugee protection.[4] Such agents could include death squads or even insurgent groups not susceptible to government control.[5]

Persecution can be economic in form. For example, economic measures such as confiscation of property or severe restrictions on the ability to earn a living, if imposed for the requisite reasons, can constitute persecution.[6] However, private disputes, general economic hardship, and lack of safety caused by civil war to innocent civilians are not generally considered forms of persecution.

Also, persecution can be based on prosecution and criminal punishment by a government, if such punishment is unusually harsh and imposed for the requisite reasons.

Does past persecution or the prospect of future persecution always warrant refugee protection?

No. Past persecution gives rise to a presumption that the individual in question will be persecuted in the future.[7] Also, for an individual to be entitled to refugee protection, the persecution in question must be on account of race, religion, nationality, membership in a particular social group, or political opinion. Two basic concepts are involved—group membership and belief. Yet, merely being a member of a race, religion, nationality, or social group is generally not sufficient to warrant refugee protection. The individual must show a connection between himself or herself and the possibility of persecution.[8] Under certain circumstances, where a group has been singled out by a persecutor for abuse, mere membership may be sufficient for purposes of refugee protection. The concept of social group is considered to be a flexible one, taking into account the peculiarities of a persecutor.[9] Such groups can include family, women, or voluntary associations.[10]

In terms of belief (religion and political opinion), it is not absolutely necessary that the individual have acted on the belief previously.[11] However, the belief must be one that the authorities in the home country will not tolerate, and it must be held with sufficient strength so that it is likely to be expressed in the future even if it has not been expressed in the past.[12] Under certain circumstances, refugee protection is warranted where the authorities impute a political opinion to an individual, even if the person does not possess the actual belief.[13]

Is only a fear of persecution required for protection?

No. The refugee's fear of return must be "well-founded."[14] This means that the fear must be plausible and correspond to conditions in the home country.[15] The treatment by the authorities in the home country of individuals who are similarly situated, including family, friends or peers, is a useful indication of whether a refugee's fear is "well-founded."[16]

If possible, a refugee should seek to document and corroborate his or her claim, for example, with written statements from others, in order to persuade the authorities of the need for protection. Most refugees, however, arrive without such evidence or documentation. All they can present are their own statements, which they should give clearly and with specific detail.

When may a refugee be granted asylum in the United States?

Individuals who meet the requirements for refugee status may be granted asylum as long as they are physically present in the United States and without regard to the nature of their immigration status.[17] They can be in valid nonimmigrant status, have overstayed their permitted stay in the United States or even have entered the United States surreptitiously by crossing the border without documentation or with fraudulent documentation. Working without authorization generally does not diminish an asylum claim.

However, just because one meets the refugee definition, that does not mean that the individual must be granted asylum. Asylum is a discretionary remedy that involves an assessment of whether the individual is worthy of refugee protection.[18] Generally, those who have a well-founded fear of persecution should be granted asylum. But if the individual in question has persecuted others in the past, committed a serious nonpolitical crime abroad or a particularly serious crime within the United States, or is firmly resettled in a third country, then the authorities may consider him or her unworthy of refugee protection.[19] A refugee is "firmly resettled" when he or she has obtained residence or the basic human rights of nationals in the country of asylum.[20] Other grounds of unworthiness could include, for example, engaging in "terrorist" activities on behalf of antigovernment guerrillas in the home country (e.g., bombing civilians or other wanton behavior in disregard of the lives of innocent noncombatants).[21]

How does a refugee apply for asylum in the United States?

A refugee applies for asylum by submitting an application form (I-589) to the office of the local district director of the Immigration and Naturalization Service (INS) with a biographic information form (G-325A), a fingerprint chart (FD-258), and any supporting materials.[22] If the claim is denied, there is no appeal. But the claim may be re-presented to an immigration judge in exclusion or deportation proceedings.[23]

If the refugee has already been placed under exclusion or deportation proceedings, then the claim is presented to the immigration judge in those proceedings.[24] Thereafter, the claim is reviewed in connection with the final order of exclusion or deportation.[25] Review occurs administratively at the Board of Immigration Appeals near Washington, D.C., and judicially thereafter in the appropriate federal court.[26]

The burden of proof is generally on the applicant for asylum to show entitlement to refugee protection.[27] No filing fee is required. The Department of State's Bureau of Human Rights and Humanitarian Affairs has an opportunity to present its views in each asylum case in the United States. Where the views of the Department of State were given previously to a district director, they need not be solicited again by an immigration judge.

Can a refugee work in the United States or travel abroad while he or she awaits recognition by the U.S. authorities?

Yes. While an asylum claim is pending, a refugee is to receive employment authorization by the INS, as long as the claim is "nonfrivolous."[28] Also, "advance parole" can be granted by INS in order to permit a refugee to travel abroad to a third country for humanitarian reasons (for example, to visit an ailing family member) while a claim is pending.[29]

Even if denied asylum, can an alien in the United States avoid return to the home country?

Yes. A refugee who establishes that he or she would face a threat to life or freedom in the home country can seek, in addition to asylum, withholding of exclusion or deportation from an immigration judge.[30] The standard of proof is higher than for asylum, requiring proof of a probability of serious persecution, but unlike asylum, the remedy of withholding is mandatory and not discretionary.[31] If the criteria are met, then the alien cannot be returned to the particular country, at least until the circumstances of the individual or home country have changed so as to remove the risk of persecution.

A refugee who has persecuted another, committed a serious nonpolitical offense abroad or particularly serious crime within the United States, or who jeopardizes national security, is not eligible for withholding.[32]

To determine if a crime is serious, it is necessary to take into account the nature of the persecution feared by the individual, as well as any aggravating or mitigating circumstances.[33] Particularly serious persecution, such as a threat to life or freedom, would require that the crime in question be extremely grave before the individual is deprived of refugee protection.[34]

Whether an offense committed abroad is political in character is determined by taking into account the motives of the individual and the government and the political context in which the offense is committed. For example, a refugee who destroys property or injures or even kills someone in the course of an escape from persecution would generally be considered to have committed but a political offense and therefore should not be deprived of protection in the United States.[35]

Do asylum seekers face political problems in coming to the United States?

Yes. Refugees coming to the United States are frequently subjected to measures designed to curb illegal immigration, such as the Haitian interdiction program, which involves patrols by U.S. Coast Guard cutters that intercept Haitian and unflagged vessels on the high seas, examine those on board for immigration papers, and turn back those Haitians without valid travel documents.[36] More than twenty thousand have been returned to Haiti under the interdiction program. Fewer than ten have been permitted to come to the United States to pursue asylum.

Asylum seekers are also sometimes held in administrative detention in the United States. Refugees who arrive at the border without valid passports or visas are detained unless they are old, young, sick, pregnant or beneficiaries of approved relative petitions filed by close American relatives seeking to accord them immigration status. Others who are apprehended by INS in the United States are held because they cannot afford to post the bonds necessary to gain release, even if they are eligible for release consideration. More than one thousand asylum seekers are held at any one time in detention in the United States.[37]

Probably the most pervasive problem that asylum seekers face in the United States is the differential treatment of various nationalities.[38] Since 1980, approximately 25 percent of those who have applied for asylum have been approved by the authorities. However, those who fled from Eastern Europe, the Soviet Union, or other Communist or Communist-dominated countries have experienced 50 to 80 percent approval levels. Those who have fled from regimes closely allied to the United States, such as El Salvador, or from countries where the U.S. authorities seek to deter immigration, such as Haiti, have 0 to 5 percent approval levels.[39] Foreign policy and immigration restriction impact differentially, which makes it harder in practice for some refugees to receive protection in the United States.

Can a refugee who has been granted asylum travel abroad?

Yes. Asylees can receive a refugee travel document from the INS. An application for the document must be submitted prior to the trip and a fee is required.

Can a refugee who is granted asylum obtain permanent status in the United States?

Yes. An individual who has been granted asylum, and who has been physically present thereafter for a year in the United States, is eligible to apply for permanent resident status. Visas for such status are limited to five thousand per year,[40] and there is generally a backlog of such applications. However, after being granted permanent resident status, the individual is thereafter eligible to apply for citizenship under the laws of naturalization.

Can family of asylees receive status?

Yes. Immediate family can accompany, or follow to join, those granted asylum without the need to request asylum independently. Generally, the family relationship must have existed at the time the application was granted.

Can refugees seeking asylum in the United States obtain legal assistance?

Refugees have no right to appointed counsel under U.S. immigration law, including applicants for political asylum. However, voluntary agencies, churches, and legal groups, including volunteer lawyer organizations, provide assistance either free of charge or for a nominal fee. Individuals can contact the branch office of the United Nations High Commissioner for Refugees in Washington ([202] 387-8546) in order to receive information about legal assistance programs in their locale.

Can refugees abroad be admitted to the United States?

Yes. Under the Refugee Act of 1980, Congress and the Administration each year consult to establish worldwide and regional ceilings for the admission of refugees from abroad. Generally, these are refugees admitted from a third country, although occasionally they may be admitted directly from the country of origin, including, for example, Vietnam, Cuba, or the Soviet Union. Applications are made by completing and filing forms I-590 and G-225C with the appropriate voluntary agency or United States embassy. Interviews are conducted thereafter by employees of the Immigration and Naturalization Service. There is no formal administrative appeal of adverse decisions nor any opportunity for judicial review. The burden is on the individual to show entitlement to refugee status.[41]

Refugees approved for admission into the United States can, a year after admission, become permanent residents in the United States with the right to naturalize thereafter.[42] Refugees, unlike those who seek asylum in the United States, have rights to certain social benefits upon arrival in the United States.[43] These benefits include language training and job placement programs.

Are there any alternatives for an alien who is not a refugee to seek admission to the United States on humanitarian grounds?

Yes. An alien who is not eligible for refugee admission from abroad may nonetheless seek "parole" into the United States on humanitarian grounds.[44] Such grounds include the need for medical treatment, family reunification, or avoidance of extreme hardship. Application for immigration parole is made to the Central Office of the Immigration and Naturalization Service in Washington, D.C. The remedy is extremely limited. Only a few hundred individuals each year are "paroled" into the United States on such humanitarian grounds.

NOTES

1. Pub. L. No. 96–212, 94 Stat. 102 (1980) (hereinafter cited as the Refugee Act of 1980). *See INS v. Cardoza-Fonseca*, 480 U.S. ____, 107 S. Ct. 1207 (1987).
2. The Protocol relating to the Status of Refugees, 19 U.S.T. 6223, T.I.A.S. No. 6577, 606 U.N.T.S. 267.
3. *See* G. S. Goodwin-Gill, *The Refugee in International Law* (1983), at 41.
4. *Maldonado-Cruz v. U.S. Department of I&N*, ____ F.2d ____, No. 88–7036 (9th Cir. Aug. 24, 1989); *Rosa v. INS*, 440 F.2d 100 (1st Cir. 1971); *In re Eusaph*, 10 I. & N. Dec. 453 (BIA 1964), *In re Diaz*, 10 I. & N. Dec. 199 (BIA 1963).
5. *See, e.g., McMullen v. INS*, 658 F.2d 1312, 1315 (9th Cir. 1981). *See also Bolanos-Hernandez v. INS*, 767 F.2d 1287 (9th Cir. 1984) (assertion of neutrality can be basis for persecution).
6. *Dunat v. Hurney*, 297 F.2d 744 (3d Cir. 1962); *Kasravi v. INS*, 400 F.2d 675 (9th Cir. 1968).
7. Office of the United Nations High Commissioner for Refugees, *Handbook on Procedures and Criteria for Determining Refugee Status Under the 1951 Convention and 1967 Protocol relating to the Status of Refugees*, Geneva (1979), para. 45 (hereinafter cited as *Handbook*).
8. *See* A. C. Helton, *Manual on Representing Asylum Applicants*, at 6. (The *Manual* can be ordered from the Lawyers Committee for Human Rights, 330 Seventh Avenue, New York, N.Y. 10001, ([212] 629-6170.) Opportunities for protection sometimes vary for certain nationality groups. *See, e.g., Manual for Representing Cubans in Gaining Release and Immigration Status* (1989) and *Manual on Gaining Immigration Status for Chinese Nationals in the United States* (1989), also available from the Lawyers Committee.
9. Helton, *Persecution on Account of Membership in a Social Group as a Basis for Refugee Status*, 15 Colum. Hum. Rts. L. Rev. 39 (1983).
10. *Id.*
11. *Handbook*, para. 82.
12. *Id.*
13. *See Maldonado-Cruz v. U.S. Department of I&N*, *supra* note 4; *Hernandez-Ortiz v. INS*, 777 F.2d 509 (9th Cir. 1985).

14. Pub. L. No. 82-414, 66 Stat 163 (1952) (codified at 8 U.S.C. § 1101–1525); 8 U.S.C. § 1101(a)(42)(A).
15. *Handbook*, para. 42.
16. *Id.*
17. 8 U.S.C. § 1158(a).
18. 8 U.S.C. § 1159(b); *see Matter of Pula*, Interim Decision 3033 (BIA 1987), *Matter of Salim*, Interim Decision 2922 (BIA 1982).
19. 8 U.S.C. § 1182.
20. 8 C.F.R. § 208.14; *Matter of Soleimani*, Interim Decision 3118 (BIA 1989).
21. *See McMullen v. INS*, 658 F.2d 1312 (9th Cir. 1981).
22. 8 C.F.R. § 208.2. Fingerprint charts are not required for asylum applicants in detention.
23. 8 C.F.R. §§ 208.8(c) and 208.9.
24. 8 C.F.R. § 208.9.
25. 8 C.F.R. § 3.1(b).
26. 8 C.F.R. § 208.3(b).
27. 8 C.F.R. § 208.5.
28. 8 C.F.R. § 274a.12(c)(8).
29. 8 U.S.C. § 1182(d)(4).
30. 8 U.S.C. § 1253(h).
31. *INS v. Stevic*, 467 U.S. 407 (1984).
32. 8 U.S.C. § 1253(h)(2).
33. *See supra* Goodwin-Gill, at 25.
34. *Id.*
35. *See supra McMullen v. INS.*
36. Helton, *Political Asylum Under the 1980 Refugee Act: An Unfulfilled Promise*, 17 U. Mich. J. L. Ref. 243, 252 (1984).
37. Helton, *The Legality of Detaining Refugees in the United States*, 14 N.Y.U. Rev. L. & Soc. Change 353 (1986).
38. Helton, *Political Asylum Under the 1980 Refugee Act: An Unfulfilled Promise*, at 253.
39. *Id.*
40. 8 U.S.C. § 1159(2)(b).
41. 8 C.F.R. § 208.8(d).
42. 8 U.S.C. §§ 1159(a)(1) and (2).
43. Refugee Act of 1980, § 412(b)(1)(B)(2).
44. 8 U.S.C. § 1157(b).

IV

The Rights of Aliens to Enter the United States, and in Exclusion Proceedings

Of all the mighty nations in the East or in the West
This glorious Yankee nation is the greatest and the best;
We have room for all creation and our banner is unfurled,
Here's a general invitation to the people of the world.

Come along, come along, make no delay,
Come from every nation, come from every way.

Nineteenth-Century ballad

During its first one hundred years as a nation, the United States encouraged immigration. No laws were enacted by the federal government affecting the right of aliens to enter the country. The laws adopted by the states were designed for the most part to promote the settlement of immigrants. The first federal laws to exclude aliens, beginning in 1875, were "qualitative" restrictions to bar convicts and prostitutes.[1] In 1882, Congress added "any convict, lunatic, idiot or any person unable to take care of himself or herself without becoming a public charge" to the list of aliens not eligible to enter.[2] Other grounds for exclusion were added through the years to cover aliens described as having physical, mental, and moral defects; as advocating subversive doctrines; as suffering economic disqualifications; or as being illiterate.[3]

In 1882, Congress for the first time excluded aliens on the basis of their country of origin. First, the Chinese were barred.[4] Subsequently the Japanese were barred,[5] and thereafter Congress created an "Asiatic barred zone" designed to exclude all Asians from immigrating to the U.S., with the exception of those from certain areas of Afghanistan and Russia and natives of Persia.[6]

Restrictions limiting the total number of immigrants to be admitted to the U.S. were first tentatively adopted in 1921 and were keyed to a system of quotas for each country, based upon the "national origins" of the population in the United States.[7] Under this system, the number of aliens who could immigrate to the United States was limited to 3 percent of the U.S. residents of that nationality living in the country in 1910. The clear intent of the 1921 law was to preserve the then-existing ethnic makeup of the United States by limiting immigration as much as possible to persons from Western and Northern Europe. The law also imposed a numeric limit of 350,000 on the total number of immigrants from the Eastern Hemisphere. The 1921 law virtually eliminated immigration from Mediterranean and Eastern European countries, which since the 1880s had been the source of a large number of immigrants to the United States.

In 1924, the National Origins Quota system was made permanent.[8] It imposed a ceiling of 150,000 for Eastern Hemisphere immigrants, established quotas for each nationality group at 2 percent of the total number of persons of that nationality residing in the U.S. in 1890, and imposed a complete prohibition on Japanese immigration. In 1952, Congress enacted the McCarran-Walter Act, known as the Immigration and Nationality Act of 1952, which consolidated previous immigration laws into a single unified statute.[9] The 1952 Act preserved the national origins quota system, repealed the Japanese exclusion provisions, established a small quota for Asians, expanded the ideological and political grounds as base for denying entry, and established a system for immigration giving preference to family members of citizens and legal residents and to workers with job skills in short supply.

In 1965, Congress passed a bill significantly amending the 1952 Act. The Immigration and Nationality Act Amendments of 1965[10] finally abolished the national origins formula. In its place, the law established a seven-category preference system but imposed a limit of 20,000 persons per country with subquotas of 200 persons for a colony and an overall ceiling of 170,000 from Eastern Hemisphere countries. It also, for the first time, imposed a limit of 120,000 on Western Hemisphere immigration, with no individual country limit.

In 1976, the colony subquota was increased to 600, but the 20,000 per country limit and the preference system were applied to the Western Hemisphere as well.[11] In 1978, the hemisphere limits were combined into a single 290,000-person worldwide limit, with the same preference system and per country limits applied in both hemispheres.[12] In 1980, the Congress also passed the Refugee Act of 1980 to bring American refugee policy into conformity with international law and to provide a "permanent and systematic procedure" for admitting refugees to the United States.[13] The Refugee Act of 1980 also reduced the worldwide annual limit on preference immigration to 270,000.[14] Persons who qualify as "immediate relatives" of United States citizens are eligible to immigrate without regard to country ceilings or hemisphere quotas.[15]

In addition to the overall quotas governing the admission of aliens who wish to immigrate to the United States as permanent residents, a statutory scheme exists for determining an individual alien's right to enter the United States (either as an immigrant or a nonimmigrant), the procedures that must be followed for admission, and the grounds and methods for challenging unfavorable decisions.

Who may come to the United States?

Any citizen or national of the United States may enter this country as a matter of constitutional right.[16]

A person who is not a citizen or a national, that is, an alien, may enter the United States only if he or she meets the requirements of the immigration laws and regulations.[17] Aliens are classified as either "nonimmigrants" or "immigrants."[18] The rules governing entry to the United States are different for each of these two groups, but an alien is presumed to be an immigrant unless he can prove that he is a nonimmigrant.[19]

Who decides whether an alien can be admitted to the United States?

Any one (or several) of the following five government agencies may be involved: the Immigration and Naturalization Service, which is part of the Department of Justice; the Department of State; the Department of Labor; the Public Health Service of the Department of Health and Human Services; and the Department of Agriculture.

The Immigration and Naturalization Service (INS) decides whether aliens are eligible to receive preferences under the immigration laws and controls the admission of all aliens into the United States. The Department of State, acting through American consuls (usually at American embassies) in foreign countries, determines whether to issue immigrant or nonimmigrant visas to aliens who are applying to enter the United States from abroad. The Department of Labor, acting through the

Employment and Training Administration is responsible for the issuance of Alien Employment Certifications required for aliens whose application for admission is based upon job skills and a purported shortage of domestic workers. The Public Health Service is responsible for ensuring that aliens meet the physical and mental qualifications for entry to the U.S.

Which aliens are nonimmigrants?

A nonimmigrant is an alien who seeks to enter the United States for a temporary period or purpose. The length of time the alien is permitted to stay depends upon the purpose of the visit.

Nonimmigrants include tourists and other visitors for business or pleasure, students, exchange scholars, diplomats and other representatives of foreign governments, employees of international governmental organizations, foreign media representatives, crewmen on vessels and airlines, certain temporary workers, aliens in transit to other countries, and aliens engaged to marry United States citizens, provided the marriage occurs within ninety days after entry.[20]

What must an alien do to enter the United States as a nonimmigrant?

An alien must show that he or she is eligible for a nonimmigrant visa and that he or she is not excludable on any of the grounds that bar entry to the U.S. Most nonimmigrant visas require only an application to the American consulate in the foreign country where the alien lives. If the applicant applies in a country of which he or she is not a resident, the consul may request a background report from the consulate in the country of the alien's residence or refer the visa applicant to the U.S. consulate in the country of residence.[21] Certain types of nonimmigrant visas, including those based on temporary employment in the United States or on engagement to an American citizen, require prior approval by INS of a "petition" submitted by the sponsoring employer or the intending citizen spouse.[22] Visitors coming as tourists must show sufficient financial means to visit the United States and must establish their intent to leave at the expiration of their authorized period of stay. A consul might, for example, require not only evidence of roundtrip travel plans but proof of a "compelling reason" for any nonimmigrant visa applicant to return to his or her home country. Business visitors must establish their business affiliation and the purpose of their trip. Students must have been admitted to an approved educational institution in the United States and must have evidence that they can maintain themselves in the United States without working.[23] Bona fide student applicants who have not yet been admitted to, or made a decision regarding, a school may be permitted to enter as a nonimmigrant "tourist/prospective student" for the purpose of selecting a school. Exchange visitors must have the sponsorship of an approved exchange visitor program.

An alien who can meet these requirements for issuance of a nonimmigrant visa may nonetheless be prohibited from entering if he or she is inadmissible under any of the grounds for exclusion.[24] If a nonimmigrant visa applicant requires the waiver of a ground of inadmissibility, as discussed below, the waiver must be recommended by the consul or the Secretary of State to the Attorney General. Certain grounds for exclusion may not be waivable.[25]

How long is a visa valid?

At the time of issuance, the U.S. consul will determine the number of times a visa may be used to enter the United States and the dates during which the visa is valid. This may vary from a visa that is valid for only a single entry during a short period of time (such as a week) to a visa that is valid for unlimited entries for an indefinite period of time. If a visa has an expiration date, that determines the last day on which the alien may enter the United States. The date does *not* specify how long the alien may remain in the U.S. once he or she has successfully entered.

Does possession of a visa issued by a U.S. consulate guarantee the alien's admission into the U.S.?

Every alien seeking to enter the country is subject to "inspection" by an INS examiner at the port of entry. The examiner must be satisfied that the alien continues to meet the requirements of the visa and is not excludable under any of the statutory grounds. If there is any doubt, the INS may ask the alien "voluntarily" to withdraw the application to be admitted to the United States and to leave immediately;

otherwise the INS may detain the alien and initiate exclusion proceedings.

How long may a nonimmigrant alien remain in the United States?

The initial period of authorized stay is determined by the INS examiner at the U.S. port of entry and is not affected by the expiration date of the visa issued by the consul. The length of time authorized depends on the type of visa that the alien has. Students are normally allowed to remain as long as they are pursuing full-time studies in the program for which they were admitted. Tourists usually are authorized to stay six months.

May an alien extend a stay in the United States as a nonimmigrant?

If a nonimmigrant alien wishes to prolong a stay, he or she may seek an extension of the authorized period of stay or seek to change to some other nonimmigrant or even immigrant status. In either case, the alien will have to seek INS permission, and the INS will designate the length of any additional authorized period of stay in this country.

In order to be eligible to apply for an extension of stay or a change of nonimmigrant status, an alien must continue to meet the requirements of his or her visa or meet the requirements of the new visa that is being requested. The alien will also have to persuade the INS that he or she still intends to return to the residence abroad at the end of the authorized period of stay. To be eligible for a change of status or extension of stay, the alien may not have violated any of the limitations and terms of the visa on which he or she entered the United States, and the alien's current authorized period of stay in the United States must not have expired.

Applications for extension of stay specify when such applications must be submitted, typically fifteen to sixty days before the current authorized stay expires. The alien must also be in possession of a passport valid for at least six months beyond the expiration date of the requested extension.

As with the initial authorized period of stay, an extension may last beyond the expiration date of the underlying visa.

Which aliens are immigrants?

Immigrants are aliens who seek to enter the United States to live as permanent residents.[26]

What qualifications must an alien establish in order to enter the United States as an immigrant?

To enter the United States as an immigrant, an alien must show both that he or she is eligible for an immigrant visa and that he or she is not excludable under any of the grounds that bar aliens from entering the United States. The initial eligibility determination is reached by deciding whether the applicant fits within one of the categories of aliens who qualify as immigrants under the Immigration Act. Under the law, the categories of eligibility fit into three general areas:

1. Relationship to a citizen or legal permanent resident of the U.S.
2. Occupation or job skills and a sponsoring U.S. employer
3. Political refugee

Some categories permit an unlimited number of qualified aliens to enter each year. However, the majority of categories, called "preferences," operate pursuant to a strict quota system that limits the total number of immigrant visas that may be issued each year, the number of visas that may be issued to persons of any one country, and the total number that can be issued pursuant to any single preference category.

The following category of aliens may enter as immigrants without regard to any numerical limitation:

1. Immediate Relatives: Spouses, unmarried children under twenty-one, and parents of adult (over twenty-one) United States citizens. A child must be under twenty-one and unmarried.[27] The eligibility criteria must be satisfied throughout the visa processing procedure. A stepchild, an illegitimate or legitimated child, or an adopted child may all qualify as children if certain conditions are met.[28] Until 1986, an illegitimate child could claim benefits through its natural mother but not through its father unless the child had been legitimated. Illegitimate children who have or have had a bona fide parent-child relationship with their natural father are recognized as children for immigration purposes.[29]

2. Returning lawful permanent residents, specified former citizens of the United States, certain aliens employed or formerly employed by the United States government, and a limited number of other aliens designated as "special immigrants."[30]

All other aliens, who must qualify under the "preference" categories, are subject to the annual quotas currently set at a worldwide total of 270,000, and a per country total of 20,000. Dependent areas and colonies have an annual quota of 5,000. (Hemisphere quotas, which previously limited the total number of immigrants from the Eastern and Western hemisphere, were eliminated in 1978.)

To qualify for an immigrant visa, these aliens must prove that they fit within one of the following preference categories:

First Preference: Unmarried, adult sons and daughters of United States citizens;[31] 54,000 annual total.

Second Preference: Spouses and unmarried sons and daughters of any age of aliens who have been lawfully admitted to the United States as permanent residents;[32] 70,200 annual total plus any unused first-preference allocations.

Third Preference: "Members of the professions" or aliens who "because of their exceptional ability in the sciences or arts" will substantially benefit the national economy, cultural interests or welfare of the United States, and whose services in the professions, sciences, or arts are sought by an employer in the United States;[33] 27,000 annual total.

INS requires a finding by the Employment and Training Administration of the Department of Labor that employment of an alien seeking a visa under this preference category will not "adversely affect the wages and working conditions" of workers in the United States.[34]

Fourth Preference: Married sons and daughters of United States citizens;[35] 27,000 annual total plus any unused allocations from the first three preferences.

Fifth Preference: Brothers and sisters of adult (over twenty-one years old) United States citizens;[36] 64,000 annual total plus unused allocations from the first four preferences.

Sixth Preference: Immigrants who "are capable of performing specified skilled or unskilled labor" for which there is a shortage of employable persons in the United States;[37] 27,000 annual total.

The Department of Labor must find that a shortage of employable and willing persons exists in the United States and that the alien's employment will not adversely affect the conditions of workers in the United States.[38]

Seventh Preference: If the total annual worldwide quotas have not been used by preference applications, the remaining number is available to "other qualified immigrants" strictly in the chronological order in which they apply.[39] This preference category has long been unavailable because of oversubscription of the other preference categories. The Immigration Reform and Control Act of 1986 provided for 10,000 such visas to be made available to nonpreference immigrants, on a one-time only basis, with availability based on the order of application after November 6, 1986. The category was immediately oversubscribed and visas were issued in two allotments of 5,000 each in 1987 and 1988. Nonpreference visas are again unavailable.[40]

Are spouses and children of immigrants counted under the numerical limitations for each category?

The spouses and children of qualifying immigrants are, in most cases, entitled to immigrant visas as "derivative beneficiaries" who are "accompanying" or "following to join" the principal immigrant.[41] However, each visa issued to a spouse or child is counted against the country and worldwide total.

What steps must an alien take in order to be admitted to the United States as an immigrant?

To apply for an immigrant visa, a relative or employer must file a "visa petition" with the Immigration and Naturalization Service (INS) to prove that the alien has the requisite family relationship or job offer and skills to be eligible for admission either as an immediate relative or under the preference system.

For those aliens whose visa petition is based on employment, the INS must normally receive an alien employment certification from the Employment and Training Administration (ETA) of the Labor Department before a visa petition can be approved.

The filing of the visa petition with the INS or the filing of an application for the alien employment certification determines the alien's "priority date." That priority date determines the order in which visas will be issued under the preference category quota system. Certain preference categories can have waiting times of many months and even years, depending upon the category and the home country of the applicant.

If the INS approves the petition, the alien and the American consulate in the alien's home country are notified. If the alien is already in the United States and is eligible for "adjustment of status," he or she may obtain permanent resident status through the local INS office, thereby obviating the need to return to the American consulate in the alien's home country. If, as is usually the case, processing is to occur at an overseas American consulate, the alien must prove to a consular official that he or she qualifies as an immigrant and is not excludable under any of the grounds barring entry into the United States. The visa application will not be processed until shortly before the priority date is current, i.e., until a visa is available for the alien applicant. Even at that point (or if the alien qualifies as an "immediate relative" and is eligible independent of any quotas), there may still be a substantial wait while the application is processed and police records are checked. If the alien has previously resided in the United States, an FBI check, which normally takes approximately sixty days, will be required.

How does the INS decide whether to approve a visa petition based on family relationships?

The petition must be filed by the qualifying relative at the INS district office in the area where the qualifying relative ("petitioner") lives.[42] Petitions by parents, sons, daughters, and siblings are usually approved on the basis of supporting documents—showing the family relationship—that are submitted with the petition. However, a petition by a spouse based on a marriage may require personal interviews and close questioning of each spouse to determine whether the marriage is bona fide or whether it was entered into for the purpose of evading the immigration laws. Questioning may include interviews of each spouse about the marriage ceremony, how the couple met, their living arrangements, the sharing of property and income, etc. If the examiner is suspicious, more detailed questioning may follow, and the case may be referred to the investigations branch of the district INS office. INS investigators may subject the couple to separate interrogation, ask about intimate details of the couple's life and living arrangements, and visit places of work and residence.

In a number of court decisions, the INS has been enjoined from asking certain types of questions.[43] In one case, applicable to the New York District, the INS stipulated that it would implement a series of procedural safeguards for the alien and the spouse in the conduct of "marriage fraud" interviews.[44]

What standards govern INS determinations of the validity of a marriage?

A bona fide marriage is a prerequisite to obtaining any immigration benefit through a marital relationship. Initially, the INS determines whether the marriage constitutes a legal marriage under the laws of the place of celebration. Secondly, the law provides that a marriage is not valid if it is determined "to have been entered into for the purpose of evading the immigration laws."[45] A marriage is valid if the "two parties have undertaken to establish a life together and assume certain duties and obligations."[46] Until recently, the INS also required that a marriage be "viable." After a series of court decisions, the INS abandoned the viability standard.[47]

Even a valid marriage does not result in automatic approval of the visa petition. For example, if the alien has ever engaged in marriage fraud in the past, a visa petition will not be approved.[48]

Does it matter if the marriage between a citizen and alien occurs during the pendency of deportation proceedings?

Section 5 of the 1986 Immigration Marriage Fraud Amendments (IMFA)[49] provides that a visa petition based on a marriage that occurred during the pendency of administrative or judicial proceedings to determine the admissibility of an alien may not be approved unless the alien has first resided outside the United States for two years.[50] This prohibition applies to every marriage that is entered into during the pendency of proceedings, without regard to the validity of the marriage. The prohibition does not apply if the marriage occurs before the proceedings commence or after the proceedings are completed. Thus, an alien who is in proceedings and intends to marry a citizen (or permanent resident) should wait until after proceedings have terminated (usually by the alien's departure from the United States) before entering into the marriage.

This provision has been subject to numerous lawsuits on the grounds that it penalizes the citizen's and alien's exercise of the fundamental constitutional right to marry, that it imposes an irrebuttable presumption of fraud on every marriage that occurs during proceedings, and that it irrationally distinguishes between marriages that occur before or after proceedings and those that occur during the pendency of such proceedings. To date, none of the challenges have been successful, though appeals are pending, and one court has denied a government motion to dismiss.[51]

How does an alien obtain an alien employment certification from the ETA?

In all cases, an alien is required to have a job offer from a prospective employer. For those designated professional occupations for which shortages have been established or for aliens who have exceptional ability in the sciences or arts, who are engaged in religious occupations, or who are executives or specialists transferred to the U.S. by international firms and organizations, alien employment certifications are automatic under regulations of the Employment and Training Administration of the Department of Labor. For all other aliens seeking permanent residence based upon their employment, employers must first seek to obtain qualified domestic workers by means of recruitment efforts through the various state employment services and other means, including advertising. The documentation of these recruitment efforts is forwarded to the regional office of the ETA for review.

A certification will be issued for an alien only if the ETA finds that sufficient workers are not available in the United States to perform the intended work and that the conditions of employment will not adversely affect working conditions in this country.[52] Each applicant must be individually certified, and approval requires a finding that there is a shortage of qualified applicants in the area at the time of the job offer. Individuals whose petitions have been approved include skilled craftsmen such as cabinetmakers, jewelers, watchmakers, machinists, mechanics, and stonecutters; foreign specialty chefs; secretaries; certain translators and interpreters; and professional occupations in medicine, nursing, engineering, and science. For certain designated professional occupations in which there is an established shortage, the ETA has issued "blanket certifications." Blanket certifications are available at present only for physicians and surgeons who are to be employed in geographic locations where there are shortages, for professional nurses, clergymen, religious teachers or workers, and physical therapists.[53]

Low-skilled occupations, with the exception of live-in domestic servants, may be ineligible for certification. Such occupations include assemblyline workers, clerks, drivers, kitchen helpers, laborers, and salespersons.[54] Certifications for live-in housekeepers will be issued only for employers whose adult family members need to be absent from the home or where round-the-clock health care is needed.

Is there a review of a denial of certification?

If a labor certification is not granted, the certifying officer of the regional ETA is required to issue a Notice of Findings setting forth the basis of the decision.

Documentary evidence to rebut the findings may be submitted within thirty-five days, otherwise the denial of the certification becomes final. Rebuttal evidence may be submitted by the employer; the alien may offer rebuttal evidence only if the employer does. If, after receiving rebuttal evidence, the certifying officer denies the application, an "administrative-judicial review" of the decision is available before a Department of Labor hearing officer if requested within thirty-five days of the certifying officer's decision.[55]

Is there judicial review of a final ETA decision to refuse to issue a certification?

Yes. Employers and aliens residing in the United States can obtain judicial review of refusals to issue Alien Employment Certifications.[56] Although the alien alone has standing to seek judicial review of a labor certification denial, the employer's failure to join with the alien in seeking administrative review of the denial is, by itself, an adequate reason to affirm the denial. The requirement that the employer join in seeking administrative review has been held to be minimally rational and thus constitutional.[57]

To reverse the decision of the ETA, the employer must show

that the denial was arbitrary or was based upon unreliable evidence, irrelevant factors, incorrect interpretation of law, or improper procedures.[58]

If the INS denies a visa petition, is the denial appealable?

Yes. Denials of visa petitions for relatives of citizens or permanent residents of the United States can be appealed to the Board of Immigration Appeals.[59] Appeals of decisions involving preference visas for employment and visas for orphans are decided by the Administrative Appeals Unit (AAU) of the Central Office of INS.[60] If the administrative appeal is unsuccessful, an action for declaratory relief may be initiated in federal court.

What is the procedure for an alien who is outside the United States to obtain a visa?

After an approved visa petition has been sent to the United States consul in the alien's home country, and the alien's priority date is close to current, the consul sends a packet of forms that must be completed by the alien applying for the visa. When all the required documents are submitted, and when the applicant's turn arrives, he or she is scheduled for a visa interview. Prior to the interview, the alien must obtain a medical examination from an approved physician.[61] The manner in which the visa interview is conducted is left largely to the consul's discretion. Also within the consul's discretion is whether the applicant's attorney will be permitted to be present at the interview.

Applicants may submit information to overcome a finding that they are not entitled to the visa,[62] but they are not given the right to examine adverse evidence. If a visa is refused, applicants are entitled to a statement of the reasons. Unless the information is classified, applicants are also entitled to receive a statement of the facts upon which the refusal is based. Applicants may request reconsideration upon the basis of further supporting information.[63]

Can a consul's refusal to issue a visa be reviewed by the Department of State?

Yes. Although the immigration statute purports to make the consular officer's decision beyond the control of the Secretary of State,[64] an applicant may request a review by the Advisory

Opinions Section of the Bureau of Security and Consular Affairs at the Department of State in Washington.[65] An advisory opinion on a "question of law" is binding upon the consul. Advisory opinions based upon questions of fact are not binding on consuls, but if a consul fails to comply with the opinion, an explanation must be submitted to the Bureau.[66]

Can a consul's decision to refuse to issue a visa be reviewed by a court?

Judicial review has generally been held to be unavailable in this situation.[67] In 1889, the Supreme Court held that the power to exclude aliens from the United States is "exercised exclusively by the political branches of government" and is not subject to review by the courts.[68]

Where the denial of a visa to a foreigner is alleged to interfere with the first amendment rights of United States citizens, at least one court has explicitly held that the government "may not, consistent with the first amendment, deny entry solely on account of the content of speech."[69] On remand, the same court reiterated: "it is still obvious to the Court, as it was previously, that 'an alien invited to import information and ideas to American citizens . . . may not be excluded solely on account of his proposed message.'"[70]

If an alien is issued an immigrant or nonimmigrant visa, does he or she then have the right to enter the United States?

No. Even though an alien may establish that he or she has been granted an immigrant or nonimmigrant (temporary) visa by a consular office, he or she may be denied admission to the United States by the INS at a port of entry if the alien is found to be "excludable."[71]

What are the grounds upon which an alien can be found to be "excludable"?

There are thirty-three broadly stated grounds. These include physical or mental disabilities, criminal conduct, advocacy of proscribed political doctrines, poverty, and improper documents.[72]

Specifically, aliens are excludable on physical, mental, or health grounds, if they are certified as having a "physical defect, disease or disability" that may affect their ability to earn a living, or if they are:

"Mentally retarded"
"Insane"
"Afflicted with a psychopathic personality or sexual deviation"
"Narcotic drug addicts"
"Chronic alcoholics"
"Afflicted with any dangerous, contagious disease," which includes HIV infection, i.e., infection with the AIDS virus

Aliens are excludable for criminal or immoral conduct if:

- They have been convicted or admitted commission of a crime of moral turpitude.
- They have been convicted of two or more offenses for which the aggregate sentences actually imposed were five years or more.
- They practice or advocate polygamy.
- They have engaged in prostitution or are coming to engage in prostitution or in any "immoral sexual act."
- They have been convicted of violating any law relating to controlled substances or are believed to be an "illicit trafficker" in such controlled substances, i.e., narcotics.

Ideological and security-based grounds for exclusion apply if:

- An alien is believed to be entering the United States to engage in activities that would be prejudicial to the public interest.
- An alien would engage in activities prohibited by the laws of the United States relating to espionage or sabotage.
- An alien is or was or ever had been a member of or affiliated with the Communist party or advocated the "economic, international and governmental doctrines of world communism."[73]

However, in 1987 Congress temporarily provided that from March 1988 until March 1989 "no alien may be . . . excluded . . . because of any past, current, or expected beliefs, statements or associations."[74] In October 1988, the ban on ideological exclusions was extended in another appropriations measure until March 1, 1991, but limited only to applications for nonimmigrant visas if submitted before January 1, 1991, and repealing the ban on applications for immigrant visas.[75]

Other aliens subject to exclusion:

- Those who are "paupers, professional beggars or vagrants" or are "likely at any time to become public charges"
- Those who are illiterate
- Those who have evaded military service in time of war
- Those who have participated in persecution in association with Nazi governments
- Those who have previously been deported or excluded
- Those who are stowaways
- Those who entered without proper documents or obtained a visa or other documentation by fraud or willful misrepresentation of a material fact

Some of the grounds for exclusion are ambiguous and elastic. Have they been interpreted and more precisely defined in decisions by administrative agencies or by the courts?

Many grounds have been subject to interpretation and refinement, but the general constitutional protection against vague, ambiguous, or overinclusive laws are not applicable to the grounds for exclusion. Similarly, aliens may be excluded on grounds, such as alcoholism, that could not be the basis for imposing criminal sanctions.

May an alien be excluded from the United States upon any ground not specified in the immigration law?

No. Consular and immigration officers are governed by the provisions of the immigration law. They have no authority to exclude an alien upon any other basis.[76]

Is there any relief for an alien who is excludable from the United States?

Yes, depending upon the ground of exclusion, the purpose for which the alien seeks to come to the United States, and the personal circumstances of the alien. Certain grounds of exclusion may be waived for a prospective immigrant who is the spouse, child, or parent of an American citizen or of an alien who has been lawfully admitted to the United States as a permanent resident. These grounds include convictions for crimes, prostitution, having obtained a visa or immigration document by fraud, and certain medical conditions. Waivers may be granted for mental disorders or tuberculosis but not ordinarily for drug addiction or chronic alcoholism or to "sexual deviates."[77]

Requirements for documents, such as passports and visas, may also be waived in various circumstances. Blanket waivers of requirements for either visas or passports have been granted by regulation for Canadians and British subjects who live in Canada, for certain visitors from Great Britain, for aliens who are in direct transit through the United States to another country, and for certain other categories of nonimmigrants.[78] Individual waivers are also available for aliens who can show an "unforeseen emergency" that made it impossible for them to obtain required documents.[79] In addition, the Attorney General has broad power to admit an alien into the United States even if he is ineligible to receive a visa.

Ineligible nonimmigrants may be admitted, with certain limitations, upon the recommendation of a consular officer or the Secretary of State. This power is typically exercised for visitors who show a need to come to the United States for medical treatment, for business reasons, to attend conventions, and in emergencies to see close relatives.[80]

Ineligible aliens may also be admitted under a procedure known as "parole" in emergencies and for reasons deemed "strictly in the public interest."[81]

The Attorney General's authority to grant parole and to fix appropriate conditions is delegated to the local INS district director in charge of the port of entry. Parole can no longer be used to admit groups of refugees.[82] Parole may be authorized prior to examination by an immigration officer, after the examination and pending final determination of admissibility, or after a finding of inadmissibility has been made.[83] Such parole ends without the need for written notice upon the alien's departure from the U.S. or upon the expiration of time for which the parole was authorized.[84] A parolee has no status as a legal resident. The grant or refusal of parole is based on the district director's discretion, although "humanitarian" parole may be authorized by the Central Office. The decision may be subject to judicial review on grounds that discretion was exercised or withheld arbitrarily.[85] When parole is terminated, the parolee reverts to the status of an applicant for admission; and his admissability is determined in exclusion proceedings as if he were still physically outside the United States regardless of the fact that he was allowed by the INS authorities to come into this country, and the time he has spent in the United States.[86]

Who determines whether an alien is excludable on medical grounds?

The United States Public Health Service. In addition to overseeing the quarantine and inspection of all incoming vessels and aircraft, the Public Health Service is responsible for the medical examination of all aliens seeking to enter the United States. The examination is usually performed prior to the issuance of a visa by private contract physicians abroad designated by the Service. Where required, arriving aliens will be subjected to further examinations by Public Health Service officers at the place of entry to the United States.[87] Medical examinations in connection with a visa are valid for one year.

"Any physical and mental defect or disease" must be reported to the INS. A factual finding that an alien is afflicted with a dangerous, contagious disease; is mentally retarded; is or has been insane, psychopathic, or a sexual deviate; has a mental defect; or is a narcotic drug addict or a chronic alcoholic is binding upon the INS. Each of these findings, except that relating to dangerous, contagious diseases, can be appealed to a Public Health Service medical board, where "one expert medical witness" may appear on behalf of the alien. No further challenge can be made of the Service's factual finding,[88] except that if the requirements for reaching the factual findings have not been followed, the findings can be set aside. The failure to conduct an independent medical examination prescribed by the regulations, has resulted in overturning the findings of fact made by the Public Health Service.[89]

Can a court review a finding by the Public Health Service that an alien is excludable upon medical grounds?

No. The language in the immigration statute that provides

that no alien shall have the right to appeal an exclusion order based upon a medical ground has been held by courts to prevent judicial review of the medical finding. This decision has been criticized, especially because the words used in the statute are not medical terms and have been challenged as being vague.[90] The fact that medical findings are conclusive in exclusion proceedings, however, has not prevented judicial review of the provisions relating to excludability in deportation proceedings. In *Fleuti v. Rosenberg*,[91] although a Public Health Service finding was relied upon as a basis for deportation, the Court of Appeals for the Ninth Circuit held the phrase "psychopathic personality," interpreted to include "sexual deviates," was unconstitutionally vague. The Supreme Court disagreed and in a subsequent case upheld the validity of the statutory language.[92]

What happens when an alien with an immigrant visa arrives in the United States?

When an alien reaches the United States, whether at a land border, an airport, or a seaport, his passport and visa are examined by an immigration inspector, and he is subject to questioning regarding his eligibility to enter the United States. The name of each alien, as well as each arriving citizen, is checked against a computerized "lookout book" the INS maintains for aliens who may be excludable and for other persons for whom other government agencies have requested a "lookout." Aliens may also be examined by a Public Health Service officer.[93]

If found admissible, aliens entering as immigrants are granted legal permanent resident status at the time they enter and are mailed an alien registration receipt card (known as "green cards," even though they are now blue).

If an alien is found not to be admissible to the United States upon initial examination, known as primary inspection, various procedures may be used, depending upon the place and means of entry and the asserted grounds of the inadmissibility.

Aliens who arrive at land borders are denied entry to the United States if there is doubt as to their admissibility, and they are advised to appear for a "secondary," more formal examination;[94] if found to be inadmissible, they are ordered excluded and their cases referred to an immigration judge for hearing in an exclusion proceeding.[95] An applicant for admission has no absolute right to be represented by counsel in either the primary or secondary inspection, unless the applicant has become the focus of a criminal investigation and has been taken into custody. The opportunity is generally afforded for counsel to be present at the interview if the examination is deterred.[96] At the exclusion hearing, the immigration judge must inform the alien of the "nature and purpose" of the hearing and advise the alien of his or her right to be represented by counsel "at no expense to the government."[97] The alien must have the opportunity to present evidence, to object to evidence presented by the government, and to cross-examine government witnesses.[98] The immigration judge's decision may be appealed, by either the alien or the government, to the Board of Immigration Appeals.[99]

Aliens who arrive by airplane or ship are frequently permitted to enter the United States and are given "deferred inspection" at INS offices near their intended destinations rather than at the airport or seaport where they first arrive. If an alien is found to be inadmissible after inspection, his case is heard by an immigration judge in the area where he is staying.[100]

Can an alien arriving in the United States be held in detention by the INS?

Yes. The INS has the statutory authority to hold an alien in custody pending a decision on whether he or she is admissible.[101] From 1954 until 1981, aliens were routinely paroled into the United States pending a determination of their admissibility. Aliens were detained only if they were likely to abscond or posed a risk to public safety or national security.[102]

In 1981, in response to the influx of aliens from Cuba and Haiti, the government abandoned its existing detention policy and adopted a new practice whereby any alien who arrives without documentation or with documentation that "appears on its face to be false, altered or to relate to another person," or who does not arrive at a designated port of entry, must be detained.[103] Those aliens who present valid travel documents (passport/visa) are subject to detention at the discretion of the inspecting officer if they are deemed likely to abscond or to pose a security risk.[104]

Aliens subject to the new 1981 detention rule[105] are eligible for release if:

- They have serious medical conditions.
- They are pregnant women.

- They are children of tender years.
- They have close family relatives who have filed a visa petition that has been approved.
- They will serve as witnesses.
- They are individuals whose continued detention is not in the public interest.

May an arriving alien who is being held in detention secure his or her release from custody? Is the detention appealable to an immigration judge or subject to habeas corpus review in a federal court?

Aliens arriving with valid travel documents but who appear to the inspecting officer to be inadmissible will ordinarily be granted parole or will be paroled for deferred inspection if the officer determines that the alien is not likely to abscond, is not a security risk, and the question of inadmissibility is contested or appears curable.[106] Aliens who arrive without valid documents will generally be detained unless parole is granted pursuant to the criteria specified above.[107]

Aliens who are released on parole may be required to furnish assurances that they will appear for a hearing and will depart from the United States if required to do so.[108] Release on bond of an alien detained in exclusion proceedings can be granted by the district director. In contrast to deportation cases, immigration judges and the Board of Immigration Appeals are not authorized to grant release on bond or to review the INS bond determinations for aliens in exclusion proceedings. A federal court habeas corpus proceeding to challenge detention must allege an abuse of discretion.[109]

Even if there has been no prolonged detention, a person denied release on parole may seek judicial review on the ground that there has been an abuse of discretion.[110]

Isn't the right of habeas corpus available to everyone, including aliens in detention?

An alien in detention under an exclusion order can bring a habeas corpus proceeding to challenge its legality.[111] Aliens excluded at a land border are not generally kept in custody, so habeas corpus proceedings may not be available unless the alien is surrendered into custody, an "accommodation" immigration officials may decline. Habeas corpus is now the exclusive remedy to contest a final exclusion order.[112]

What type of hearing is granted an alien who has been ordered excluded?

The Supreme Court has held in a much criticized 5–4 decision that for an alien seeking entry to the United States, "the procedure authorized by Congress . . . is due process as far as an alien denied entry is concerned."[113] The Immigration Act spells out the procedures to which an alien in exclusion proceedings is entitled.

When an alien is subjected to an exclusion proceeding, he or she appears before an immigration judge who must state the nature and purpose of the hearing, advise the alien of the right to be represented by counsel not at government expense, and afford the alien the opportunity to present evidence and to examine adverse witnesses and unfavorable evidence. The alien has the burden of proving that he or she is admissible to the United States. The decision by the immigration judge must be based on the record of the proceedings and must include a review of the evidence and the basis for the ruling.[114]

An alien who is a legal permanent resident is protected by the due process clause, even if he or she is entering the United States. Therefore, the exclusion proceedings to which a returning resident alien is subjected must meet the constitutional requirements of due process.[115]

Does the INS have the power to deny a hearing to an alien who is being ordered excluded?

Under certain limited circumstances, the Immigration Act allows an alien to be excluded without a hearing. Hearings may be refused under certain circumstances to aliens who are deemed excludable because they are entering "to engage in activities which would be prejudicial to the public interest, or would endanger the welfare, safety, or security of the United States," who are excludable as members of communist or anarchist organizations, or who are believed likely to engage in "espionage, sabotage, public disorder" or other subversive activity,[116] but only if the alien is deemed excludable on the basis of confidential information, disclosure of which would be prejudicial to the "public interest, safety or security."[117] Until recently, the government had not applied the summary exclusion proceeding to a permanent resident alien who was returning to a residence in the United States. Whether summary procedures may be invoked in such circumstances is currently the subject of litigation.[118]

Alien crewmen are also denied hearings regarding their eligibility to enter the United States. Crewmen, who are defined as persons employed on vessels and aircraft, are not permitted to enter the United States unless they have been granted a conditional landing permit that is valid for the period during which their vessel or aircraft remains in the United States, but in no event to exceed twenty-nine days. The conditional landing permit may be summarily revoked by an immigration officer without a hearing upon a finding that the alien is not a bona fide crewman or that he does not intend to depart from the United States on the carrier that brought him to this country. Neither a hearing nor an administrative appeal is provided for the denial or revocation of a conditional landing permit.[119]

Alien stowaways are denied permission to land in the United States and have neither the right to a hearing nor the right of appeal.[120]

Is it constitutional to deny hearings to aliens who have been ordered excluded by the INS?

The Supreme Court has upheld the denial of a hearing to an alien seeking initial admission to the United States for the same reason that the Court refused to review the decision to hold aliens in custody, i.e., because Congress has the "plenary power" to determine the conditions under which an alien may enter this country.[121]

As indicated in the discussion of the judicial review of refusals by American consuls to issue visas, this view has been sharply challenged because it assumes that the congressional power over aliens seeking to enter the United States, unlike other congressional powers, is not subject to constitutional limitations.

Is there any qualification to the ruling that excluded aliens seeking to enter the United States may be denied a hearing?

Yes. In a significant decision in 1953, the Supreme Court held that the constitutional protection of due process requires a hearing to be granted to an alien who is a "returning resident."[122] This decision was recently reaffirmed in 1982 when the Supreme Court held that a returning resident's right to reenter must be determined in a proceeding that comports with due process.[123] A returning resident who claims to be a citizen is entitled not only to an administrative hearing before the INS but also, if there is a genuine issue of material fact relating to the claim, to a trial in a court to determine his citizenship.[124]

In cases in which hearings have been granted, can a decision by an immigration judge to exclude an alien be appealed?

Yes. Except for crewmen, stowaways, and persons excluded on security grounds or for certain medical disqualifications,[125] a decision by the immigration judge can be appealed to the Board of Immigration Appeals. The immigration judge is required to notify the applicants for admission to the United States of their right of appeal. An appeal of an oral decision must be made immediately at the close of the hearing. An appeal of a written decision must be made within ten calendar days. An attorney or representative of a nonprofit social service organization may represent the applicant on appeal. Although an applicant may be represented by counsel before the Board of Immigration Appeals in connection with the appeal, the Board does not hear evidence. The function of the Board of Immigration Appeals is to review the decision of the immigration judge.[126]

What grounds may be used before the Board of Immigration Appeals to reverse a decision by an immigration judge?

An appeal can be based upon claims of improper procedures at the hearing and claims that the order of exclusion rested on mistakes of fact or errors of law. Procedural grounds include an unfair hearing and a failure to follow the statutory and regulatory requirements governing the conduct of the hearing.

The immigration judge must rule solely on evidence produced at the hearing, and the decision must have had "adequate support in the evidence." If there was a failure to consider evidence or an "unwarranted disregard of evidence," the exclusion order can be set aside.[127]

Can an appeal challenge the constitutionality of a statute that authorizes exclusion of an alien?

Neither an immigration judge nor the Board of Immigration Appeals can rule upon the constitutionality of an Act of Congress.[128]

Can an alien challenge an exclusion order in the courts?

Yes. An alien against whom a final order of exclusion has been entered is entitled to judicial review of the order solely by habeas corpus proceedings.[129]

Does the statute confining judicial review of an exclusion order to habeas corpus proceedings mean that a person who wants to challenge a decision of the INS has no other access to the courts in the United States?

No. The statute refers only to orders of exclusion. An alien or a person who claims to be a citizen may be able to challenge an adverse administrative ruling affecting his or her legal rights through other judicial remedies. The Administrative Procedure Act permits a right of review by a court to any "person suffering legal wrong because of agency action, or adversely affected or aggrieved by agency action."[130] However, the APA does not constitute an independent basis for federal court jurisdiction.[131] Examples of administrative decisions that have been reviewed by the courts include the denial of a claim of United States citizenship not presented in an exclusion proceeding;[132] the refusal to grant a waiver to an excluded alien where a substantial claim of constitutional right affects residents of the United States;[133] and denials of visa petitions.[134] Courts have also heard claims by excludable aliens challenging the legality of practices or procedures whereby the INS adjudicates aliens' claims for political asylum or parole determinations.[135]

What grounds may be raised in courts to challenge orders of exclusion and other rulings adversely affecting aliens?

There are four major grounds:

1. Questions of law
2. Procedural questions, i.e., failure to follow the legally required procedures or a denial of fair procedure

3. Failure to base the decision upon the proper standard of evidence
4. Failure to exercise any discretion, where required to do so, or an arbitrary exercise of discretion

What is meant by "questions of law"?

This refers to the meaning of the relevant statutes and regulations, and whether administrative regulations and decisions properly reflect the purpose of the statutes. As we have suggested elsewhere, the meaning of terms used in the Immigration and Nationality Act is often unclear. Where there is any doubt, a "question of law" can be raised.

Among questions of law the courts have decided are whether the term "psychopathic personality" refers to a person who is a "sexual deviate";[136] the meaning of the phrase "willfully misrepresenting a material fact;"[137] whether an alien has made a "new entry" into the United States if the entry followed a "brief" or an "involuntary" departure from this country or if the alien has returned from a round trip between the continental United States and a "territory,"[138] whether a particular criminal offense involves "moral turpitude,"[139] and when a judgment of a court is a "conviction."[140]

What is meant by "procedural questions"?

These relate to the form and conduct of the proceedings in which the rights of the alien have been decided.

Although the constitutional protection of due process does not usually appear to apply to aliens who are in exclusion proceedings, statutory protections continue to apply. Where a hearing is required, the courts have read into the statute the need for a "fair" hearing, in addition to demanding compliance with the provisions of the statutes or regulations.[141] The statute, for example, does not expressly provide for an interpreter if the alien does not understand English, nor does it expressly afford the alien the opportunity to present evidence and cross-examine witnesses. But these rights, among others, are required as essential elements of a fair hearing.[142]

The Supreme Court has also required hearings for an excluded alien when the alien is a "returning resident." Such aliens are regarded as "assimilated" into the United States for the purpose of due process.[143]

Courts have also intervened on behalf of crewmen, who are given only summary procedures under the immigration laws. Refusals to grant conditional landing permits to crewmen have been successfully challenged when the crewmen have not been given an opportunity to show their eligibility to enter the United States, when improper considerations were relied upon to deny entry, and when the procedures used were arbitrary or unfair.[144]

What is meant by "proper standard of evidence"?

An immigration judge's decision must be based upon adequate support in the record. This standard has been interpreted to mean that there must be a substantial and reasonable basis in the evidence.[145]

An alien who applies for admission to the United States has the burden of proving that he or she is entitled to enter this country. The type of evidence and the weight to be given to the evidence present many different kinds of legal questions.

What is meant by "failure to exercise discretion" or "arbitrary exercise of discretion"?

Many decisions rendered by the INS are called "discretionary." These involve measures of relief for which an alien may be eligible if he or she meets certain requirements, but which are not assured as a matter of right. Discretionary relief includes the granting of waivers of various grounds of excludability, permission for an alien who has been deported to return to the United States, and permission for an alien who has lived in the United States for seven consecutive years to obtain lawful status.[146]

The explanation ordinarily given by the INS regarding the grant of discretionary relief is usually that each case is decided on its own merits. Yet certain criteria are generally used. Typically, they include a showing of good moral character, close family ties in the United States, and hardship for the alien or close relative if the alien is deported. Negative factors that have led to denial of discretionary relief have included serious criminal offenses, violations of immigration requirements, making false statements in connection with applications, and failure to give information regarding political and other associations, notwithstanding reliance on fifth amendment protection against self-incrimination.[147]

A refusal to grant discretionary relief is regarded as "arbitrary" when no reason is shown for the decision, when it is irrational, out of keeping with an established policy, or based upon improper grounds.[148]

There are also cases in which the INS has failed to take any action on requests for discretionary relief. A court may require that some action be taken in such cases, but the court will not compel the INS to grant the requested relief.[149]

NOTES

1. Act of Mar. 3, 1875, 18 Stat. 477.
2. Act of Aug. 3, 1882, 22 Stat 214.
3. *See* Act of 1907, 34 Stat. 898; Act of 1917, 39 Stat. 874; Act of 1952, 66 Stat. 163. *See generally* 8 U.S.C. § 1182(a).
4. Act of May 6, 1882, 22 Stat. 58 (1882).
5. Gentlemen's Agreement of 1907.
6. Immigration Act of 1917, Pub. L. No. 64-301, 39 Stat. 874 (1917).
7. Act of May 19, 1921, Pub. L. No. 67-5, 42 Stat. 5 (1921).
8. Immigration Act of 1924, Pub. L. No. 68-139, 43 Stat. 153 (1924)
9. Immigration and Nationality Act of 1952, Pub. L. No. 82-414, 66 Stat. 166 (1952).
10. Immigration and Nationality Act of 1965, Pub. L. No. 89-236, 79 Stat. 911 (1965).
11. Immigration and Nationality Act Amendments of 1976, Pub. L. No. 94-571, 90 Stat. 2703 (1976).
12. Immigration and Nationality Act—Refugee Policy, Pub. L. No. 95-412, 92 Stat. 907 (1978).
13. *See infra* note 14. *See also infra* ch. 3.
14. Refugee Act of 1980, Pub. L. No. 96-212, § 203, 94 Stat. 102, 106-7 (1980). *See* 8 U.S.C. § 1151(a). The worldwide total was reduced to 280,000 for 1980 and to 270,000 for subsequent years. See § 204(b)(3)(A).
15. Under current law, immediate relatives are spouses and unmarried children under twenty-one of United States citizens and parents of citizens if the citizen is over twenty-one. 8 U.S.C. § 1151(b).
16. *United States v. Ju Toy*, 198 U.S. 253, 263 (1905).
17. *See generally* Immigration and Nationality Act of 1952, as amended, 8 U.S.C. §§ 1101 *et seq.* *See also* Title 8 Code of Federal Regulations

for rules promulgated by the Immigration and Naturalization Service and Title 22 of the Code of Federal Regulations for rules promulgated by the State Department.

18. 8 U.S.C. § 1101(a)(15).
19. 8 U.S.C. § 1184(b).
20. For the nonimmigrant categories, see 8 U.S.C. § 1101(a)(15)(A)–(N); 8 C.F.R. § 214
21. 2 C.F.R. § 41.111.
22. 8 U.S.C. §§ 1184(c)&(d).
23. However, after admission to the United States, under certain circumstances foreign students may be permitted to work after their first year of study. 8 C.F.R. §§ 214.2(f)(9), 214.2(m)(13).
24. *See* 8 U.S.C. § 1182(a).
25. *See generally* 8 U.S.C. § 1182.
26. 8 U.S.C. § 1101(a)(20).
27. 8 U.S.C. § 1101(b)(1).
28. *Id.*
29. Immigration Reform and Control Act of 1986, Pub. L. No. 99–603, § 315(a), 100 Stat. 3359, 3439 (1986).
30. 8 U.S.C. § 1101(a)(27).
31. 8 U.S.C. § 1153(a)(1).
32. *Id.* at § 1153(a)(2).
33. *Id.* at § 1153(a)(3).
34. 8 U.S.C. § 1182(a)(14); 20 C.F.R. § 656.2(e).
35. 8 U.S.C. § 1153(a)(4)
36. *Id.* at § 1153(a)(5)
37. *Id.* at § 1153(a)(6)
38. *See supra* note 34.
39. 8 U.S.C. § 1153(a)(7).
40. Immigration Reform and Control Act of 1986, Pub. L. No. 99-603, § 314(a), 100 Stat. 3359, 3439 (1986).
41. 8 U.S.C. § 1153(a)(8).
42. *See* INS Central Office cable reproduced at 61 Interpreter Releases 374 (May 16, 1984).
43. *See, e.g., Ali v. INS*, 661 F. Supp. 1234 (D. Mass 1986).
44. *See Stokes v. United States*, 393 F. Supp. 24 (S.D.N.Y. 1975). The procedural safeguards are:
    1. Written notice to the parties of their rights, including the right to an attorney
    2. The right to present evidence, including live witnesses to cross-examine, and to rebut adverse evidence
    3. The right to inspect the record of proceedings
    4. The right to subpoena witnesses and documents

5. Verbatim record of the proceeding (done by recording)
6. Referral back to the presiding officer for further adjudicatory proceedings after an investigation, if any
7. A decision based solely on evidence of record

45. 8 U.S.C. § 1154(c).
46. *Lutwak v. United States*, 344 U.S. 604, 611 (1953).
47. *See Bark v. INS*, 511 F.2d 1200 (9th Cir. 1975); *Chan v. Bell*, 464 F. Supp. 125 (D.D.C. 1978); *Dabaghian v. Civiletti*, 607 F.2d 868 (9th Cir. 1979). *See also Matter of McKee*, 17 I. & N. 332 (Int. Dec. 2782) (1980).
48. 8 U.S.C. § 1154(c).
49. Immigration Marriage Fraud Amendments of 1986, Pub. L. No. 99-639, 100 Stat. 3537 (1986).
50. 8 U.S.C. §§ 1154(h), 1251(c)(2).
51. The courts that have considered (and upheld) the constitutionality of Section 5 to date include *Escobar v. INS*, 700 F. Supp. 609 (D.D.C. 1988), *appeal filed* Feb. 2, 1989; *Anetekhai v. INS*, 685 F. Supp. 601 (W.D. La. 1988), *appeal pending*, No. 88–3191; *Smith v. INS*, 684 F. Supp. 1113 (D. Mass. 1988); *Almario v. INS*, 111 F.2d 111 (No. 88–1134)(6th Cir, April 7, 1989).

    Other courts have challenges pending and have not yet decided the issue. *See, e.g., Azizi v. Meese*, No. H-87-957 (D. Conn.); *Behbahani v. INS*, No. 88-0711-A (W.D.N.Y.); *Yogar v. INS*, No. 88-0711-A (W.D.N.Y.). One district court has denied a government motion to dismiss: *Manwani v. INS*, No. C-C-88-41-M (W.D.N.C.). No doubt the issue will be subject to considerably more litigation.
52. 8 U.S.C. § 1182(a)(14).
53. 20 C.F.R. § 656.10.
54. *Id.* at § 656.11.
55. *Id.* at § 656.25.
56. *Pancho Villa Restaurant v. Dept. of Labor*, 796 F.2d 596 (2d Cir. 1986); *Production Tool Corp. v. ETA*, 688 F.2d 1166 (7th Cir. 1982); *Silva v. Secretary of Labor*, 518 F.2d 301 (1st Cir. 1975); *Yong v. Regional Manpower Administrator*, 509 F.2d 243 (9th Cir. 1975); *Pesikoff v. Secretary of Labor*, 501 F.2d 757 (D.C. Cir. 1974); *Secretary of Labor v. Farino*, 490 F.2d 885 (7th Cir. 1973); *Ratnayake v. Mack*, 499 F.2d 1207 (8th Cir. 1973); *Lewis-Mota v. Secretary of Labor*, 337 F. Supp. 1289 (S.D.N.Y. 1972). An alien not in the United States may sue in a federal court to obtain review of a denial of an alien employment certification, but the right to do so is not certain.
57. *Sieminski v. Donovan*, 589 F. Supp. 790 (N.D. Ill. 1984).
58. *See supra* note 56.

59. 8 C.F.R. §§ 204.1(a)(3), 3.1(b)(5).
60. 8 U.S.C. § 1104.
61. C. Gordon & H. Rosenfield, *Immigration Law and Procedure*, § 3.7(h) (1988).
62. 22 C.F.R. § 42.81.
63. *Id.*
64. 8 U.S.C. §§ 1181, 1225.
65. 8 U.S.C. § 1104.
66. 22 C.F.R. § 130(b), (c).
67. *Forinthian House of Beauty, Inc. v. Shultz*, No. 82 Civ. 6944 (S.D.N.Y. Oct. 21, 1983).
68. *Chae Chan Ping v. United States* (*The Chinese Exclusion Case*), 130 U.S. 581, 609 (1889).
69. *Abourezk v. Reagan*, 592 F. Supp. 880, 887 (D.D.C. 1984), *rev'd and remanded on other grounds*, 785 F.2d 1043 (D.C. Cir. 1986), *aff'd by an equally divided Court*, 108 S. Ct. 252 (1987).
70. *Abourezk v. Reagan*, C.A. No. 83-3739 (D.D.C. June 7, 1988), slip. op. at 7 n.8, *appeal filed* (No. 88-5235, July 14, 1988). *See also Allende v. Shultz*, 605 F. Supp. 1220 (D. Mass. 1985), *aff'd* 845 F.2d 1111 (1st Cir. 1988). Bernsen, *Consular Absolutism in Visa Cases*, 63 Interpreter Releases 388 (1986).
71. 8 U.S.C. § 1182(a).
72. *Id.* at §§ 1182(a)(1)–(31), (24) *repealed.*
73. *See id.* at § 1182(a)(28)(I); 22 C.F.R. § 42.91(a)(28).
74. *See* Section 901(a) of the Foreign Relations Authorization Act for Fiscal Years 1988 and 1989, Pub. L. No. 100-204, § 901, 101 Stat. 1331, (1987) (amended Oct. 1, 1988).
75. Pub. L. No. 100–461, 102 Stat. 2268 (1988), *enacted* Oct. 1, 1988.
76. *See Jean v. Nelson*, 472 U.S. 846 (1985).
77. 8 U.S.C. §§ 1182(g), (h), (i).
78. 8 C.F.R. § 212.1.
79. *Id.* at § 212.1(g).
80. 8 U.S.C. § 1182(d)(3).
81. *Id.* at § 1182(d)(5).
82. *Id.*
83. 8 C.F.R. § 212.5.
84. To be distinguished from "advance parole," which is granted to certain aliens in this country otherwise inadmissible for reentry to the United States, for the purpose of traveling to another country and returning. 8 C.F.R. § 212.5(d)(2) *as amended by* 47 Fed. Reg. 30,044 (1982).
85. *United States ex rel. Kasel v. Savoretti*, 139 F. Supp. 143 (S.D. Fla. 1956); *Varga v. Ryan*, 160 F. Supp. 113 (D. Conn. 1957).

86. *Luk v. Rosenberg*, 409 F.2d 555 (9th Cir. 1969); *Matter of Dobiran*, 13 I. & N. 587 (1970).
87. 8 U.S.C. § 1201(d); 22 C.F.R. § 42.113; 8 U.S.C. § 1224; 42 C.F.R. §§ 71.46 *et seq.*
88. 8 U.S.C. §§ 1224, 1226(d); 42 C.F.R. § 34.
89. *United States ex rel. Johnson v. Shaughnessy*, 336 U.S. 806 (1949).
90. *Id. United States v. Esperdy*, 277 F.2d 537 (2d Cir. 1960). *See* Comment, 68 Yale L.J. 931 (1959).
91. 302 F.2d 652 (9th Cir. 1962), *aff'd on other grounds*, 374 U.S. 449 (1963).
92. *Boutilier v. INS*, 387 U.S. 118 (1967).
93. 8 C.F.R. §§ 234, 235.
94. *See United States v. Henry*, 604 F.2d 908 (5th Cir. 1979).
95. 8 C.F.R. § 235.6.
96. 8 C.F.R. § 292.5(b), *as amended by* 45 Fed. Reg. 41,629 (1980)
97. 8 C.F.R. § 236.2(a).
98. *Id.*
99. 8 U.S.C. § 1226(b); 8 C.F.R. § 3.1(b).
100. 8 C.F.R. § 235.6.
101. 8 U.S.C. § 1225(b); *See generally Shaughnessy v. Mezei*, 345 U.S. 206 (1953); *Garcia-Mir v. Meese*, 788 F.2d 1446 (11th Cir. 1986). *But see Rodriguez-Fernandez v. Wilkinson*, 654 F.2d 1382 (10th Cir. 1981). However, the blanket authority to detain is modified by statutory discretion, vested in the Attorney General, to "parole" any alien into the United States "for emergent reasons or for reasons deemed strictly in the public interest." 8 U.S.C. § 1182(d)(5).
102. *See Leng May Ma v. Barber*, 357 U.S. 189 (1958).
103. *See* 8 C.F.R. § 235.3(b). The INS adoption of a new detention policy was successfully challenged as violating the Administrative Procedure Act and on the grounds that it was initially applied in a discriminatory manner against Haitians. *See Jean v. Nelson*, 472 U.S. 846 (1985).
104. 8 C.F.R. § 235.3(c).
105. 8 C.F.R. § 212.5.
106. 8 C.F.R. § 235.3(c).
107. 8 C.F.R. § 235.3(b).
108. 8 C.F.R. § 212.5(c).
109. *See Rodriguez-Fernandez v. Wilkinson*, 654 F.2d 1382 (10th Cir. 1981) (judicial review narrowly limited); *Application of Pierre*, 604 F. Supp 265 (E.D. Pa. 1985) (while extended incarceration of entry applicant does not necessarily entitle him to habeas corpus relief, court will look at total picture and will expect the decision process to move expeditiously). *But see supra* note 101.

110. *Bertrand v. Sava*, 684 F.2d 204 (2d Cir. 1982); *St. Fleur v. Sava*, 617 F. Supp 403 (S.D.N.Y. 1985).
111. *Chin Yow v. United States*, 208 U.S. 8 (1908).
112. 8 U.S.C. § 1105a(b).
113. *United States ex rel. Knauff v. Shaughnessy*, 338 U.S. 537, 544 (1950).
114. 8 U.S.C. § 1226.
115. *See Landon v. Plasencia*, 459 U.S. 21 (1982); *Chew v. Colding* 344 U.S. 590 (1953).
116. 8 U.S.C. § 1225(c). This provision may be invoked when an alien is excluded pursuant to 8 U.S.C. § 1182(a)(27), (28), or (29).
117. 8 U.S.C. § 1225(c). Executive Order No. 11,652, 37 Fed. Reg. 5209 (1972).
118. *Rafeedie v. INS*, 688 F. Supp. 729 (D.D.C. 1988), *appeal pending* No. 88–5240. *See Chew v. Colding*, 344 U.S. 590 (1953).
119. 8 U.S.C. § 1282(b); 8 C.F.R. § 252.2.
120. 8 U.S.C. § 1323(d). *See generally Augustin v. Sava*, 735 F.2d 32 (2d Cir. 1984).
121. *Shaughnessy v. Mezei*, 345 U.S. 206 (1953).
122. *Chew v. Colding*, 344 U.S. 590 (1953).
123. *Landon v. Plasencia*, 459 U.S. 21 (1982). *See also Rafeedie v. INS*, 00 F.2d 000 (D.C.C., July 21, 1989) (No. 88-5240).
124. 8 U.S.C. § 1105(a)(5).
125. 8 U.S.C. §§ 1225(c), 1182(b), 1323(d). *See also* 8 C.F.R. § 252.2.
126. 8 U.S.C. § 1226(b); 8 C.F.R. § 3.1(b).
127. *Kwock Jan Fat v. White*, 253 U.S. 454 (1920).
128. *Califano v. Sanders*, 430 U.S. 99 (1977).
129. 8 U.S.C. § 1105a(b). The alien need not be in custody to file a habeas writ.
130. 5 U.S.C. § 702.
131. *Califano v. Sanders*, 430 U.S. 99 (1977).
132. *Rusk v. Cort*, 369 U.S. 367 (1962).
133. *Kleindienst v. Mandel*, 408 U.S. 753 (1972).
134. *Montgomery v. French*, 299 F.2d 730 (8th Cir. 1962); *Skiftos v. INS*, 332 F.2d 203 (7th Cir. 1964).
135. *See HRC v. Smith*, 676 F.2d 1023 (5th Cir. 1982) (where complaint alleged wholesale violation of alien's constitutional rights through procedures adopted by immigration officials, federal question jurisdiction properly resided in district court); *Jean v. Nelson*, 472 U.S. 846 (1985).
136. *Boutilier v. INS*, 387 U.S. 118 (1967).
137. *Ablett v. Brownell*, 240 F.2d 625 (D.C. Cir. 1957); *Leibowitz v. Schottedt*, 94 F.2d 263 (7th Cir. 1938); *Iorio v. Day*, 34 F.2d 920 (2d Cir. 1929).

138. *Rosenberg v. Fleuti*, 374 U.S. 449 (1963).
139. *Jordan v. De George*, 341 U.S. 223 (1951).
140. *Pino v. Landon*, 349 U.S. 901 (1955).
141. *See supra* note 127.
142. *Augustin v. Sava*, 735 F.2d 32 (2d Cir 1984); *Chin Yow v. United States*, 208 U.S. 8 (1908).
143. *Landon v. Plasencia*, 459 U.S. 21 (1982); *Chow v. Colding*, 344 U.S. 590 (1953). *But see Rafeedie v. INS*, 688 F. Supp. 729 (D.D.C. 1988), *appeal pending*, No. 88–5240.
144. *United States ex rel. Colovis v. Watkins*, 170 F.2d 998 (2d Cir. 1948); *Savelis v. Vlachos*, 248 F.2d 729 (4th Cir. 1957).
145. *O'Connell v. Ward*, 126 F.2d 615 (1st Cir. 1942).
146. 8 U.S.C. §§ 1181(b), 1182(d)(3), 1182(d)(5); 1182(g), (h), (i); 1182(a)(16), (17); 1182(c); 1254. *See Francis v. INS*, 532 F.2d 268 (2nd Cir. 1970).
147. *United States ex rel. Kalondis v. Shaughnessy*, 180 F.2d 489 (2d Cir. 1950); *Kimm v. Rosenberg*, 363 U.S. 405 (1960).
148. *McGrath v. Kristensen*, 340 U.S. 162 (1950); *Mastrapasqua v. Shaughnessy*, 180 F.2d 999 (2d Cir. 1950); *Kovac v. INS*, 407 F.2d 102 (9th Cir. 1969).
149. *Fong v. Brownell*, 215 F.2d 683 (D.C. Cir. 1954).

V
The Right of Aliens to Remain in the United States

[D]eportation may result in the loss of "all that makes life worth living."
—*Bridges v. Wixon*, 326 U.S. 135, 147 (1945)

[N]or is . . . deportation a punishment; it is simply a refusal by the Government to harbor persons whom it does not want.[1]
—Justice Oliver Wendell Holmes in *Bugajewitz v. Adams*, 228 U.S. 585, 591 (1913)

[D]eportation is . . . a dreadful punishment, abandoned by the common consent of all civilized peoples.
—Judge Learned Hand in *U.S. ex rel. Klonis v. Davis*, 13 F.2d 630 (2d Cir. 1926)

Judge Learned Hand's scathing denunciation of deportation as a national policy, expressed in a decision enforcing the expulsion of a Polish alien who was twice convicted of burglary and "was as much our product as though his mother had borne him on American soil," has had scant influence on the American Congress. Five times since his observation that deportation has been abandoned by the common consent of civilized peoples, Congress has chosen to increase the number of reasons for deportation, so that by 1960 there were more than seven hundred different grounds for deporting aliens from the United States.[2]

Despite the many grounds the government has for "refusing to harbor persons whom it does not want," by far the overwhelming number of aliens who are required to leave are those who have entered the country surreptitiously. About 97 percent of the 1,767,400 deportable aliens located in 1986 "entered without inspection." Roughly the same percentage—a total of 1,661,997—were aliens who had crossed the border from Mexico. The apprehension of 1,767,400 aliens represents the highest number in our history, which has been dramatically increasing since the mid 1970s.[3]

These aliens have at most the right to remain in the United States until the lawfulness of their presence has been decided.

In fact, the INS reports that more than 98 percent of the aliens who were required to depart left the country without a decision made in any formal proceedings or hearings under what is described as "Voluntary Departure with Safeguards."[4]

Most of the remaining deportable aliens had been admitted to the United States as nonimmigrants—visitors for pleasure or for business, students, crewmen, transit visitors, and other categories of aliens coming to this country for a temporary stay. These aliens, as nonimmigrants, generally have the right to remain only for a limited period of time to accomplish the purpose of their visit. The grounds usually invoked for their deportation are either that they did not leave when required or that they failed to comply with the conditions required of them in their nonimmigrant visa status.[5]

It is anomalous that most of the seven hundred grounds for deportation are applicable to the fewest number of deportable aliens. These are aliens who live in the United States as permanent residents and who generally have become deportable for conduct occurring after their entry to this country. In 1986, of a total of 1,611,471 aliens who were required to leave the United States (of which 22,937 were ordered deported, 28,007 were required to depart under docket control, and 1,560,527 who left under "voluntary departure with safeguards"), only 451 were permanent residents.[6] The small number does not lessen the impact on the individual alien. To the person expelled, it is often exile from the country where he has spent his life and formed a family. Between 1892, when deportation was initiated against aliens found to be illegally in the United States, and 1986, more than 920,000 aliens were deported.[7]

If the purpose of expelling alien residents is to cleanse the country of wrongdoers, the records of the INS indicate that deportation of offending aliens does not justify either its cost or its impact upon aliens and their families. The following table lists the number of aliens deported during the period of time from 1908 to 1986, the span of years for which records are available:[8]

Aliens Deported by Selected Grounds

Grounds	*1908–1986*	*1981–1986*
Criminal	51,711	3,390
Morality	16,615	33

Mentally or physically disqualified	27,320	15
Narcotic law violators (includes marijuana)	11,140	2,805
Subversive	1,543	15
Public charge	22,565	9

The question whether aliens who have settled in the United States as permanent residents should be deported has been judicially debated ever since the Supreme Court held in 1893 that Congress has the power to expel Chinese aliens because as persons of "a distinct race and religion . . . [they] might endanger good order and be injurious to the public interests."[9] In the numerous decisions that have followed, the Court has reiterated that Congress has plenary power over which aliens shall be admitted to the United States but has also explicitly held that the Court has a "limited judicial responsibility" to review Congress' power to regulate the admission and exclusion of aliens.[10] The Court has also drawn a sharp distinction between the deportation of aliens already in the United States and the "exclusion," or denial of entry, to aliens who are outside the United States.[11] In recent decisions the Supreme Court has reiterated that immigration procedures are subject to due process;[12] has implied that there are first amendment rights involved in the immigration statutes;[13] has said of a statute that permits immigration officers to make warrantless searches of automobiles that "no Act of Congress can authorize a violation of the Constitution";[14] has required strict construction of deportation provisions; and has imposed heavier burdens of proof for establishing grounds of deportability.[15]

Nonetheless, the major role in relieving the harshness of the deportation laws has been played by Congress. Congress, which initially required that aliens who had entered the United States illegally be deported within a period of one year,[16] removed all time limitations in 1952. But in a series of statutes, it has provided for the "suspension of deportation" of certain otherwise deportable aliens who have been physically present in the United States for either seven or ten years,[17] for waivers of certain grounds of exclusion and deportation in cases involving hardship or family unity.[18] The INA has also long contained a "registry" provision permitting an alien who has resided continously in the United States since a particular date, who is of good moral character, who is eligible for citizenship, and who meets other minimal requirements, to become a lawful permanent resident. In 1986 the registry provision was amended to apply to any alien who entered the United States prior to January 1, 1972.[19] Similarly, as has been discussed in chapter II, the Immigration Reform and Control Act of 1986 (IRCA) provided a special legalization provision for certain Cubans and Haitians[20] and a one-time legalization program for aliens who have resided in the United States illegally since before 1982 or who have been engaging in agricultural work.[21] In contrast, Congress has also occasionally increased the restrictions or penalties to which aliens are subject before entering the United States. For example, the Immigration Marriage Fraud Act of 1986 (IMFA) provides that any alien who seeks an immigrant visa based on a marriage entered into within two years of the visa application obtains only conditional status and must return for a second interview after two years.[22] If the marriage was entered into during the pendency of deportation proceedings, the aliens must reside outside the United States for two years.[23]

What right does an alien who has been admitted to the United States have to remain and live in this country?

As noted earlier, aliens may be admitted to the United States either temporarily as visitors ("nonimmigrants") or as permanent residents ("immigrants"). The right to remain in the United States is different for the two categories.

How is the right of a "nonimmigrant" visitor to remain in the United States determined?

The right of a visitor, that is, a nonimmigrant alien, to remain in the United States depends upon the purpose of the visit to the United States and upon the alien's particular nonimmigrant status.

Generally, a nonimmigrant may remain in the United States for the period of time required to accomplish the purpose of the visit—a transit visitor for the time it takes to pass through the country; a tourist for the time reasonably required to travel and visit (usually six months unless special circumstances exist);[24] a business visitor for the time needed to conduct his or her business; a student for so long as he or she maintains student status; a diplomat so long as he or she is accredited as a diplomat from a foreign government; an employee of an international organization for the duration of such employment; and specified types of temporary workers and trainees for the time approved for employment and training.[25]

How long can a nonimmigrant remain in the United States?

The length of a visitor's authorized stay may be as short as one to three days for a transit visitor, or as long as many years for nonimmigrants such as diplomats, employees of international governmental organizations, media representatives, and treaty traders. Visitors for pleasure, i.e., tourists, who enter on a B–2 visa are admitted for a minimum of six months, regardless of whether less time is requested. Exceptions to the minimum six-month admission may be made only in individual cases upon the specific approval of the district director for good cause.[26]

Nonimmigrant students (F–1 visas) who are enrolled full-time in an academic institution are automatically granted "duration of status" (D/S). This means that so long as the student pursues a full course of study and does not violate any other condition of the visa, he or she may remain until thirty days after the completion of study in the educational program for which the visa was obtained, or after completion of any subsequent period of approved practical training.[27] Students admitted to the United States pursuant to an M–1 visa to study at an established vocational or other recognized nonacademic institution will be authorized to remain for the period of time necessary to complete the course of study (plus thirty days) or for one year, whichever is shorter.[28]

What are the requirements a nonimmigrant must satisfy to be permitted to remain in the United States?

A nonimmigrant is allowed to remain in the United States so long as (1) he or she does not violate any of the terms or conditions of the nonimmigrant visa, which includes not engaging in employment unless the visa category permits it or obtaining permission from the INS district director at the place of the alien's temporary residence; (2) he or she agrees to depart from the United States before the expiration of the authorized period of stay (or any extension).

May a nonimmigrant extend the authorized period of stay?

A nonimmigrant who has not violated his or her visa status may apply for an extension of stay. In the absence of special circumstances, the application must be submitted fifteen to sixteen days before expiration of the authorized period of stay.[29]

Can nonimmigrant students extend their stay?

Academic students (F–1) are granted admission to the U.S. for duration of status and do not need to request an extension of stay so long as they remain in the same educational program. The F–1 students must apply for extensions of stay if they have completed one educational program and want to start another. To obtain the extension of stay, a student must show that he or she continues to be a bona fide student currently maintaining status who intends and is able to maintain status for the duration of the requested extension.[30]

What happens to nonimmigrants who stay in the United States beyond their authorized time?

Nonimmigrant aliens often remain in the United States beyond the time authorized by the Immigration and Naturalization Service. "Overstaying" does not preclude subsequently obtaining legal status, but the alien is subject to deportation if he or she is found by INS officers. INS officers have the choice either of placing the alien, when located, under deportation proceedings to compel departure or of permitting him or her to depart the United States voluntarily.[31] Unless the alien is believed likely to abscond, is financially unable to arrange for his or her departure, has previously violated the immigration laws, is a criminal, is not of good moral character, or evidences other similar characteristics, the nonimmigrant will likely be granted permission to leave the United States voluntarily within a fixed time, usually no more than thirty days.[32] There are certain categories of aliens who may be authorized to remain in the United States for extended periods, even though they may have violated their nonimmigrant status. For example, students and exchange visitors may be granted one-year extensions of their dates for voluntary departure, upon the condition that they maintain the terms on which they entered the U.S.; qualified applicants for immigrant visas with applications pending before American consulates abroad, who are expected to have interview appointments scheduled imminently, may be permitted to remain in the United States in increments of thirty days until the American consul schedules an appointment, and only so long as an immigrant visa remains available.[33] Nationality groups not protected in another status are permitted to remain in the United States in increments not exceeding one year. Any alien for whom "there are compelling factors warranting grant of voluntary departure," such as aged persons, children, and others for whom humanitarian considerations are involved, are also granted extended voluntary departure in increments not exceeding one year.[34]

Aliens who are placed under deportation proceedings and seek voluntary departure are usually required to leave voluntarily within thirty days but may obtain extensions of time depending upon the circumstances.[35] Following deportation proceedings, further stays may be granted by the INS district director, who is responsible for enforcing the departure of the alien from the United States. No administrative appeal may be taken from the district director's decision setting the length of time for voluntary departure.[36] (For a discussion of deportation procedures, *see* ch. VI.)

Who decides how long a nonimmigrant may remain?

The initial decision is made by the immigration inspector when an alien arrives in the U.S.[37] Applications for more time are made at the INS office in the area where the alien is staying. All applications must be submitted between fifteen and sixty days before the expiration of the alien's currently authorized stay.[38] If made afterward, the application will be denied unless good reason, such as illness, is shown for the delay. The applications are decided by the Travel Control Section in the district offices of the INS in the name of the district director. The decision cannot be appealed to a higher officer, although a request for reconsideration by the district director can always be made. The final decision can be reviewed by a court and may be set aside if based upon an improper legal ground, the result of discrimination, or if no fair consideration was given to the request.[39] Also, if the INS refuses to adjudicate an application at all, a court may order it to do so.

Can nonimmigrants change their status from one category to another?

Usually yes. Aliens who want to change their nonimmigrant status must show that they are in lawful nonimmigrant status at the time of the request, and that they are eligible for the new status. If a nonimmigrant has overstayed his or her authorized period of stay in the United States or has violated his or her visa status (for example, by working without permission or by working full-time when permission was authorized only for part-time employment), a change of nonimmigrant status will not be granted.[40] An alien applying for a change to student status will not be considered ineligible for such a change solely because the applicant may have started attendance at school before the application was submitted.[41] In addition, an alien who has entered as a visitor for pleasure will not usually be granted a change to student status unless his intention to attend school in the United States was previously disclosed to the American consul.[42]

Decisions are generally made on the basis of documents submitted to the INS, but interviews are conducted where questions are raised regarding the status of the alien, his or her purpose in changing status, or his or her intention to leave the United States upon completion of the purpose of the authorized period of stay in this country. When the application is denied, the applicant will be notified of the decision and the reasons for the denial. There is no appeal from the denial of the application.[43]

Can nonimmigrant aliens apply for an "adjustment of status" to permanent residence?

Yes, under certain specifically enumerated circumstances. "Adjustment of status" is the process by which an alien who is already in the United States may obtain legal permanent residence (or immigrant status) without leaving the country.[44]

Normally, aliens must return to their home countries to obtain an immigrant visa.

Eligibility for adjustment of status depends in part on whether an alien is obtaining lawful permanent residence status as a spouse, parent, or child of a United States citizen ("immediate relative") or as a beneficiary of one of the six preference categories.

Preference category immigrants are eligible for adjustment if (1) they were inspected and admitted or paroled into the United States, (2) they are eligible for an immigrant visa, (3) an immigrant visa is immediately available,[45] (4) they are in legal immigration status at the time of their application for adjustment, and (5) they have continuously maintained legal immigration status since entering the United States.[46] Thus, a preference category alien who has overstayed his or her authorized period of stay or worked without authorization is not eligible for adjustment.

Immediate relatives of United States citizens must meet the first two criteria but remain eligible for adjustment even if they have violated their visa status prior to applying for adjustment.[47]

Aliens who entered without inspection,[48] entered as crewmen, were admitted in transit without visa,[49] or seek adjustment based on a marriage entered into during the pendency of administrative or judicial proceedings regarding the alien's right to remain in the United States[50] are statutorily barred from adjusting status under any circumstance no matter what the basis is for their application.

Adjustment of status to permanent residence is a discretionary decision by the INS.[51] Although most eligible applicants are granted adjustment, if the INS believes that a nonimmigrant entered the United States with the concealed intent to become a permanent resident, the application may be rejected in the "exercise of discretion," or, if the facts warrant, because the nonimmigrant visa was obtained by making false statements. The Board of Immigration Appeals has held that a student who failed to complete school and who immediately engaged in unauthorized employment evidenced a "preconceived intent" to remain in the United States indefinitely.[52] Similarly, aliens who accept employment or marry citizens or permanent residents within three months of their initial entry are subjected to especially probing interrogations to determine their purposes in entering the United States.

What are the advantages of application for adjustment of status?

There are numerous advantages to adjustment of status whereby an alien may apply for immigrant status without leaving the United States. The most significant is that the applicant can be represented and advised by counsel throughout the process, and that administrative and judicial reviews are available if the immigrant visa is denied. In addition, the process may be more expeditious and the applicant has the right to remain and work in the United States while the adjustment application is being processed. As noted, denial of the adjustment application does not preclude renewal of the application in deportation proceedings before an immigration judge, with opportunities for administrative and judicial reviews,[53] nor does a denial preclude applying to an American consul abroad for an immigrant visa.

What is the procedure for determining an application for adjustment of status to permanent residence?

The application is decided by an immigration examiner in the Travel Control Section of the INS office where the alien resides. The procedure for adjustment of status is similar to admissions procedures and requires compliance with all entry requirements except for possession of an immigrant visa. First, the alien must be the beneficiary of an approved immigrant visa petition. A petition may be submitted either prior to the application or, in cases where a visa is immediately available, simultaneously with the application. Some INS district offices utilize a "one-step" procedure, which permits an applicant to appear at the immigration office (without advance scheduling) to submit his or her application together with the necessary visa petition, the filing fee, fingerprints, photographs, record of the medical examination, and any supporting documents. After the application is accepted, the necessary interview is conducted the same day.[54] Most offices do not use the one-step procedure. These offices receive the application, which must be accompanied by supporting documents specified on the form I-485 with form G-325, and thereafter send notices of a specific appointment date for the adjustment interview. A medical examination of each applicant must be conducted, usually by physicians approved by the Public Health Service at the time specified by the INS office.

The interview is conducted by an immigration officer. Appearance at the interview is mandatory for all adjustment of status applicants. Applicants may have counsel present, but the role of the attorney is limited to advising the alien. Unfavorable information, unless classified, is disclosed and the alien has the right to offer rebuttal.[55] The purpose of the interview is to determine whether the visa petition should be approved, verify the identity of the applicant, clarify and update the required information, review the applicant's eligibility for status as a permanent resident, and examine any other relevant factors. In the case of a marriage-based visa, the interview will also be used to determine the validity of the marriage.[56] The timing of the decision on the application varies among local INS offices, depending upon procedures for obtaining clearances and, where required, allocation of visas by the State Department, or upon a perceived need for additional investigation.

Although eligible applicants are usually granted permanent resident status, the approval may be withheld in the "sound discretion" of the district director.[57] The denial of the application for permanent residence by an immigration examiner, who acts for the district director, cannot be appealed, but the alien has the right to renew his application before an immigration judge in a deportation proceeding.[58] While only the district director may approve a visa petition,[59] the immigration judge may grant adjustment of status even if it was denied by the district director.

What are the rights of a permanent resident alien to remain in the United States?

As the phrase implies, an alien who is a "permanent resident" is entitled to remain in the United States permanently. However, this right is not guaranteed. The immigration laws provide that under certain conditions, permanent resident aliens may be deported from the United States. Eighteen sections of the Immigration and Nationality Act of 1952 define various classes of aliens who can be deported and are estimated to cover some seven hundred different grounds.[60]

Upon what grounds can an alien be deported?

The grounds cover violations of law involving the alien's initial entry to the United States as well as conduct after entry. Grounds relating to entry include entering without inspection, entering with documents obtained by fraud or by willful misrepresentation, and ineligibility for receipt of an immigrant visa or for admission to the United States for any of the grounds for exclusion discussed in chapter II.

Conduct after entry for which an alien can be deported includes conviction for a crime involving moral turpitude within five years after entry;[61] failing to register as an alien;[62] becoming an anarchist or a Communist or personally advocating, or belonging to, an organization that advocates opposition to all organized government, the overthrow of the United States government by force and violence, or the doctrines of communism;[63] becoming a public charge within five years after entry;[64] becoming a narcotics addict at any time after entry or being convicted of any offense involving the possession of, or traffic in, a controlled substance, at any time and in any country; being a prostitute or being connected with the management of a house of prostitution or "any other immoral place";[65] being convicted of possessing or carrying a sawed-off shotgun or an automatic weapon;[66] or being found by the Attorney General to be an "undesirable resident" because of violation of certain statutes relating to neutrality, espionage, selective service, trading with the enemy, and other statutes involving wartime prohibitions; participating in the persecution of any person because of race, religion, national origin, or political opinion in association with the Nazi government or its military forces.[67]

No statutes of limitations have been adopted to bar the INS from deporting aliens, although various remedies have been provided to relieve aliens from deportation in different circumstances.

Is there a constitutional basis for challenging any of these statutory grounds for deportation?

Yes, but so far the courts have not generally agreed with the challenges.[68]

The Constitution does not expressly give Congress power to deport aliens. The Supreme Court has implied it from the power granted to Congress to regulate foreign commerce and in the assumed, but not expressly stated, "inherent power of sovereignty."[69]

On the basis of this concept, the Supreme Court, usually by divided votes, has upheld the absolute power of Congress to determine the grounds for deporting aliens. The first ruling on this issue in 1893 upheld a statute requiring the deportation of Chinese laborers found in the United States without a Certificate of Residence unless they were able to establish lawful residence "by at least one credible white witness."[70] The Supreme Court held that "Chinese laborers residing in the United States continue to be aliens, and remain subject to the power of Congress to expel them, or order them to be removed and be deported from the country, whenever in its judgment their removal is necessary or expedient for the public interest."[71] Three dissenting justices denied that there is any "unrestrained power to banish . . . resident aliens," questioned whether it was "possible that Congress can, at its pleasure, in disregard of the guarantees of the Constitution, expel at any time the Irish, German, French and English who may have taken up their residence here," and observed that the deportation was a "legislative sentence of banishment and, as such, is absolutely void."[72]

The Supreme Court has upheld statutes requiring deportation of aliens because they became members of the Communist party,[73] were convicted of crimes "involving moral turpitude,"[74] or engaged in other conduct that may have been neither criminal nor grounds for deportation at the time they engaged in it.[75] The Court has reasoned that Acts of Congress in this field are a "political" decision and are, therefore, subject only to limited review by the courts.[76]

The doctrine that deportation laws are "political" and somehow not subject to the express guarantees provided by the Constitution has been much criticized and is dubious. It originated in a 6–3 Supreme Court decision that equated the expulsion of aliens living in the United States with the exclusion of incoming aliens.[77] It suggests that a resident alien is not protected by the constitutional protection of "substantive due process," since "[h]e may claim protection against our Government unavailable to the citizen. . . . he retains a claim upon the state of his citizenship to diplomatic intervention on his behalf."[78] In one case, the absolute congressional right to set the conditions for remaining in this country and the grounds for expulsion were attacked on equal protection grounds. An irrational classification that distinguished among similarly situated aliens was overturned.[79] The Supreme Court has, so far, declined to do so.[80]

In 1954, although neither he nor the majority of the Supreme Court was willing to reverse earlier decisions, Justice Felix Frankfurter observed that "much could be said for the view, were we writing on a clean slate, that the Due Process Clause qualifies the scope of political discretion heretofore recognized as belonging to Congress in regulating the entry and deportation of aliens."[81]

Although the Court has not yet overturned a congressional statute distinguishing among classes of aliens, the Court has invalidated INS or other agency action that discriminates against aliens, or among classes of aliens, without express congressional authorization.[82] Likewise, the Court has held that a state law depriving undocumented alien children of a free public education violates equal protection.[83] In addition, the Supreme Court has long recognized that the Constitution and Due Process Clause do apply to the procedures afforded aliens in the United States whom the government seeks to deport. The Court has repeatedly emphasized that all aliens, regardless of their status, are "persons" within the meaning of the fifth and fourteenth amendments and are protected by procedural due process.[84]

Does the first amendment's prohibition of laws "abridging the freedom of speech or the press or the right of the people peaceably to assemble" protect an alien who exercises such rights from being deported?

In *Bridges v. Wixon*, the Supreme Court recognized that freedom of speech and the press are guaranteed to aliens residing in this country.[85] But the Court has not decided whether the power of Congress to deport aliens is subject to the first amendment. In *Harisiades v. Shaughnessy*, the only full discussion of the issue, the Court explicitly tested the deportation of aliens in the United States against the first amendment but rejected the challenge on the merits because the Court regarded Communist party membership as equivalent to advocacy of "the practice or incitement of violence" and therefore not protected by the first amendment.[86] However, this case predates substantial developments in first amendment jurisprudence. As discussed below, in more recent exclusion cases, the Court skirted the issue of whether speech alone constituted a valid basis for barring an alien from entering the United States.[87]

In other cases, the Court has required evidence showing that an alien's involvement with the Communist party constituted "meaningful membership." In *Rowoldt v. Perfetto*,[88] the Court defined "meaningful association" to be a conscious knowledge of membership in a "distinct and active political organization." It held that a member who had joined the party "to fight for something to eat," and who operated its bookstore may have been a member solely to get "the necessities of life," and ruled that he was not a "member of the Communist Party" in the sense intended in the deportation law. In *Gastelum-Quinones v. Kennedy*, the Supreme Court placed the burden of proving the "meaningful membership" upon the government in a case where Communist party membership had been established, but where the alien chose to remain silent and failed to explain the circumstances of his membership.[89]

In *Kleindienst v. Mandel*, the Court observed that "First Amendment rights are implicated" in the exclusion provisions of the immigration law that deny visas to Marxists.[90] The first amendment rights at issue in that case were those of persons in the United States who wished to hear a visitor from abroad. At least one court has subsequently held that the first amendment does not permit denying a visa to an alien solely on account of his proposed message.[91] Even though this decision like *Mandel* is based on the citizen's right to receive information, the principle would appear to apply equally, if not more forcefully, to an alien residing in the U.S. who is protected by due process. Presumably, the right of a person residing in the United States to hear an alien visitor from abroad can be no greater than the right of a permanent resident alien in the United States to speak his mind freely, to associate with whom he chooses, and to believe in whatever religious, economic, or political doctrine moves him. The Court upheld the exclusion on the grounds that there were "facially legitimate and bona fide" reasons unrelated to speech for denying entry to the aliens. The recognition by the Supreme Court of the right of people in the United States to hear views from abroad as a right protected by the first amendment could be an opening for a more definitive future ruling by the Court that no alien can be deported for the views he holds. In 1989 a district court declared unconstitutional those provisions of the Immigration Act that authorized the deportation of aliens based on their political speech or beliefs.[92]

Significantly, courts have recognized the right of citizens to bring suit challenging denial of entry to aliens whom American citizens and organizations have invited for lectures and conferences.[93]

Does the Constitutional prohibition against *ex post facto* laws apply to deportation?

No. The Supreme Court has held that the *ex post facto* laws banned by the Constitution are only those imposing "criminal punishment."[94] This term has been interpreted to mean the imposition of a jail sentence or a fine. But, the prohibition has also been applied to cases that were "civil in form" but criminal in substance. These cases involved persons not jailed or fined, but for whom there was no way of inflicting punishment except by depriving them of their "offices and trusts."[95]

The logic of these decisions suggests that the constitutional prohibition of *ex post facto* laws should apply to the deportation of aliens who have been admitted to the United States as permanent residents. In many opinions the Supreme Court has observed that deportation of an alien who has resided in the United States is a form of punishment and may result for the deported alien "in the loss of all that makes life worth living."[96] But so far the Court has held to the view that deportation is a "civil act" that merely removes an undesirable alien from the United States and, as such, is not "an act of punishment."[97]

Does the Due Process Clause of the Constitution protect aliens?

Yes. Although, as noted earlier, the Court will employ only limited judicial scrutiny to test the validity of a deportation statute, an alien is entitled to "procedural due process" to assure a fair hearing of the charges against him. Moreover, the Court has held that congressional classifications regarding admission of aliens are subject to equal protection review under the rational basis or "legitimate and bona fide reason" standard.[98] State classifications, in contrast to federal enactments, are subject to strict scrutiny if they classify on the basis of alienage. For example, state laws restricting aliens from certain kinds of jobs have long been held unconstitutional.[99] Thus, the Supreme Court has held that aliens may not be barred from the state civil service, from practicing law, and from being notaries public.[100] But recently the Court has also held that aliens may be barred from jobs that are "ultimately related to the process of democratic self-government," a doctrine that is known as the "public function exception."[101] State laws discriminating against undocumented aliens in other contexts are also subject to heightened scrutiny under the Equal Protection Clause.[102] Thus, for example, a state may not deny aliens, including undocumented alien children, a free public education.[103]

The due process right in criminal proceedings that protects persons from vague laws has also been extended to deportation statutes, but so far no deportation law has been declared invalid on this ground.[104]

The long-established decisions have maintained a distinction between substantive grounds for admission, exclusion and expulsion on the one hand, and procedures governing the deportability of an alien on the other.[105]

Does the existence of war affect the status of aliens in the United States?

Yes, for "enemy aliens." When there is a "declared war" or a threatened, attempted, or actual invasion of U.S. territory, aliens fourteen years of age or older who are "natives, citizens, denizens, or subjects of the hostile nation" may be arrested, confined, removed from the country, or placed under special controls while living in the United States.[106] In 1948, a 5–4 decision by the Supreme Court construed this statute, enacted in 1798 and still in effect, as permitting the deportation of an alien enemy following the end of hostilities but before the termination of the "declared war." It also held that the decision to deport an enemy alien is a war power not subject to review by the courts. Although the record in the case indicated that the alien had received a "fair hearing" when he was interned during the war as an enemy alien and when he was being "repatriated," the decision authorizes summary internment and deportation of "enemy aliens" without hearings normally required under the Due Process Clause.[107]

War can also affect the rights of citizens who have "enemy alien ancestry." During World War II, the Supreme Court upheld the military decrees and Executive Orders that placed all persons of Japanese ancestry, United States citizens as well as aliens, under curfew restrictions and permitted their confinement in internment camps, without hearings and without any right of appeal. Under these orders, 120,000 persons of Japanese ancestry, of whom two-thirds were American citizens, were removed from their homes and held in custody until the end of the war on the basis that "pressing public necessity" may "justify . . . legal restrictions which curtail the civil rights of a single racial group."[108] (The decision has been much criticized, and it has been frequently suggested that it would no longer be followed, but the Court has not disavowed the World War II holding.) Four and one-half decades later, the lower federal courts have overturned the convictions of the two petitioners, American citizens of Japanese descent, for violating the military orders. The courts found that the U.S. government had suppressed or destroyed evidence that contradicted the military necessity rationale relied on by the government.[109] In a suit brought against the United States by former Japanese-American internees, or their representatives, the Court of Appeals affirmed in part the lower court's dismissal of the case but reversed with respect to the Takings Clause claims.[110] Congress has also implicitly disavowed the Court's holding. In 1988, a law was enacted that provided compensation to Japanese Americans who were interned during World War II.[111]

Do aliens have the right to leave the United States?

Aliens, as well as citizens, are subject to travel controls "[w]hen the United States is at war" or during any period of national emergency.[112] Aliens may also be forbidden to leave the United States whenever there is a state of war between two or more countries.[113] Both aliens and citizens are subject to travel controls.[114] A 1978 amendment of the immigration statute authorized the imposition of special control over the entry and departure of aliens and citizens by the President at any time.[115] The 1978 amendment eliminated the specific sanction for violation of the special controls. Current regulations authorize the prevention of the departure of designated classes of aliens whose departure would be inimical to the national security interests of the United States, who have not complied with selective service requirements, who are fugitives from justice, or who are needed as witnesses or parties in any pending criminal investigation or prosecution, or who are needed in connection with any official executive, legislative, or judicial inquiry.[116]

It is well established that departure can only be prohibited after a full and fair hearing.[117] Administrative regulations have been set forth that define the grounds on which exit may be inhibited, confer primary authority on departure-control officers (usually immigration officers), and provide for a formal hearing before an immigration judge.[118] The immigration judge is authorized only to make recommended decisions, and the power of decision resides in the regional commissioner without further appeal.[119] The regulations permit determination of the case based on confidential information when found necessary for security considerations.[120] Aliens in the United States, whether resident or nonresident, may not depart until they obtain a tax clearance certificate from the Internal Revenue Service. Certain aliens in temporary status are exempt from this requirement.[121]

In the past, the authority to control the departure of aliens was used to prevent aliens in the United States from traveling to China, Cuba, Vietnam, North Korea, and other countries and to require permanent resident aliens to obtain advance permission from the State Department for such travel.[122] Permanent resident aliens who traveled to certain Eastern European countries could not return unless they had obtained reentry permits in advance of their departure from the United States.[123] Permanent residents could reenter the United States after travel to other countries upon presentation of the Alien Registration Receipt Card, "green card," issued when they first became permanent residents.[124] After a temporary absence abroad,[125] the permanent resident could also present a valid, unexpired, duly issued reentry permit in lieu of an immigrant visa.

NOTES

1. This pithy quotation has been often relied upon by Supreme Court Justices, who have said that they are not "wiser or more sensitive to human rights than our predecessors." *Galvan v. Press*, 347 U.S. 522, 531–32 (1954) (Frankfurter, J.). Justice Holmes was referring solely to the power of Congress to "retain control over aliens long enough to make sure of the fact . . . [that they have not entered illegally]. . . . To this end it may make their admission conditional for three years." *See Keller v. United States*, 213 U.S. 138, 149–50. Hesse, The *Constitutional Status of the Lawfully Admitted Permanent Resident Alien*, 68 Yale L.J. 1575, 1605–8 (1959), contains a penetrating analysis of the Supreme Court's decisions on this question. *See also* Nafziger, *The General Admission of Aliens Under International Law*, 77 Am. J. Int. Law 804–47 (1983); Schuck, *The Transformation of Immigration Law*, 84 Colum. L. Rev. 1 (1984).
2. The Commissioner of Immigration and Naturalization Service told the Senate Appropriations Committee in 1953 that the 1952 Act increased the number of grounds from 485 to 700. Appropriations for the Departments of State, Justice, and Commerce for the Fiscal Year Ending June 30, 1954. Hearings before the Subcomm. of the Senate Comm. on Appropriations, 83rd Cong., 1st Sess., 250 (1953) (statement of A. R. Mackey, Commissioner, INS).
3. 986 Statistical Year Book of the INS, Table 55, at 96, and Table L, at xxxvi.
4. *Id.* Tables 65, 64, at 112, 111. The number of aliens "required to depart" is 1,588,534. By subtracting the number of aliens "under docket control," which is 28,007, and dividing that total (1,560,527) by the number "required to depart," we arrive at a percentage which is over 98 percent. The term "required to depart" by definition excludes those aliens who have been deported.
5. *Id.* Table 63, at 110.
6. *Id.* Tables 65, 64, at 112, 111. To determine the number of permanent residents (451), add the categories entitled "Immigrant" under each "status" described on Table 64, at 111.
7. *Id.* Table 54, at 95.
8. *Id.* The other grounds for deportation include entry without inspection or by false statements, 422,858; without proper documents, 157,424; failure to maintain nonimmigrant status, 135,466; all other categories, 75,210
9. *Fong Yue Ting v. United States*, 149 U.S. 698, 717 (1893).
10. *Fiallo v. Bell*, 430 U.S. 787, 793 n.5 (1977). *See also id.* at 796 n.6 ("congressional determinations . . . are subject only to limited judicial

review"); *Landon v. Plasencia*, 459 U.S. 21, 32 (1982); *INS v. Chadha*, 462 U.S. 919, 940–41 (1983).

11. *Compare Shaughnessy v. United States ex. rel. Mezei*, 345 U.S. 206, 212 (1953) *with Landon v. Plasencia*, 459 U.S. 21 (1982). *See also Yamataya v. Fisher (Japanese Immigrant Case)* 189 U.S. 86 (1903).
12. *Landon v. Plasencia*, 459 U.S. 21 (1982); *Fiallo v. Bell*, 430 U.S. 787 (1977); *The Japanese Immigrant Case (Yamataya v. Fisher)*, 189 U.S. 86 (1903); *Wong Wing v. United States*, 163 U.S. 228 (1896); *Yick Wo v. Hopkins*, 118 U.S. 356 (1886). *Cf. INS v. Chadha*, 462 U.S. 919 (1983).
13. *Kleindienst v. Mandel*, 408 U.S. 753 (1972). *See also Abourezk v. Reagan*, 592 F. Supp. 880 (D.D.C. 1984), *rev'd and remanded on other grounds*, 785 F.2d 1043 (D.C. Cir. 1986), *aff'd by an equally divided court*, 108 S.Ct. 252 (1987).
14. *Alameida-Sanchez v. United States*, 413 U.S. 266 (1973).
15. *Jordan v. DeGeorge*, 341 U.S. 223 (1951); *Rowoldt. v. Perfetto*, 355 U.S. 115 (1957); *Gastelum-Quinones v. Kennedy*, 374 U.S. 469 (1963); *Woodby v. INS*, 385 U.S. 276 (1966).
16. Act of Mar. 3, 1891, ch. 551, 26 Stat. 1084 (1981) (current version at 8 U.S.C. §§ 1101, 1251).
17. 8 U.S.C. § 1254(a).
18. *See, e.g.*, 8 U.S.C. § 1182(b) (interacy waiver for certain family members or where alien is fleeing religious persecution); § 1182(g) (tuberculosis waiver); § 1182(h) (marijuana conviction waiver); § 1182(i) (fraud waiver). *See also* 8 U.S.C. § 1251(f) (fraud waiver).
19. 8 U.S.C. § 1259.
20. Immigration Reform and Control Act of 1986, sec. 202, Pub. L. No. 99–603, 100 Stat. 3405 (1986).
21. *See* 8 U.S.C. § 1160; 8 U.S.C. § 1255a.
22. 8 U.S.C. § 1186(a).
23. Immigration Marriage Fraud Amendments of 1986, sec. 5, Pub. L. No. 99–639, 100 Stat. 3537 (1986); 8 U.S.C. § 1154(h).
24. 8 C.F.R. § 214.2(b)(2).
25. *See generally* 8 C.F.R. § 214.2.
26. 8 C.F.R. § 214.2(b).
27. 8 C.F.R. § 214.2(f)(5)(ii)–(iii).
28. 8 C.F.R. § 214.2(m)(5).
29. 8 C.F.R. § 214.1(c)(2).
30. 8 C.F.R § 214.2(f)(7)(ii). For M-1 vocational students, *see* 8 C.F.R. § 214.2(m)(10).
31. 8 C.F.R. §§ 242.2, 242.5(a)(2).
32. 8 U.S.C. §§ 1252(b), 1254 (e); *see also* 8 C.F.R. §1242.5 (a)(3); O.I. 242.

33. *See* 8 C.F.R. § 242.5.
34. *See* 8 C.F.R. § 242.5(a)(2)(vii).
35. 8 C.F.R. § 242.5(a)(2)&(3).
36. 8 C.F.R. § 244.2. The regulation does permit an immigration judge or the Board to reinstate voluntary departure in a deportation proceeding that is reopened for another purpose.
37. 8 C.F.R. § 214.1(a).
38. 8 C.F.R. § 214.1(c)(2).
39. *Mehta v. Attorney General*, No. 4-71 Civ. 504 (D. Minn, June 30, 1972).
40. *See* 8 C.F.R. § 248.1(b).
41. 8 C.F.R. § 248.1(c).
42. O.I. 248.7d.
43. 8 C.F.R. § 248.3(g).
44. 8 U.S.C. § 1255.
45. 8 C.F.R. § 245.1(f). The INS may interpret "currently available" to mean that this preference category is within sixty days of being current. *Cf.* 81C.F.R. §1242.5(a)(2)(vi).
46. 8 U.S.C. § 1255(a) & (c). For a detailed list of aliens not eligible for adjustment, see 8 C.F.R. § 245.1(b). Certain technical violations of visa status do not render an alien ineligible for adjustment. *See* 8 U.S.C. § 1255(c)(2).
47. 8 U.S.C. § 1255(c)(2).
48. 8 U.S.C. § 1255(a). 8 U.S.C. § 1255(c)(1).
49. 8 U.S.C. § 1255(c)(3).
50. 8 U.S.C. § 1255(e).
51. 8 U.S.C. § 1255(a).
52. *Patel v. INS*, 738 F.2d 239 (7th Cir. 1984) The Board of Immigration Appeals has also ruled that intent alone is an insufficient basis on which to deny adjustment of status in cases where INS Operating Instructions provide that an alien beneficiary could remain in the U.S. while awaiting an immigrant visa. *Matter of Cavazos*, 17 I.& N. 215 (1980). This has been strictly interpreted to apply only in cases of immediate relatives. Thus, intent alone might be a sufficient basis for denial of adjustment in the cases of all other preference or quota beneficiaries.
53. *See* 8 C.F.R. § 242.17.
54. O.I. 245.3b.
55. 8 C.F.R. § 242.17.
56. *See, e.g., Ali v. INS*, 661 F. Supp. 1234, 1238 (D. Mass 1986).
57. *Menezes v. INS*, 601 F.2d 1028 (9th Cir. 1979); *Wing Ding Chan v. INS*, 631 F.2d 978, (D.C. Cir. 1980), *cert. denied*, 450 U.S. 921 (1981).
58. 8 C.F.R. § 242.17; 8 C.F.R. § 245.2(a) (1987). *See also Jain v. INS*, 612 F.2d 683 (2d Cir. 1979), *cert. denied*, 446 U.S. 937 (1980).

59. Denial of petition may be administratively appealed (8 C.F.R. 204.1(a)3) and challenged in district court through a declaratory judgment action. *Cheng Fan Kwok v. INS*, 392 U.S. 206 (1968); *Colato v. INS*, 531 F.2d 678 (2d Cir. 1976).
60. Hearings, *supra* note 2. *See* 8 U.S.C. § 1251(a) for a listing of the grounds for deportation.
61. 8 U.S.C. § 1251(a)(4).
62. *Id.* at § 1251(a)(5).
63. *But see Bridges v. Wixon*, 326 U.S. 135, 148 (1945) ("Freedom of speech and of press is accorded aliens residing in this country"). *See also Bridges v. California*, 314 U.S. 252 (1941); *Harisiades v. Shaughnessy*, 342 U.S. 580 (1951).
64. 8 U.S.C. § 1251(a)(8).
65. 8 U.S.C. § 1251(a)(11) & (12).
66. 8 U.S.C. § 1251(a)(14).
67. 8 U.S.C. § 1251(a)(17).
68. A federal judge in Chicago, perceiving "recent developments in this once-dormant area of the law," suggested that it is cruel and unusual punishment forbidden by the eighth amendment to deport a twenty-eight year-old alien, who had come to the United States from Italy when he was fifteen, for selling three marijuana cigarettes to a roommate, and used "equitable powers" to prevent the alien's deportation although he held that the INS was "legally correct." *See Lieggi v. INS*, 389 F. Supp. 12 (N.D. Ill. 1975), *rev'd mem.*, 529 F.2d 530 (7th Cir. 1976).
69. *Fong Yue Ting v. United States*, 149 U.S. 698 (1893). *Harisiades v. Shaughnessy*, 342 U.S. 580, *reh'g denied*, 343 U.S. 936 (1952).
70. *Fong Yue Ting. v. United States*, 149 U.S. 698, 700 (1893).
71. *Id.* at 698.
72. *Id.* at 732 (Fuller, C.J., Brewer & Field, J.J., dissenting).
73. *Galvan v. Press*, 347 U.S. 522 (1953); *Harisiades v. Shaughnessy*, 342 U.S. 580, *reh'g denied*, 343 U.S. 936 (1952).
74. *Jordan v. DeGeorge*, 341 U.S. 223 (1951), *reh'g denied*, 341 U.S. 956 (1951).
75. *Marcello v. Bonds*, 349 U.S. 302 (1955), *reh'g denied*, 350 U.S. 856 (1956).
76. *Fong Yue Ting v. U.S.*, 149 U.S. 698 (1893). *But see Fiallo v. Bell*, 430 U.S. 787 (1977).
77. *Chae Chin Ping v. United States (The Chinese Exclusion Case)*, 130 U.S. 581 (1889).
78. *Harisiades v. Shaughnessy*, 342 U.S. 580, 585 (1951).
79. *Francis v. INS*, 532 F.2d 268 (2d Cir. 1976). See also *Tapia-Acuna v. INS*, 640 F.2d. 223 (9th Cir. 1981); *Newton v. INS*, 736 F.2d 336 (6th Cir. 1984).

80. *See Fiallo v. Bell*, 430 U.S. 787 (1977).
81. *Galvan v. Press*, 347 U.S. 522, 530–31 (1954)(Frankfurter, J.).
82. *Jean v. Nelson*, 472 U.S. 846 (1985); *Hampton v. Mow Son Wong*, 426 U.S. 88 (1976).
83. *Plyler v. Doe*, 457 U.S. 202 (1982).
84. *Plyler v. Doe*, 457 U.S. 202, 210 (1982) ("Aliens, even aliens whose presence in this country is unlawful, have long been recognized as 'persons' guaranteed due process of law by the Fifth and Fourteenth Amendments"). *See also Wong Wing v. United States*, 163 U.S. 140 (1896); *The Japanese Immigrant Case (Yamataya v. Fisher)*, 189 U.S. 86 (1903); *Johnson v. Eisentrager*, 339 U.S. 763 (1950).
85. 26 U.S. 135, 148 (1945) citing *Bridges v. California*, 314 U.S. 252 (1941). *See also Parcham v. INS*, 769 F.2d 1001 (4th Cir. 1985).
86. 42 U.S. 580, 591–92 (1951).
87. *Kleindienst v. Mandel*, 408 U.S. 753 (1972) (legitimate and bona fide reasons in addition to political views of alien justified exclusion). *See also Abourezk v. Reagan*, 592 F. Supp. 880 (D.D.C. 1984), *rev'd and remanded on other grounds*, 785 F.2d 1043 (D.C. Cir. 1986), *aff'd by an equally divided Court*, 108 S. Ct. 252 (1987).
88. 55 U.S. 115 (1957).
89. 74 U.S. 469 (1963).
90. 408 U.S. 753, 765 (1972).
91. *Abourezk v. Reagan*, 785 F.2d 1043 (D.C. Cir. 1986) *aff'd by an equally divided Court*, 108 S. Ct. 252 (1987).
92. *American-Arab Anti-Discrimination Committee v. Meese*, No. CV 872D02107-SVW (C.D. Cal.) (January 26, 1989) declaring 8 U.S.C. § 1251(a)(6)(D), (F)(iii), (G)(v), and (H) unconstitutional under the first amendment.
93. *Abourezk v. Reagan*, 785 F.2d 1043 (D.C. Cir. 1986) *aff'd by an equally divided Court*, 108 S. Ct. 252 (1987); *Allende v. Shultz*, 845 F.2d 1111 (1st Cir. 1988).
94. *Marcello v. Bonds*, 349 U.S. 302 (1955).
95. *Cummings v. Missouri* 71 U.S. 277 (1866); *Ex parte Garland*, 71 U.S. 333 (1867).
96. *See Bridges v. Wixon*, 326 U.S. 135, 147 (1944); *Jordan v. DeGeorge*, 341 U.S. 223 (1950); *Delgadillo v. Carmichael*, 332 U.S. 388 (1947); *Ng Fung Ho v. White*, 259 U.S. 276, 284 (1922).
97. *Harisiades v. Shaughnessy*, 342 U.S. 580, 594–95 (1951); *INS v. Lopez-Mendoza*, 468 U.S. 1032, 1038 (1984) (exclusionary rule not applicable because deportation proceedings are civil in nature).
98. *Fiallo v. Bell*, 430 U.S. 787, 794. *See also United States v. Barojas-Guillen*, 632 F.2d 749 (9th Cir. 1980); *Narenji v. Civiletti*, 617 F.2d 745 (D.C. Cir. 1980), *cert. denied*, 446 U.S. 957 (1980). However, in a

significant decision, the Second Circuit in *Francis v. INS*, 532 F.2d 268 (2d Cir. 1976), held that it was a denial of equal protection to deny relief to deportable aliens who have lived in the United States for seven consecutive years but to grant such relief to aliens with similar residence who were returning to this country from a temporary visit abroad.

99. *Truax v. Raich*, 239 U.S. 33, (1915); *Takahishi v. California Fish & Game Comm'n*, 334 U.S. 410 (1948).
100. *See Sugarman v. McDougall*, 413 U.S. 634 (1973) (state civil service); *In re Griffiths*, 413 U.S. 717 (1973) (attorneys); *Bernal v. Fainter*, 467 U.S. 216 (1984) (notary public).
101. *See Cabell v. Chavez-Salido*, 454 U.S. 432 (1982) (state may require probation officers to be citizens); *Ambach v. Norwick*, 441 U.S. 68 (1979) (same *re* teachers); *Foley v. Connelie*, 435 U.S. 291 (1978) (same *re* police officers).
102. *Plyler v. Doe*, 457 U.S. 202 (1982).
103. *Id.*
104. *Boutilier v. INS*, 387 U.S. 118 (1967); *Jordan v. DeGeorge*, 341 U.S. 223 (1950); *Fleuti v. Rosenberg*, 302 F.2d 652 (9th Cir. 1962), *aff'd on other grounds*, 374 U.S. 499 (1963).
105. *Landon v. Plasencia*, 459 U.S. 21 (1982); *Paointhara v. INS*, 708 F.2d 472 (rational basis upheld), *modified*, 721 F.2d 651 (9th Cir. 1983); *Newton v. INS*, 736 F.2d 336 (6th Cir. 1984) (upholds denial of suspension of deportation for alien doctors). *Cf. INS v. Chadha*, 462 U.S. 919 (1983).
106. 50 U.S.C. § 21.
107. *Ludecke v. Watkins*, 335 U.S. 160 (1948).
108. *Korematsu v. United States*, 323 U.S. 214 (1944), *reh'g denied* (1945); *Hirabayashi v. United States*, 320 U.S. 81 (1943).
109. *Hirabayashi v. United States*, 828 F.2d 591 (9th Cir. 1987); *Korematsu v. United States*, 584 F. Supp. 1406 (N.D. Cal. 1984).
110. *Hohri v. United States*, 782 F.2d 227 (D.C. Cir. 1986).
111. Civil Liberties Act of 1988, Pub. L. No. 100–383, 102 Stat. 903 (1988).
112. 8 U.S.C. § 1185(a); The National Emergencies Act of 1976, Pub. L. No. 94–412, 90 Stat. 1255 (1976), provides for the termination of any "declaration of National Emergency" now in effect in two (2) years. The procedures and time periods for future declarations of national emergencies are made subject to Congressional veto under certain specified conditions.
113. *Id.*
114. 8 U.S.C. § 1185(a)–(b).
115. Foreign Relations Authorization Act, Fiscal Year 1979, Pub. L. No. 95–426, § 707, 92 Stat. 963, 992 (1978), *amending* 8 U.S.C. § 1185.

116. 2 C.F.R. § 46.3 (1987); *Matter of Nimmons*, 11 I. & N. 599 (1966) (no showing that alien needed as witness).
117. *Mao v. Brownell*, 207 F.2d 142 (D.C Cir. 1953); *Polovchek v. Meese*, 774 F.2d 731 (7th Cir. 1985).
118. 2 C.F.R. § 46 (1987).
119. 2 C.F.R. § 46.5 (1987).
120. *Id.*
121. 6 U.S.C. § 6851(d); 8 U.S.C. § 1185; 22 CFR §§ 46, 53.
122. 2 C.F.R. § 46.3(k)&(*l*) (1962).
123. 8 C.F.R. § 211.1 (1962).
124. 8 C.F.R. § 211.1(b).
125. 8 C.F.R. § 211.1(b)(2) (1987).

VI
THE RIGHTS OF ALIENS IN DEPORTATION PROCEEDINGS

> [I]t is not competent for . . . any executive officer . . . arbitrarily to cause an alien, who has entered the country . . . and has become a part of its population, although alleged to be illegally here, to be taken into custody and deported without giving him all opportunity to be heard upon the questions involving his right to be and remain in the United States.
>
> —The United States Supreme Court in the *Yamataya v. Fisher*, (*Japanese Immigrant Case*), 189 U.S. 86, 100–101 (1903)

"Aliens, even aliens whose presence in this country is unlawful, have long been recognized as 'persons' guaranteed due process of law by the Fifth and Fourteenth Amendments."[1] Although the Supreme Court has maintained its position that Congress' power to set the substantive grounds for which aliens may remain in the United States is subject to only very limited judicial review,[2] the Court has held that "not even Congress may expel [an alien] without allowing him a fair opportunity to be heard."[3] Any expulsion must be executed in compliance with due process.[4]

What "process is due"[5] has been a recurrent issue. It is settled, not without debate, that an alien may be permanently banished from the United States with less process than would be required to sentence him or her temporarily to jail.[6] A formal judicial trial, with the protection of specific constitutional guarantees, is compelled before a person may be sentenced to confinement; a "fair administrative proceeding," never precisely defined, is sufficient to sustain deportation.

The war between the INS and the alien under threat of deportation has been a continuous campaign of legal battles to secure for the alien the same full measure of due process that is provided in other situations in which the liberty of a person is at stake. Among the first aliens to be subject to banishment from the United States were Chinese laborers in 1893 who, lacking a Certificate of Residence, could be deported unless they could prove with the testimony of at least "one credible white witness" that they were lawful residents.[7] Almost one hundred years later, sensitivity to the rights of aliens has been heightened and there are more "certain benchmarks to guide"[8] decision makers in their application of due process. Yet persons who "look like Orientals," or look as "if they are Spanish-speaking," among others, are not free from illegal searches and seizures,[9] and the alien who is in the process of losing, in the words of the Supreme Court, "all that makes life worth living"[10] is not afforded all the procedures that seem due for such a drastic governmental action. A continuing trend of judicial decisions and administrative reform, however, has brought an increasing measure of due process to the alien in the deportation proceeding.[11]

What is deportation?

Deportation is a proceeding by the Immigration and Naturalization Service to expel an alien from the United States who has been found to be in this country illegally. Except for very limited circumstances, no one can be deported from the United States without first being given an opportunity for a hearing before an immigration judge.

Deportation proceedings are to be distinguished from (1) "exclusion proceedings," which apply to aliens who are regarded as not being "in the United States," notwithstanding the fact that they may have entered the country (see ch. IV); (2) administrative actions by the Immigration and Naturalization Service to permit members of a designated nationality who are unlawfully in the United States the opportunity to leave this country "voluntarily"; (3) procedures that result in the removal of aliens from the United States under a procedure known as "required departure"; and (4) the removal of an alien "who falls into distress or who needs public aid from causes arising subsequent to his entry, and is desirous of being so removed," which results in a bar to reentry to the United States except with the prior approval of the Immigration and Naturalization Service.

The grounds upon which an alien may be deported from the United States are discussed in chapter VI. The procedures for subjecting an alien to deportation proceedings are discussed on the following pages, together with other procedures for requiring aliens to leave the United States.

How does the INS find aliens who are illegally in the United States?

By a variety of methods.

When aliens are arrested, state and local police, as well as the FBI, may report them to the nearest INS office.[12] When aliens seek help from welfare agencies, hospitals, and similar institutions, public or private, these organizations may notify immigration investigators when there are questions regarding the applicant's status in the United States.[13] The courts, however, have acknowledged the rights of undocumented aliens to certain public services, such as public education for undocumented children[14] and in some cases health care,[15] and a number of cities and counties have instructed law enforcement officers and social service providers not to inquire about immigration status or cooperate with the Immigration Service unless required to by law.[16]

Educational institutions are required to report to the INS when foreign students, who are in the U.S. on student visas, have completed their courses or dropped out of school.[17] Aliens who receive Social Security cards that are not authorized for employment—e.g., for establishing a bank account, for stock investments, for school records, or for other reasons—may be reported to the INS if Social Security taxes are subsequently paid into their accounts.[18]

Information may be furnished to immigration investigators by former employers, fellow employees, deserted spouses, in-laws, people with personal grudges, and others who for personal, economic or political reasons decide to report the unlawful presence of aliens in the United States. Credit bureaus and collection agencies have been known to threaten to report aliens to the INS as a means of collecting debts. It is difficult to know which, if any, of these "tips" are acted upon by the INS.[19]

Despite these other methods, the overwhelming number of aliens found illegally in the United States are detected by INS officers, primarily near the Mexican border, by inspecting vehicles at traffic "checkpoints," using "roving" Border Patrol officers to stop and search automobiles at random, conducting searches of farms and ranches, and undertaking "area control operations"[20] such as raids of factories or other workplaces where there are believed to be a large number of illegal aliens.

Approximately 60 percent of the aliens apprehended by INS agents outside of border areas during 1982 were apprehended through such factory raids,[21] which have been the subject of considerable litigation.[22]

In addition, Congress enacted the Immigration Reform and Control Act of 1986 with its employer sanctions provisions (*see* p.9 *et seq.*). INS I-9 forms, which employers and new employees are required to complete, attesting that the employee is authorized to work, are subject to periodic INS and Department of Labor inspection. Given this new authority to inspect I-9 forms, and employers' fears of criminal penalties should they be found to be employing unauthorized workers, it is unclear how much the Immigration Service will continue to rely on the traditional practice of factory raids or how that practice may be modified.[23]

How is an area control operation conducted?

An area control operation is a dragnet search of a particular area or neighborhood that the INS believes has a high concentration of undocumented aliens. Such areas include not only the regions abutting the Mexican and Canadian borders but also the neighborhoods of major cities that have a high proportion of recent immigrants or concentrations of Spanish-speaking and Chinese-speaking persons. In these operations, INS agents station themselves on busy streets, at subway entrances and bus stops, or enter "ethnic" restaurants and social clubs frequented by immigrants. The agents stop every person who "looks like an alien," questioning them about their identity, place of birth, and right to be in the United States. Those people who cannot convince the immigration officer that they are citizens of the United States or in this country legally will usually be taken into custody, compelled to submit to formal interrogation, and, if they appear to be in the United States illegally, placed under deportation proceedings.[24]

How is a factory raid conducted?

Factory raids—also referred to as factory "surveys"—have been conducted by the INS because of their effectiveness in quickly apprehending large numbers of undocumented aliens. Typically, a raid is commenced when the INS receives information, often anonymous, that a workplace is employing undocumented aliens. A surveillance is conducted to verify the information. If the immigration officers determine that there is an adequate basis for believing that undocumented aliens are employed in the factory, they ask the owner or manager for consent to enter the workplace, question suspected aliens, and arrest any undocumented aliens found there. If consent is not given, the officers are required to obtain a search warrant to enter the premises.[25] The raid or "sweep" is then conducted as some agents enter and systematically move through the factory, questioning workers while other agents are stationed at each exit of the building or outside the building.[26] The raid usually results in disruption and panic as some workers attempt to hide or flee from the INS officers.

The fourth amendment protects the right to be free from unreasonable searches and seizures by law enforcement officials. However, police questioning, by itself, is not a violation of the fourth amendment. In an opinion that implicitly condoned factory raids as an important INS enforcement technique, the Supreme Court, in *INS v. Delgado*, held that "unless the circumstances of the encounter are so intimidating as to demonstrate that a reasonable person would have believed he was not free to leave if he had not responded, one cannot say that the questioning resulted in a detention under the Fourth Amendment."[27] Despite the surprise nature of the factory raid in that case, and the stationing of INS agents at each exit of the factory while workers were questioned, the Court determined that the workers had "no reason to believe that they would be detained if they gave truthful answers to the questions put to them or if they simply refused to answer." Thus their encounters with the INS were "consensual," and the raid did not constitute a detention in violation of the fourth amendment.[28] In the aftermath of *Delgado*, all factory raids must be challenged on their facts as involving indicia of coercion not present in *Delgado* or on the grounds that the warrant requirement was not satisfied.[29]

What is a checkpoint?

It is a point on a highway where INS Border Patrol officers require vehicles to stop in order to question occupants. Automobiles and other vehicles are stopped at random without probable cause to believe that the occupants are aliens, are illegally in the United States, or have committed a crime. Such traffic checkpoints have been used by the INS since 1927 and are located primarily near the U.S.-Mexican border. They are to be distinguished from controls at the border—known as "line watches"—and inspections at places that are "functional equivalents" to the border. Traffic checkpoints are usually more than twenty-five but less than one hundred miles distant from the border and are used to intercept illegal aliens who are leaving the border areas.[30]

What is a "roving" patrol?

It is the practice of Border Patrol officers, at indeterminate and ever-changing points on the highway, to track, stop, and question people regarding their status in the United States. In 1975, the Supreme Court gave the following description of a "roving border patrol operation":

> [T]wo officers were observing northbound traffic from a patrol car parked at the side of the highway. The road was dark and they were using the patrol car's headlights to illuminate passing cars. They pursued respondent's car and stopped it, saying later that their only reason for doing so was that its occupants appeared to be of Mexican descent. The officers questioned respondent and his two passengers about their citizenship and learned that the passengers were aliens who had entered the country illegally.[31]

As a result of this case, the Court held that stops based solely on the ethnic appearance of a vehicle's occupants were unconstitutional. To permissibly stop vehicles as part of a "roving" patrol, INS officials must have reasonable suspicion that the vehicle contains aliens illegally in the United States.[32]

What authority does the INS assert for the procedures it uses to detect aliens illegally in the United States?

The Immigration and Nationality Act confers broad powers on INS officers to search for, apprehend, interrogate, search, arrest, and initiate deportation proceedings against aliens who are illegally present in the United States.[33]

The Act gives immigration officers the authority to question, without a warrant, any "person believed to be an alien as to his right to be in the United States." The Act also provides that "for the purpose of patrolling the border to prevent the illegal entry into the United States of aliens," INS officers may search vehicles "within a reasonable distance" and may have "access to private lands, but not dwellings," within twenty-five miles of any external boundary.[34]

INS has defined "reasonable distance" to be one hundred air miles from the border but also permits a regional commissioner to declare any distance from the border "reasonable" if justified by "unusual circumstances."[35] An amendment in the Immigration Reform and Control Act of 1986 requires that the INS must obtain a search warrant before agents may enter any "open field" in search of undocumented aliens.[36]

Although the broad powers conferred on immigration officers by statute are unqualified, due process and standards of fundamental fairness apply to INS investigations, interrogations, and other preliminary procedures through which an alien may be deprived of his or her liberty.[37] In addition, courts have held that the fourth amendment imposes some limits on INS enforcement activities. The extent of those limits, however—and the degree of protection afforded—depends on the specific circumstances in each situation.

What authority do immigration and customs officers have to question, detain, and search persons at the border seeking to enter the United States?

Virtually unlimited. The Supreme Court has said that any traveler crossing an international boundary may be required "to identify oneself as entitled to come in, and his or her belongings as effects which may be lawfully brought in," and that the power to exclude aliens "can be effectuated by routine searches and seizures of individuals and conveyances seeking to cross our borders."[38] This means that INS officers are apparently unrestricted in their right to interrogate and search individuals seeking to enter the United States, in order to determine their eligibility for admission.[39] The same authority extends to those locations considered "functional equivalents" of the border.[40]

What authority do INS officers have to stop and question persons believed to be aliens after they have entered the United States?

Once aliens have entered the United States, they are covered by the fourth amendment's protection against unlawful searches and seizures. The degree of fourth amendment protection, however, depends on the specific nature of the INS activity and where it takes place. In a series of decisions since 1973, the Supreme Court has ruled on INS operations *in border areas*:

Permanent checkpoints may be used if they are "reasonably located," if the stops of persons in automobiles are "routinely conducted," and if the questioning is "brief." In its 1976 decision, *United States v. Martinez-Fuerte*, the Supreme Court held that such investigatory stops do not need to be supported by any particularized suspicion, and vehicles may even be stopped "selectively" "largely on the basis of apparent Mexican ancestry" of their occupants.[41]

The checkpoints in the case before the Court were within ninety miles of the Mexican border—at San Clemente, California, and Serita, Texas. They were justified by Justice Powell, writing the majority opinion, upon the ground that "the need to make routine checkpoint stops is great" because "interdicting the flow of illegal entrants from Mexico poses formidable law enforcement problems," and the "intrusion on Fourth Amendment interests is quite limited," since "it involves only a brief detention of travelers during which all that is required of the vehicle's occupants is a response to a brief question or two and possibly the production of a document evidencing a right to be in the United States."[42] Justice Powell emphasized that the holding was limited to the facts in this particular case in which no suggestion was made that "the stopping officers exceeded [the] limitations" set forth in the opinion.

Nonetheless, Justice Brennan in dissenting from the decision argued that since the INS' "objective is almost entirely the Mexicans illegally in the country, checkpoint officials . . . free to stop any or all motorists without explanation or excuse . . . will perforce target motorists of Mexican appearance. The process will then inescapably discriminate against citizens of Mexican ancestry and Mexican aliens lawfully in this country."[43]

Roving patrols, in contrast to fixed checkpoints, may not be used to stop vehicles and question their occupants unless there is reasonable suspicion that the vehicle contains aliens illegally in the United States. Only one year before its decision in *Martinez-Fuerte* regarding fixed checkpoints, the Supreme Court in its 1975 decision *United States v. Brignoni-Ponce* held that random roving-patrol stops could not be tolerated because they would "subject the residents of . . . [border] areas to potentially unlimited interference with their use of the highways, solely at the discretion of Border Patrol officers. . . . [They] could stop motorists at random for questioning, day or night, anywhere within 100 air miles of the 2,000 mile border, on a city street, a busy highway, or a desert road."[44] The Court held that such random stops would not be reasonable under the fourth amendment despite claims by the INS that they were necessary to detect illegal aliens in the United States. Instead, the Court held that roving patrol stops were permissible only "when an officer's observations lead him reasonably to suspect that a particular vehicle may contain aliens who are illegally in the country."[45]

As to what constitutes the "reasonable suspicion" necessary to justify a roving patrol stop, the Court emphasized that Hispanic appearance of a vehicle's occupants is insufficient by itself to justify such a stop, although ethnic appearance can be considered in combination with other factors. Those factors include the characteristics of the area, proximity to the border, appearance of the vehicle, and behavior of the driver.[46] Six years later, the Supreme Court upheld an investigatory "roving patrol" stop of a large camper in the Arizona desert despite the fact that the INS agents did not see anyone inside the camper.[47] The camper was the only vehicle in an area known to be heavily trafficked by aliens illegally entering the country, and several sets of footprints had been found following a path parallel to the border. The Court held that trained and experienced Border Patrol agents may draw permissible deductions from facts that would be meaningless to the average person, and that such deductions may form a basis for the reasonable suspicion needed to justify an investigative stop.[48]

Temporary checkpoints, which are used occasionally by the INS in strategic locations, have not yet been examined by the Supreme Court. In *Martinez-Fuerte* the Court expressly reserved this question[49] but noted that temporary checkpoints "operate like permanent ones."[50] Thus it could be argued that as long as the "temporary checkpoint" is "reasonably located"—a choice the Court said "must be left largely to the discretion of Border Patrol Officials" in accordance with applicable statutes and regulations—then investigative stops would be authorized without any reasonable suspicion just as they are at fixed checkpoints. However, at least one court has ruled that the fixed checkpoint exception of *Martinez-Fuerte* does *not* extend to temporary checkpoints, and that stops at temporary checkpoints must be based on the same founded suspicion of illegal alienage that is required for roving patrol stops.[51]

What authority do INS officers have to interrogate "persons believed to be aliens" beyond the "border areas" of the United States?

As already mentioned, INS officers have broad statutory authority to "interrogate any alien or person believed to be an alien as to his right to be or to remain in the U.S."[52] However, to the extent that any INS interrogation involves the "seizure" of an alien, the fourth amendment requires that it be based on some degree of articulable suspicion (except for the brief questioning at fixed checkpoints already discussed).[53] What level of suspicion is required, however—suspicion only that the person is an alien or suspicion that the person is an alien unlawfully in the United States—remains unsettled. The Supreme Court expressly reserved this question in its 1975 *Brignoni-Ponce* decision.[54] And in *Delgado*, the Court was able to skirt the question entirely by determining that the INS questioning of workers was "consensual" and thus that no fourth amendment seizure had occurred.[55]

Lower court answers to the question remain inconsistent. A number of circuits have held that the degree of suspicion required depends on the type of questioning. Thus casual questioning without any threat of detention is justified solely on the basis of alienage. However, questioning in circumstances that are somewhat detentive in nature requires reasonable suspicion that the person is illegally in the United States.[56]

This approach has been rejected, however, by a federal district court in New York that found the distinction between casual questioning without detention and questioning involving some detention, factually unworkable.[57] The Court held that whenever an immigration agent approaches an alien for questioning, the alien is being stopped and detained. Thus in order for INS officials to *approach* a person for questioning, they must have a reasonable suspicion that the alien is *illegally* in the country.

A third approach has been taken by the Third Circuit, which articulated a single standard for such interrogatory stops: whether they are "reasonably related in scope to the justification for their initiation."[58]

Because there is no consistent national standard for reasonable suspicion, it is arguable that suspicions of both alienage and illegal alienage apply in dictating the extent of a permissible stop for questioning. The presence of a reasonable suspicion will be determined on a case-by-case basis.

However, the Supreme Court's *Delgado* decision condoning workplace raids (see discussion above) may have some effect on this issue. In *Delgado* the Court ruled that INS agents did not need to have individualized suspicion to support their questioning of workers in a factory because the workers were "free to move about the factory" and to refuse to answer questions, and thus there was no detention under the Fourth Amendment.[59] This finding of no detention was strongly criticized by Justices Brennan and Marshall who concurred in part and dissented in part. They argued that in light of the large number of officers who participated in the factory raid, the interrogation of all the workers in the factory, the handcuffing and arrest of many of the workers, and the conspicuous stationing of officers at the factory exits, a worker could not have believed that he was at liberty to refuse to answer an agent's question and walk away.[60] The majority, however, found that INS's questioning of the workers constituted "classic consensual encounters" and thus was able to avoid the requirement of reasonable suspicion altogether.[61]

Delgado represents perhaps the most dramatic example of how the courts have created exceptions to their holdings that "aliens in this country are sheltered by the fourth amendment, in common with citizens,"[62] and that the fourth amendment applies to all seizures of the person, including seizures that involve only a brief detention short of a traditional arrest.[63] In *Delgado*, despite the indicia of coercion—the large number of officers and their stationing at exits—the Supreme Court held that no seizure had occurred and therefore the fourth amendment was inapplicable.

Even where courts have found a detention occurred, however, the requirement of "reasonable suspicion" has in practice provided less constitutional protection of aliens believed to be in the United States illegally than, with narrowly limited exceptions, is afforded to citizens and aliens who have committed other offenses. Law enforcement officials investigating criminal conduct are not permitted to engage in detentive interrogation without a reasonable belief that the persons detained have violated or are about to violate the law.[64] In contrast, the courts have upheld questioning and detention of aliens on far more questionable grounds. For example, the United States Circuit Court of Appeals for the District of Columbia upheld the authority of INS officers to question and detain aliens in "suspicious circumstances" on the streets of Washington, in a hotel restaurant, and on hospital grounds. "Suspicious circumstances" were found when a person of "Oriental appearance" did not appear to speak English, when "Chinese persons" "immediately got up from their seats" in a hospital waiting room and "departed" when an INS officer entered to speak with another "Chinese patient," and when "a person of Chinese extraction, dressed in a blue denim uniform," was seen "scurrying through the dining room" of a restaurant "to the main entrance door."[65]

The United States Court of Appeals for the Second Circuit found that a variety in English dialect was enough to arouse a suspicion that a woman was an alien, when in a bus station in Buffalo, she pronounced the name of the city as "Boofalo."[66] The First Circuit cited "conversation in Chinese," "mode of dress," proximity to a restaurant known to have employed illegal aliens, and the attempt to walk away when approached by INS agents, as factors taken in combination that justified an INS agent's stop and interrogation.[67] And the Third Circuit held that "nervousness and an attempt to flee justified a brief detention."[68]

These cases further demonstrate the unworkability of distinguishing between "detentive" and "nondetentive" questioning. If a person's attempt to walk away from questioning by INS agents provides the basis for his or her subsequent detention, as a number of these cases hold, then the person was hardly free to walk away from the initial encounter and that too should be viewed as detentive.[69]

Given this, as well as the willingness of courts to find "suspicious" circumstances justifying interrogation and detention, it is highly doubtful that under present judicial holdings the "right of the people to be secure in their persons . . . against unreasonable searches and seizures" applies to a person whom an INS officer believes is an alien illegally in this country.[70]

How do immigration officers decide who "looks like an alien?"

Immigration officers have stated that they have arrested persons who "look like Orientals" or "look Chinese," or who are "Mexican-American-appearing males" or "of obvious Mexican descent," or who "look as if they are Spanish-speaking" or like a "Mexican cowboy."[71] In addition to racial or ethnic characteristics (insufficient standing alone),[72] "mode of dress and haircut" are often relied on as distinguishing features, along with foreign cultural characteristics, "furtive" conduct, and speech—"conversation in Chinese," or speaking with a "distinct Spanish accent" and having "trouble understanding English."[73]

May INS officers stop and question persons because they "look" Spanish-speaking, of "Mexican descent," "Chinese," or some other ethnic origin?

No, except as noted earlier near the border at permanent checkpoints as part of a routine procedure. The Supreme Court previously forbade stops of automobiles near the Mexican border to question the occupants' citizenship solely because they appeared to be of "Mexican descent."[74] The Court held that the officers on roving patrol could not stop vehicles unless there were specific articulable facts, which along with rational inferences, afforded a reasonable suspicion that the vehicle contained aliens who might be illegally in the country.

Although the case involved areas adjacent to the Mexican border, the decision would apply equally to persons of other ethnic origins anywhere in the United States. However, it is important to note that the decision forbids reliance upon the appearance of "Mexican ancestry" as the *only* factor in determining whether a person is an alien.[75] The opinion stated that such ancestry could be a "relevant factor" and suggested that it could be combined with other circumstances to justify a "reasonable suspicion" that a person is an undocumented alien. Other factors mentioned were the "characteristics of the area," "obvious attempts to evade officers," and "mode of dress and haircut." In view of the grounds the courts have accepted as "reasonable" for determining that a person may be an illegal alien, it is questionable whether the Supreme Court's decision offers much fourth amendment protection to persons, including citizens, who are stopped for questioning because of their ethnic appearance.

A more recent case applies *Brignoni-Ponce* to determine whether the INS had a reasonable suspicion to stop an alien. The court of appeals held that an uneven paint job on an early-model car and the fact that the car's occupants appeared to be Hispanic were not sufficient to provide the INS officer with a reasonable suspicion to stop the car, which was spotted over three hundred miles north of the border. The officer did not have a reasonable suspicion to question the car's occupants regarding their citizenship, despite the presence of other factors, such as the significance of the particular highway as a smuggling conduit, the significance of the particular vehicle in trafficking aliens, the fact that the driver of the car was not wearing a shirt, and the officer's eighteen years of experience.[76]

Do INS officers have the power to search vehicles for illegal aliens?

As noted earlier, the immigration statute confers authority on INS officers to search vehicles for illegal aliens at and near the border. At the border—when vehicles are entering the United States—or at those locations deemed "functional equivalents" of the border, this authority is virtually unlimited. In all other cases, however, this authority is subject to the probable cause requirements of the fourth amendment. This means that INS officers can search vehicles only with consent, or if they have probable cause to believe that illegal aliens are in the vehicle. A warrantless search of a vehicle for aliens, however, extends only to those parts of the vehicle where an alien could be hidden.[77]

Prior to 1973, the INS took the position that the immigration statute that authorizes a "search for aliens" in any vehicle "within a reasonable distance from any external boundary of the United States" permitted INS officers to stop and search any vehicle in the border area without a warrant; without probable cause to believe that the vehicle contained aliens, legally or illegally in the United States; and without probable cause to believe that the vehicle had made a border crossing. In 1973 the Supreme Court rejected this view, stating in *Almeida-Sanchez v. INS* that "[n]o Act of Congress can authorize a violation of the Constitution."[78] The Court held that a warrantless search of an automobile by a roving patrol on a road twenty miles from the Mexican border, without probable cause or consent, violated the fourth amendment's protection from unreasonable searches and seizures.[79]

The Supreme Court extended this decision two years later to prohibit searches at traffic checkpoints as well, unless justified by probable cause. The Court held that "a search, even of an automobile, is a substantial invasion of privacy," and that it does "not appear to make any difference in the search" whether a car is stopped by a roving patrol or at a checkpoint.[80]

This means that although INS agents may freely stop vehicles at fixed checkpoints for brief questioning of their occupants—absent any suspicion at all[81]—they may not conduct searches of those vehicles without consent or probable cause. There is no hard-and-fast rule, however, for what constitutes probable cause in such a situation. The Court suggested that probable cause might be warranted based on factors such as "appearance and behavior" of the vehicle's occupants, "their inability to speak English," and "the nature of the vehicle, and indications that it may be heavily loaded." Furthermore, INS officers are "entitled to draw reasonable inferences from these facts" based on their knowledge and experience with alien smugglers.[82] Thus the Ninth Circuit has held that an automobile's appearance and subsequent flight when asked to stop at a checkpoint supplied probable cause for search.[83]

Some other issues remain sources of confusion, among them the question of what constitute "functional equivalents" to the border. Some courts have construed certain fixed checkpoints as "functional equivalents," thereby permitting INS agents to conduct vehicular searches without probable cause, as they can at the border.[84] In a recent case, however, the Fifth Circuit overturned its prior designation of a fixed checkpoint fourteen miles from the Mexican border as a "functional equivalent" of the border.[85] The court explained that the functional equivalency status of a checkpoint depends on the nature of the traffic passing through it—that such checkpoints must be essentially "international" in character and thereby intercept no more than a negligible number of domestic travelers. Despite the fact that the checkpoint was only fourteen miles from the border, it did not meet this test.[86]

A second question that remains unresolved pertains to the use of "area warrants" to permit vehicular searches at checkpoints, or even by roving border patrols, in the absence of a particularized showing of probable cause. In 1973, five justices of the Supreme Court appeared to endorse this view, proposed by Justice Powell, that the illegal alien problem in the border region justified the use of such "area warrants." Justice Powell suggested that these warrants be issued upon a *general* showing of probable cause established through a variety of factors, such as the frequency of illegal entries in the area, proximity to the border, and probable degree of interference with the rights of innocent persons. The warrant would then authorize vehicular searches in a particular area for a reasonable period of time, possibly several days or weeks.[87] The Supreme Court explicitly declined to reach this question in 1975 when it was considering the propriety of checkpoint searches, as the case before it did not involve such a warrant.[88]

Do immigration officers have the right to enter residences or private places of employment to search for aliens illegally in the U.S.?

Yes, but only with a warrant or consent, unless the officer is in "hot pursuit" of a person believed to have committed a crime of violence that endangers life and security and it is not possible to obtain a warrant in advance.[89] The standard for a warrant, however, differs for workplaces and residences because of the different level of privacy protection accorded to each of these by the courts.

In the case of *workplaces*, a number of courts have now held that an administrative warrant is sufficient to authorize INS searches of workplaces. While probable cause must still be satisfied, the probable cause standard is less rigorous than would be required for a criminal warrant.[90] The warrant must provide sufficient specificity "with respect to the persons sought, the place to be searched, and the time within which the search might take place" so as to prevent unbridled discretion on the part of the INS officers. But it need not name or even particularly describe the aliens being sought.[91]

In a recent decision, however, the Ninth Circuit drew a distinction between search warrants that authorize only *entry* by INS agents into a workplace and those that authorize *seizure* of employees believed to be illegal aliens. In the case of the former, the warrant allows INS officers to enter a factory, but any subsequent arrest of a worker must be independently supported by probable cause. In the case of a seizure warrant, however, the warrant actually authorizes INS officers to seize individuals without any additional justification. Thus the court held that while the relaxed probable cause standard is appropriate for an entry warrant, a warrant authorizing seizure must meet the more rigorous probable cause requirements of a criminal warrant.[92]

It is worth noting that those courts that have held that an administrative warrant is sufficient to authorize INS workplace searches have in part relied on the fact that INS activities are "not analogous to a criminal investigation. . . . [T]here are no sanctions of any kind, criminal or otherwise, imposed by law upon a knowing employer of illegal aliens."[93] This is no longer the case, however. Because of the 1986 Immigration Reform and Control Act's employer sanctions provision, it is now a criminal offense for employers to engage in a pattern and practice of knowingly hiring or continuing to employ aliens not authorized to work.[94] Thus since such warrants may now aid the police in enforcing criminal laws, it is arguable that they should meet the higher probable cause requirements of criminal warrants.

With regard to *residences*, it is somewhat less clear what type of warrant is necessary to justify an INS search for illegal aliens. The courts have recognized that the fourth amendment protection accorded to the home is qualitatively different from that accorded to the workplace.[95] Thus, absent consent, it would seem that INS agents can enter residences to search for illegal aliens only with a warrant that meets the particularized probable cause requirement of criminal warrants.

There has been some controversy concerning this issue,

however, particularly in the context of INS searches of farm worker housing, where the question most frequently arises. For example, residents of migrant farm housing in Washington challenged the INS practice of surrounding farm and ranch housing communities without a warrant, sealing off access roads surrounding each residence unit, using flashlights to look inside each unit's windows and doors, and then getting "consent" to interrogate the residents. The INS maintained that such practices did not constitute a "seizure" of the residents anymore than the workplace raids upheld by the Supreme Court in *Delgado*. The Ninth Circuit disagreed, however, noting both the lack of a warrant and the greater protection accorded to residences.[96]

In other raids of agricultural operations, the INS has relied on administrative warrants to justify their searches of farm worker housing. A federal court in Illinois held that administrative warrants were insufficient for such residential searches.[97] However, the Sixth Circuit recently held that the use of an administrative warrant in such circumstances did not violate any "clearly established" statutory or constitutional right, and thus the INS agents were entitled to qualified immunity for their role in such actions.[98]

May a person refuse permission to an immigration officer to enter a private dwelling or place of employment?

Yes. However, the question of consent is a tricky one. Government agents are under no obligation to warn people that they have a right to refuse consent.[99] Furthermore, there have been numerous situations in which immigration and other enforcement officers have walked into private dwellings without specific consent—when the doors were open or unlocked—or where there has been other disagreement over whether consent was granted. In these circumstances, the testimony of immigration officers that consent has been granted is usually accepted as true.[100] It also remains unclear whether consent by one individual confers authority to question all individuals found in a residence.[101]

Does the fourth amendment prevent the INS from using evidence obtained illegally?

No. The fourth amendment rights of aliens (and citizens

whom INS officers suspect of being aliens) suffered a major setback in 1984 when the Supreme Court ruled that under most circumstances the fourth amendment exclusionary rule does not apply in deportation hearings.[102] By a 5–4 majority, the Court held that the social and judicial costs incurred by applying the exclusionary rule—allowing an ongoing violation (the alien's continued illegal presence in the U.S.) and complicating the character of deportation proceedings—outweighed any benefits to be gained in terms of increased deterrence of unlawful INS conduct. The majority cited with approval existing INS efforts to curb fourth amendment violations and concluded that any additional deterrence to be gained from applying the exclusionary rule would be insignificant.[103]

The net effect of this holding is that immigration agents can engage in fourth amendment violations, and the courts can use the evidence obtained illegally as the basis for an alien's deportation. However, there are a number of important exceptions to this rule. For example, where the fourth amendment violations are so "egregious" that to rely on the resulting evidence would offend due process, suppression of the evidence is warranted.[104] Although there is no clear standard as to when INS conduct is sufficiently "egregious" to warrant this remedy, it can be argued that suppression is called for whenever INS agents violate clearly established fourth amendment principles.[105] For example, the Ninth Circuit recently held that a roving Border Patrol officer's detention of an individual based solely on his Hispanic appearance constituted a fourth amendment violation sufficiently egregious to require suppression, since it "flout[ed] the well-established pronouncement of *Brignoni-Ponce* that Hispanic appearance alone is insufficient to justify a stop."[106]

A second basis for suppression of evidence obtained in violation of the fourth amendment is when the INS conduct also violates specific INS rules or regulations regarding search, interrogation, or arrest that were intended to protect the alien's interests.[107]

Finally, a third avenue for suppression exists under the Due Process Clause when statements are obtained "involuntarily." Fourth amendment violations such as illegal arrests and searches may contribute to a coercive environment so as to make subsequent statements "involuntary."[108]

Are immigration officers permitted to enter private land without a warrant to search for illegal aliens?

Yes, but only within twenty-five miles of an external boundary of the United States. This power, granted by the Immigration and Nationality Act, is limited to the sole purpose of "patrolling the border to prevent the illegal entry of aliens into the United States" and explicitly does not extend to dwellings that are on the land.[109]

Does this authority permit immigration officers to enter farms to search for illegal aliens in parts of the United States that are more than twenty-five miles from the external boundaries?

Prior to November 1986, this was an issue of great controversy, with the Immigration Service maintaining that it had this authority under the "open fields" exception to the fourth amendment acknowledged by the Supreme Court. The INS admitted that its officers enter private lands every day in order to interrogate farm workers in areas where they have reason to believe that illegal aliens may be employed.[110] These areas included sections of the United States that are far beyond the twenty-five mile zone in such states as Colorado, Illinois, and Idaho, as well as in the border areas in California, Texas, Arizona, and New Mexico.

The issue was finally put to rest by Congress with an amendment enacted as part of the 1986 Immigration Reform and Control Act expressly prohibiting this practice. The amendment requires that, except for areas within twenty-five miles of a border, the INS must obtain a search warrant before agents may enter "a farm or other outdoor agricultural operation for the purpose of interrogating a person believed to be an alien as to the person's right to be or remain in the United States."[111]

Does a person have the right to refuse to answer an immigration officer's questions?

Yes. Although immigration officers are empowered by statute to question any "person believed to be an alien," no law requires anyone to answer such questions unless a subpoena has been issued to compel testimony to be given before an immigration officer.[112]

As a practical matter, however, individuals who are approached by INS officers for questioning are in a double bind when it comes to deciding whether or not to answer these questions. As already discussed, the attempt to avoid questioning is one factor that, combined with others, might lead to a finding of "reasonable suspicion" sufficient to justify a person's detention. Thus where other "suspicious" circumstances are present—among these foreign appearance, seeming inability to speak English, or nervousness—an individual who refuses to answer an INS officer's questions may be risking arrest by providing the added ground for his or her subsequent detention. On the other hand, to answer the INS officer's questions may also mean giving information that will lead to arrest.

In addition, any information or statement given to an INS officer during interrogation can later be used against a person during his or her deportation proceeding. Because deportation proceedings are civil proceedings, as opposed to criminal proceedings, the majority of courts have held that there is no duty to give *Miranda* warnings.[113] This means that an individual who is interrogated by INS agents—even in custody—does not need to be warned of his or her right to remain silent. Only at the point of actual arrest do INS regulations require that individuals be warned that the statements they give may be used against them.[114] But usually there is no official "arrest" until well after the individuals have been detained and interrogated, and have signed statements that will later be used against them.

The Due Process Clause of the fifth amendment does, however, provide some protection for aliens facing deportation proceedings. The courts have held that only those statements that are "voluntarily" given can be admitted into evidence in a deportation proceeding.[115] Thus whenever a statement is a result of coercion, stress, or inducement, it is not "voluntary" and should be suppressed.[116] Often the circumstances of an individual's apprehension and interrogation by the INS (lack of food, sleep, threats, denial of right to use a telephone) as well as his or her personal characteristics (youth, lack of education, lack of prior contact with law enforcement officials) can be cited as evidence that the individual's statement was involuntary.[117] Similarly, even where the law does not require that an individual be warned of the right to remain silent, the failure to give such a warning may also be relevant in showing that a statement was involuntarily given.[118]

Finally, the fifth amendment's protection against self-incrimination also applies to aliens in deportation proceedings. Thus to the extent that aliens are asked to give testimony that could be used in a criminal case against them, they can assert their fifth amendment right to remain silent. This applies to questions that might not even seem to incriminate an alien in some crime, such as "Where were you born?" Because alienage is an essential element of a number of crimes—among these, entry without inspection, or reentry after deportation[119]—it can be argued that forcing an alien to testify as to alienage is a form of compelled self-incrimination.[120] In addition, even if the answers would not themselves incriminate the alien, as long as they are links in a chain of circumstantial evidence that could lead to a conviction, the fifth amendment right may be asserted.[121]

Because deportation proceedings are civil, as opposed to criminal, however, courts have held that an adverse reference may be drawn from an alien's invocation of the fifth amendment in deportation proceedings.[122] No court has held that failure to testify is sufficient by itself to find an alien deportable. But where the Immigration Service provides some evidence of alienage, an alien's refusal to testify on this issue may help the government meet its burden of proving alienage.[123] Furthermore, once the government establishes alienage, the burden is on the alien to show place and manner of entry.[124] Thus refusal to testify on these points will result in a finding of deportability, despite the fact that such testimony cannot be compelled under the fifth amendment.

Who has the power to issue a subpoena compelling testimony?

Before the beginning of a deportation proceeding, the district director and certain other officials are authorized to issue a subpoena at their discretion to compel a person to give testimony before an investigating officer.[125] If a witness fails to appear or refuses to answer questions during an investigation, the INS may apply to a federal court to compel compliance with the subpoena.[126] Objections to the subpoena may be presented to a court. If the court directs the witness to answer INS questions, failure to comply may result in a citation for contempt of court. As already noted, however, the fifth amendment may be asserted for any question that could incriminate the witness.

How do persons invoke their right not to speak to an immigration officer?

In view of the skill and experience of immigration officers in conducting investigations, it requires the most resourceful persons to protect their right of privacy regarding where they live and where they work. Those who choose not to speak to immigration or law enforcement officers who do not have search warrants or warrants of arrest should (1) decline to give any information; (2) state that they refuse to speak to the officer until they have had an opportunity to consult an attorney; and (3) state that they refuse to let any officer enter their premises without a warrant.

Under no circumstances should persons physically resist any effort by an officer to question them or to enter the premises. Neither should a person try to run away or elude the officer. This action will itself be regarded by immigration officers as a reason for arrest.

What authority do immigration officers have to arrest aliens?

The Immigration and Nationality Act permits the issuance of a warrant of arrest for any alien determined to be illegally in the United States. It also permits an immigration officer to arrest, without a warrant, "any alien . . . if he has reason to believe that the alien so arrested is in the United States in violation of . . . law . . . and is likely to escape before a warrant can be obtained for his arrest."[127]

The courts have interpreted "reasonable belief," under constitutional standards, to mean probable cause.[128] Probable cause exists when the facts and circumstances within the arresting officer's knowledge are sufficient in themselves to warrant a prudent person's belief that an offense has been or is being committed.[129] Thus to arrest without a warrant requires not only probable cause of illegal alienage but also probable cause that the individual is likely to flee before a warrant can be obtained.

As with "reasonable suspicion," however, there are no rigid criteria for when "probable cause" has been met. In practice it is unusual for a court to question the INS officer's determination. Once an admitted alien is unable to submit documents showing legal presence in the United States, courts are generally ready to find probable cause both that the alien was illegally in the United States and likely to flee.[130] If the alien is a legal permanent resident but unable to produce a green card, there still may be probable cause for arrest pursuant to the statute that requires all aliens over eighteen to carry their registration papers at all times.[131]

Does the INS use arrest warrants to bring aliens under deportation proceedings?

Rarely. Most aliens who are taken into custody are arrested without warrants upon the decision of the arresting officer that the alien is illegally in the United States and is likely to escape. The "decision" that the alien is "likely to escape" is usually based upon no more than the belief that he or she is in the United States illegally. In such cases, the warrant of arrest is obtained later to formalize the custody and to provide legal authority for keeping the alien in detention.

Few aliens illegally in the United States are taken into custody[132] except for Mexican aliens in areas near the United States-Mexican border and other selected parts of the country, alien crewmen, aliens with no fixed address, aliens with criminal records or past histories of disappearing. Most deportation cases are initiated without warrants of arrest by the issuance of an "order to show cause" why the alien should not be deported. This document provides the alien with notice of charges against him and fixes a date for a deportation hearing.[133]

What rights does an alien have when he or she has been taken into custody?

If an alien is questioned by immigration officers, he or she has the right to refuse to answer any questions and the right to seek assistance from the consulate of the country of which the alien is a citizen. If an alien is being held for a hearing to determine whether he or she can be deported, the alien has the right to apply for release from custody on bond. If the alien is unable to obtain release on bond, he or she has the right to a hearing before an immigration judge on eligibility for release.[134]

What arrangements are required for the release upon bond of an alien who is held in custody?

Although bond is fixed and aliens are eligible for release in most cases, the statute permits the INS to keep aliens in custody pending "final determination of deportability" at the "discretion of the Attorney General."[135] The authority to detain aliens has been delegated to INS district directors and specified assistants. The decision to keep the alien in custody without bond, the amount of bond, and any other conditions for release imposed can be reviewed by an immigration judge; thereafter the alien can appeal to the Board of Immigration Appeals and finally seek review by a court in a federal habeas corpus proceeding.

In most cases, the bond is fixed at $1,000. For crewmen, other than those who voluntarily surrender to immigration authorities, the bond ranges from $2,500 to $3,500. In exceptional cases involving aliens for whom there are criminal grounds for deportation, the bond may range from $5,000 to $10,000.

Commercial bonding companies will not usually post bond for aliens unless the full cash amount of the bond is deposited in advance. The typical arrangement is for the arrested alien or his friends to post a United States Treasury Bond or cash (a cashier's check) with the Immigration and Naturalization Service.

What are the grounds for challenging a district director's decision?

If the amount of the bond is "excessive," the immigration judge, the Board of Immigration Appeals, or a federal court can reduce the bond. Since its purpose is to assure the alien's presence at hearings, when required, courts will not permit the bond determination to be used as an indirect method of preventing the alien's release. Courts have usually limited bonds to $5,000, although aliens with substantial assets, or those who are believed to be "likely to abscond" because of a past criminal record or previous flight, are subject to bonds in amounts ranging as high as $100,000.

Conditions imposed for the alien's release upon bond can also be challenged. The usual condition is that the alien appear when and where required. Requirements to prevent association with Communists or employment by a Communist newspaper have been ruled to be unrelated to the purpose of the bond.[136] However, in 1974, the Attorney General, reversing the Board of Immigration Appeals, ruled that aliens could be barred from "unauthorized employment" as a condition of release from custody. The condition is not to be imposed uniformly but will depend upon such factors as the impact on unemployment in the United States, the number of aliens performing the intended employment, the nature of the charges against the alien, his prior immigration record, and personal considerations such as the presence of dependents.[137]

Challenges of INS decisions to keep aliens in custody while their deportation proceedings are pending have had mixed results. A 5-4 Supreme Court decision, *Carlson v. Landon*, held that it is constitutional to give the Attorney General the "discretion" to decide whether to keep aliens in custody without the opportunity to be released by posting bond. The Supreme Court has characterized deportation proceedings as "civil" rather than "criminal," and the fifth amendment's assurance of due process and the eighth amendment's protection against excessive bail are said not to be applicable.[138] An alien will be released from custody only upon a showing that there has been a "clear abuse" of discretion.[139]

The operations instructions issued by the INS authorize district directors to detain aliens in custody when "any available information indicates that an alien's freedom at large would clearly represent a present danger to public safety or security, or when an alien's lack of funds or fixed address supports a finding that he is likely to abscond."[140]

In *Carlson v. Landon*, the Supreme Court upheld continued detention when INS officers believed that "an alien communist may so conduct himself as to aid in carrying out the objectives of the world communist movement."[141]

A bizarre case in 1974 resulted in a holding by a federal court of appeals that "[t]here is no question of the Attorney General's discretion . . . to continue [holding] an alien in custody during deportation proceedings upon a properly made determination that the release of an alien would be a danger to the national security of the United States."[142] The refusal to release the alien was held to be "properly made," although it was based upon confidential information furnished to the Board of Immigration Appeals that was never disclosed to the alien, and despite the fact that the district court, which reviewed the confidential information in camera, found that it failed to establish that the alien was a "security risk." While stating that the determination can be overridden where "it is clearly shown [to be] without reasonable foundation," the court of appeals rejected the alien's argument that he was given no opportunity to refute the secret material given to the Board of Immigration Appeals and held that release from custody is a "form of discretionary relief [which] may be denied on the basis of confidential information, the disclosure of which would be prejudicial to the public interest, safety, or security."[143]

Other court decisions have held it arbitrary to deny bail to an alien as a security risk where there was no showing of recent Communist activity, or because an alien had refused to answer the questions of a congressional committee.[144]

What rights does an alien have in a deportation hearing?

Aliens are entitled to a full and fair "due process" hearing. This includes notice of the charges against them, an opportunity to examine the evidence against them and to cross-examine adverse witnesses, the right to present evidence on their own behalf, and a decision by an unbiased judge based solely on the evidence presented in the hearing.[145]

The alien has "the privilege of being represented[,] at no expense to the government[,]" by counsel of his or her choice.[146] "However, there is no [absolute] right to appointed counsel in deportation proceedings. . . . 'the fact that an alien is without counsel is not considered a denial of due process, if he does not show that he was prejudiced thereby.' "[147]

The INS has the burden of proving that the person in the proceeding is an alien and that the alien is deportable.[148] The alien has the burden of showing that he entered the United States lawfully.[149] A finding by the immigration judge that an alien is deportable must be based upon "clear, unequivocal and convincing evidence."[150]

Although an alien involved in a deportation hearing is afforded certain due process rights, he or she is not afforded all the protections available to citizens in criminal proceedings. For example, in *INS v. Lopez-Mendoza*, the Supreme Court held that the exclusionary rule need not be applied in civil deportation hearings.[151] The exclusionary rule precludes the admission of evidence that has been obtained in violation of the fourth amendment. An alien's admission of unlawful presence in this country made subsequent to an allegedly unlawful arrest may therefore be admitted into evidence in his or her deportation hearing.

What provision does the INS make for counsel for aliens who are indigent?

None. The Immigration and Nationality Act provides specifically that the right of aliens to counsel shall be without cost to the government.[152] If the alien does not have a lawyer, as a matter of policy the INS in most cases makes no effort to assist in obtaining one. However, certain local INS offices may advise aliens under arrest to contact the referral service of the local bar association, the local chapter of the American Immigration Lawyers Association (AILA), or various social service organizations, such as the U.S. Catholic Conference. These organizations may provide aliens with advice on obtaining legal assistance.

Is the government's failure to provide counsel in deportation proceedings for indigent aliens a violation of their constitutional rights?

No court has so far overturned a deportation order against an indigent alien because of failure of the INS to provide counsel, but a decision has stated that "fundamental fairness" requires that "a lawyer at the Government's expense" should be provided to unrepresented indigents in deportation proceedings. The court divided on the question of whether the alien "has an unqualified right to the appointment of counsel," urged by the dissenting opinion, or, as held by the majority, is entitled to a lawyer only if it can be shown that legal representation "could have obtained [a] different administrative result."[153]

The Supreme Court has held that the government must provide counsel to all indigents in criminal cases involving both misdemeanors and felonies and in juvenile court hearings.[154] The dissenting opinion in *Aguilera-Enriquez* urged that since the consequences to a resident alien are at least "as grave" and constitute "punishment in the form of banishment," "fundamental fairness" requires the appointment of counsel at government expense for all unrepresented indigent resident aliens.[155]

Although the government is under no obligation to provide aliens with representation, it cannot interfere with the aliens' access to counsel, and various cases have upheld aliens' due process rights to counsel. In *Castro-Nuno v. INS*, the court determined that the alien had been denied his statutory right of representation. The judge had twice continued the deportation hearing when the alien was present with counsel, but the INS officer failed to appear. On the third occasion, when the alien's counsel was not present, the judge proceeded with the hearing.[156] In *Rios-Berrios v. INS*, the court held that the immigration judge should have continued the deportation hearing to provide the alien with a reasonable amount of time to locate counsel and permit his counsel to prepare for the hearing; the court found that the judge's failure to do so was prejudicial to the alien.[157] In *Nunez v. Boldin*, the court held that prison officials not only must refrain from interfering with communication between prisoners and their attorneys but are obligated to provide prisoners with access to legal assistance and resources.[158]

Does the Immigration and Naturalization Service have the power to deport an alien without a hearing?

No, not in most cases. However, an alien who has been admitted to the United States as a crewman on a conditional landing permit may be deported without a hearing upon a summary revocation of his permit; a similar situation prevails for aliens who have deserted from foreign armed forces while in the United States, where treaties authorize summary removal from this country.[159] Certain aliens who have been previously deported but who have reentered the United States illegally may also be deported without a hearing.[160]

Do aliens who are in the United States illegally have the opportunity to leave the country without being deported?

Yes. If the aliens are not under detention, they usually have the opportunity to leave the United States voluntarily at their own expense. In most cases, INS prefers that the alien leave voluntarily. Unless an alien has a criminal record, has previously been ordered deported, or has a record of repeated immigration law violations, the INS will issue an alien who is illegally in the United States a "voluntary departure" letter that permits him or her to leave the country voluntarily on or before a certain date. The letter is issued prior to the deportation hearing.[161]

Must an alien who is issued a voluntary deportation letter leave the United States on the date fixed for his or her departure?

No. The purpose of granting aliens a deadline for voluntary departure is to permit them to leave on their own. If the alien does not depart by the specified date, he or she is subject to deportation proceedings and, if judged to be illegally in the United States, can be deported. However, an alien who leaves the United States at any time before the entry of an order of deportation is regarded as having departed "voluntarily."

Does an alien have the right to obtain postponement of his or her deportation hearing?

Yes, if he or she has a good reason, but not if the purpose is merely to obtain delay. If the alien does not have an attorney when the first hearing is scheduled, one postponement will be granted to allow time to obtain a lawyer, but after a hearing is delayed for this purpose, further postponements are usually refused. If the alien has no lawyer, he or she may be required to proceed with the hearing.

Postponements will also be granted, at the discretion of the immigration judge, if witnesses are not available or, in some circumstances, to permit the alien to obtain administrative benefits from the district director or other types of relief that would result in the termination of the deportation proceeding. Such benefits include, for example, decisions by a district director to reinstate a student to lawful status, although he or she may have become deportable by working or by failing to attend school. Aliens who are under deportation proceedings because they have been convicted of crimes have also obtained postponement of their hearings to permit them to obtain executive pardons that would wipe out their convictions and grant them immunity from deportation.

Does an alien who is found to be deportable have any relief from deportation?

Yes. An alien may apply during the deportation proceeding

for any relief from deportation for which he or she is eligible. It is the duty of the immigration judge to inform the alien of the various types of relief that may be appropriate to his or her particular circumstances.[162]

What kinds of relief are available?

Voluntary departure. An alien can be granted permission to leave the United States voluntarily under an "order of voluntary departure." This right is important because, unlike an alien who has been ordered deported, an alien who leaves voluntarily is not required to obtain special permission from the INS in order to return to the United States. To obtain an order of voluntary departure, aliens must demonstrate that they are ready, willing, and able to leave the country at their own expense according to the conditions set forth by the immigration judge, and that they have been of good moral character for the past five years.[163]

Adjustment of status to permanent resident. An alien may apply for permanent residence if he or she meets the requirements for obtaining an immigrant visa (*see* ch. IV), and if a visa is currently available. The availability of adjustment of status has been severely limited to exclude crewmen, aliens who entered the United States without inspection, aliens other than specified immediate relatives who have worked without permission, and any alien not in legal immigration status on the date of application for adjustment. Essentially, adjustment of status is available only to those aliens who have not violated their status.[164]

Suspension of deportation. Aliens may apply for suspension of their deportation order provided that they have been physically present in the United States for a continuous period of at least seven years, have been persons of good moral character, and that their deportation would result in extreme hardship to themselves or to members of their immediate families who are citizens or permanent residents. The grant of an order to suspend deportation is, in effect, the approval of status as a permanent resident.

The requirement of continuous physical presence in the United States does not require constant presence for a seven-year period. An alien may make brief departures from the country without interrupting his or her continuous presence. As long as the alien's absence from the United States is brief, casual, and innocent, the alien will not have failed to maintain the necessary continuous physical presence.[165]

In determining whether "extreme hardship" exists, courts may consider the various factors that were outlined by the Board of Immigration Appeals in a 1978 case.[166] These factors include the alien's age and health, family ties in the U.S. and abroad, length of residence in the United States, the political and economic conditions in the country to which he or she would be deported, occupational, financial, and business status, ability to earn a living and support a spouse or children who are American citizens, immigration history, and whether he or she offers any special contribution to this country or the community within it.

The decision to suspend deportation is within the discretion of the Attorney General. In a recent Supreme Court case, the Court held that it was within the Attorney General's discretion to deny a motion to reopen a case of application for suspension even though the petitioning aliens, due to intervening circumstances, had achieved the seven-year presence and had established a *prima facie* case of eligibility for suspension. The Attorney General denied the motion because the couple had obtained the seven-year residence by filing frivolous appeals and had shown disregard for the immigration laws by using a professional smuggler to enter the country and by refusing to leave the country voluntarily after promising to do so.[167]

Aliens who are deportable on criminal, subversive, immoral, and certain other grounds must show that they have been present in the United States and have been persons of good moral character for a period of ten years following the commission of the act that made them subject to deportation. A decision to suspend the deportation of an alien must be reported to Congress to obtain approval for ten-year suspensions and to permit disapproval of seven-year suspensions.[168]

Registration as a permanent resident. A deportable alien may also apply for registration as a permanent resident if he or she has resided in the United States continuously since January 11, 1972, and meets certain other conditions such as being a person of good moral character and being eligible for citizenship.[169] An alien who meets the prescribed requirements for refugees may apply for refugee status. (*See* ch. III.)

Waivers of deportability. Waivers of deportability may be granted to certain categories of aliens. These include aliens who have been lawfully admitted to the United States, have had seven years of consecutive residence, but who left the country temporarily and are deportable upon any ground except that of subversion.[170] Waivers have been granted to aliens who are deportable for insanity, narcotics addiction,[171] or convictions, criminal offenses, or avoidance of military service.

In order to obtain a waiver, aliens must usually establish that deportation will result in hardship either for themselves or their families, and that at the time of the application they are of good moral character.

A mandatory waiver must be granted to an alien who entered the United States upon the basis of a fraudulent misrepresentation if that alien is the spouse, parent, or child of a citizen or permanent resident of the United States.[172] This provision has been construed to include only those aliens who entered the United States as immigrants, not those who entered as nonimmigrants or under false claims of citizenship.[173]

Withholding of deportation. The Immigration and Nationality Act requires the Attorney General to withhold the deportation of aliens who demonstrate that their "life or freedom would be threatened" in the country to which they would be deported.[174] In order to qualify for such relief, the alien must establish a clear probability of persecution. According to the Supreme Court in *INS v. Stevic*, the alien, in order to avoid deportation, must show that "it is more likely than not that the alien would be subject to persecution."[175] Such mandatory relief is only temporary and is subject to annual review.

Political asylum. The Refugee Act of 1980 established a broader form of relief.[176] The statute grants the Attorney General the discretion to grant asylum to an alien who is unable or unwilling to return to the alien's country of origin "because of persecution or a well-founded fear of persecution on account of race, religion, nationality, membership in a particular social group, or political opinion."[177] A more liberal standard is to be applied to asylum cases than to cases seeking to have deportation withheld. The Supreme Court recently held in *INS v.*

Cardoza-Fonesca that in order to show a well-founded fear of persecution, an alien need not meet the "clear probability of persecution" standard required for withholding deportation.[178]

In determining eligibility for asylum, the Ninth Circuit has stated that the "well-founded fear of persecution" standard includes both a subjective and objective component. An alien satisfies the subjective component by showing that the fear of return is genuine; the objective element is satisfied if there is "reasonable possibility" of persecution.[179] (*See* ch. III for a more expansive treatment of this issue.)

Deferred action status. As a matter of discretion, the INS may elect not to enforce the departure of an alien for humanitarian or other reasons in the public interest.[180] The remedy is rarely granted and generally should be considered a last resort.

What type of hearing is provided for applicants for relief from deportation?

The hearings in which the applications are decided are the same as those that determine whether the alien shall be deported. However, a legal distinction is maintained by the INS between the first step of the hearing, which determines whether the alien is deportable, and the second step, which decides whether the alien shall be granted relief from deportation. The deportation hearing, as indicated earlier, must provide the alien with the basic rights of due process. The discretionary phase of the hearing does not accord all of these rights.[181]

In the phase of the hearing to consider relief from deportation, the immigration judge "may consider and base his decision upon information not contained in the record" and not disclosed to the alien.[182] This power was sustained by a 5–4 Supreme Court decision in 1956, which held that confidential information could be used to deny relief from deportation if "its disclosure would be prejudicial to the public interest, safety, or security."[183] The power to use confidential information has been retained "provided the Commissioner has determined that such information is relevant and is classified . . . as requiring protection from unauthorized disclosure in the interest of national security."[184] The use of confidential information to deny discretionary relief has been rare in recent years.

Apart from this limitation, courts have assumed that an alien has the right to a "full hearing" on his or her eligibility for discretionary relief, and it has been suggested by the Supreme Court[185] that a finding regarding an alien's eligibility may be required to be based upon "substantial evidence in the record."

As indicated in the discussion regarding the exercise of discretion in applications to enter the United States (*see* ch. IV), aliens must show that they are of good moral character, that they have close family ties in the United States, that there are other humanitarian reasons for approval, or that a favorable decision would be beneficial to the United States. The policy of the INS, reinforced by a decision by the Board of Immigration Appeals, has been to grant an application for discretionary relief unless there are specific reasons for its rejection.[186] These reasons have included entering the United States as a visitor but with the intention to remain permanently,[187] making misrepresentations to consular or immigration officers,[188] failing to support a family,[189] avoidance of foreign military duty,[190] and violating an agreement to return to the alien's home country to perform services.[191] The factors relied upon will vary according to the nature of the relief. An application for permission to leave the United States voluntarily[192] will be granted more liberally than a change of status to permanent residence.[193]

Does a deportable alien have any voice in determining the country to which he or she is to be deported?

Yes. The INS has the power to require the deportation of an alien to the country of the alien citizenship, birth or last residence, but the alien first has the opportunity to designate a country of his or her own choice.[194]

An alien also has the right to request a stay of deportation to any country in which the alien would be subject to persecution on grounds of race, religion, nationality, social group, or political opinion.[195]

May aliens determine the place of their detention while awaiting their deportation hearing?

No, it is within the Attorney General's discretion to select the place of detention for aliens in custody. In *Committee of Central American Refugees v. INS*, the aliens complained that the INS policy of transferring aliens to remote detention facilities effectively deprived them of their right to counsel. The court held that the government was not obligated to detain aliens where their access to legal representation was the greatest, and that the transfer in question did not deny the aliens access to counsel because an attorney-client relationship had not yet been established.[196]

Does an alien have the right to appeal unfavorable decisions regarding deportability or relief from deportation?

Yes. All decisions may be appealed to the Board of Immigration Appeals.[197] Grounds for appeal are similar to those set forth in the discussion in chapter IV relating to appeals of exclusion orders: questions of law, procedural questions, standards of evidence, and arbitrary exercise of discretion.

Can an alien obtain review of a deportation order in the courts?

Yes. All deportation orders, as well as decisions made in deportation proceedings regarding discretionary relief from deportation, can be reviewed in a United States court of appeals. The petition to review the deportation order must be filed within six months following a final ruling by the Board of Immigration Appeals.[198] Alternatively, review can be obtained in an action for a writ of habeas corpus in a United States district court at any time before the alien is deported.[199]

The grounds for judicial review in a court must be those raised in the administrative proceedings, except that a challenge can be made to the constitutionality of the statute whether or not that argument was raised at the hearings.[200] In addition, a person who claims to be a citizen has the right to a trial in a U.S. district court on the issue of citizenship if the court of appeals finds that he or she has a "substantial claim" to citizenship.[201]

Can the INS deport an alien while the alien's case is pending in a court?

Not in most actions. A petition for review of a deportation order in a federal circuit court of appeals provides for an automatic stay of deportation until the court acts upon the petition.[202] A stay of deportation is also assured in habeas corpus proceedings brought in federal district court.[203] However, if an appeal is taken of an adverse decision by the district court, the alien must usually obtain a further stay of deportation from the circuit court of appeals.[204] Similarly, in any action brought in a federal district court for a declaratory judgment involving an alien, a stay of deportation must be obtained from the court unless the INS is willing to withhold deportation voluntarily without court action.[205]

Is other relief available for aliens who have exhausted their remedies before the INS and in court?

Yes. Members of the House of Representatives and of the Senate may introduce private bills in Congress to relieve an alien from deportation, to permit an alien to remain in the United States, or to render an alien eligible to become a citizen.[206] The Immigration and Naturalization Service will postpone the deportation of any alien for whom a private bill has been introduced in Congress, but only if the Judiciary Committee, to which private immigration bills are referred, requests a report on the legislation from the INS. The Senate Judiciary Committee routinely requests reports on all private immigration bills introduced in the Senate, but unless there is unusual hardship, the House Judiciary Committee will not request reports for aliens who entered the United States without inspection as stowaways, or for crewmen who have deserted their vessels. The stay of deportation granted by the INS is withdrawn if the private bill is voted down, tabled, withdrawn, or not acted on favorably at the close of Congress and therefore dies. However, the INS allows thirty days for a bill to be reintroduced in a succeeding Congress if there was no prior adverse action on the legislation. Few private immigration bills are enacted into law.

NOTES

1. *Plyler v. Doe*, 457 U.S. 202 (1982).
2. *Fiallo v. Bell*, 430 U.S. 787 (1977). This principle is, however, subject to important limitations.
3. *Landon v. Plasencia*, 459 U.S. 21 (1982); *Kwong Hai Chew v. Colding*, 344 U.S. 590, 596–98 (1953). An exception to these holdings has been carved out for foreign military and naval deserters when treaties with other governments provide for summary removal of the deserter. *See Narlidis v. Sewell* 524 F.2d 371 (9th Cir. 1975).

4. *Yamataya v. Fisher (The Japanese Immigrant Case)*, 189 U.S. 86 (1903).
5. *Morrissey v. Brewer*, 408 U.S. 471, 484 (1914). *See also Gagnon v. Scarpelli*, 411 U.S. 778 (1973); *Arnett v. Kennedy*, 416 U.S. 134 (1974).
6. *Turner v. Williams*, 194 U.S. 279 (1904), held that jury trials are not required in deportation proceedings. *See also Zakonaite v. Wolf*, 226 U.S. 272 (1912). Discussions of these and other cases are contained in Louis Boudin, *The Settler Within Our Gates*, 26 N.Y.U. L. Rev. 266–90, 452–74, 632–62 (Apr–Oct. 1951); *Resident Aliens and Due Process*, 8 Vill. L. Rev. 566 (1963); and *Developments in the Law: Immigration Policy and the Rights of Aliens*, 96 Harv. L. Rev. 1286, 1384–95 (1983).
7. *Fong Yue Ting. v. United States*, 149 U.S. 698 (1893).
8. *Mullane v. Central Hanover B. & T. Co.*, 339 U.S. 306 (1950).
9. *See infra* text at note 65 *et seq.*
10. *Ng Fung Ho. v. White*, 259 U.S. 276, 284 (1922).
11. *See* Charles Gordon, *Due Process of Law in Immigration Proceedings*, 50 A.B.A.J. 34–40 (Jan. 1964); *Developments in the Law, supra* note 6.
12. This practice appears to be on the rise in light of recent legislation mandating that the INS "promptly" place detainers on aliens detained on drug charges. *See* § 11751(d) of Pub. L. No. 99-570, the 1986 Anti Drug Abuse Act, adding new subsection "(d)" to § 1287 of the Act, 8 U.S.C. § 11357. In addition, the 1986 Immigration Reform and Control Act requires the Service to "expeditiously deport criminals." § 1242(i), 8 U.S.C. § 11252(i), as added by § 1701 of Pub. L. No. 99-603, effective Nov. 6, 1986.
13. *Matter of Lane*, 13 I. & N. 632 (1970). *See also* Dallek, *Health Care for Undocumented Immigrants: A Story of Neglect*, 14 Clearinghouse Rev. 407 at 412–13 (1980). Some medical institutions, such as the Orange County Medical Services Administration in California, have required indigents to apply for Medicaid and reported to the INS those who refused or who applied without proof of citizenship.
14. *Plyler v. Doe*, 457 U.S. 202 (1982).
15. *Lewis v. Gross*, 663 F. Supp. 1164 (E.D.N.Y. 1986), authorizing payment of Medicaid benefits to undocumented aliens living in New York State.
16. New York, Berkeley, and Chicago are three cities that have issued such instructions.
17. 8 C.F.R. § 1214.3(g).
18. 20 C.F.R. § 1422.107(e).

19. The Supreme Court held in *Sure-Tan, Inc. v. NLRB*, 467 U.S. 883 (1984), in a 7–2 split decision, that undocumented aliens were "employees" covered by the National Labor Relations Act (NLRA), and when employers report undocumented alien employees in retaliation for their participating in union activities, they are committing an unfair labor practice under the NLRA. Since the enactment of employer sanctions as part of the Immigration Reform and Control Act of 1986, there have been attempts to use employer sanctions as a rationale to undermine this position. Thus far those attempts have failed and the principle of *Sure-Tan* has been reaffirmed. *See Patel v. Quality Inn South*, 846 F.2d 700 (11th Cir. 1988); and Memorandum of the National Labor Relations Board (NLRB) General Counsel, dated Sept. 1, 1988, regarding reinstatement and back-pay awards for undocumented aliens.
20. *See infra* text at note 24.
21. *INS v. Delgado*, 466 U.S. 210, 222 n.2 (Stevens, J., concurring) (1984).
22. *See, e.g., INS v. Delgado*, 466 U.S. 210 (1984); *Int'l Molders' and Allied Workers' Local Union v. Nelson*, 799 F.2d 547 (9th Cir. 1986); *Babula v. INS*, 665 F.2d 293 (3d Cir. 1981); *Blackie's House of Beef v. Castillo*, 659 F.2d 1211 (D.C. Cir. 1981); *Martinez v. Nygaard*, 831 F.2d 822 (9th Cir. 1987).
23. Implementation of IRCA's employer sanctions provisions did not go into full force until May of 1988, and for agricultural operations it only began on Dec. 1, 1988.
24. O.I. 242. *See Illinois Migrant Council v. Pilliod*, 540 F.2d 1082 (7th Cir. 1976), *modified en banc*, 548 F.2d 715 (1977). In recent years, the INS appears to have abandoned the widespread use of area control operations, with the exception of traffic stops at or near the border and raids at places of employment.
25. *LaDuke v. Nelson*, 560 F. Supp. 158 at 161 (E.D. Wash. 1982). *See also Blackie's House of Beef v. Castillo*, 659 F.2d 1211 (D.C. Cir. 1981).
26. *See generally INS v. Delgado*, 466 U.S. 210 (1984); *Martinez v. Nygaard*, 831 F.2d 822 (9th Cir. 1987); *Int'l Molders' and Allied Workers' Local Union v. Nelson*, 799 F.2d 547 (9th Cir. 1986).
27. *INS v. Delgado*, 466 U.S. at 216.
28. *Id.* at 218, 221.
29. See *infra* text at note 91 *et seq.* for discussion of the warrant requirement for factory raids. For recent cases where courts have held that INS conduct during a factory raid violated the fourth amendment, see *Int'l Molders and Allied Workers v. Nelson*, 674 F. Supp. 294

(N.D. Cal. 1987), and *Martinez v. Nygaard*, 831 F.2d 822 (9th Cir. 1987).

30. See *United States v. Ortiz*, 422 U.S. 891 (1975), *Almeida-Sanchez v. United States*, 413 U.S. 266 (1973), and *United States v. Brignoni-Ponce*, 422 U.S. 873 (1975), for extended description of INS procedures at traffic checkpoints and the method of operation of "roving" Border Patrol officers. *See also infra* text at notes 41–43.
31. *United States v. Brignoni-Ponce*, 422 U.S. at 874–75.
32. *Id.* at 881. *See infra* text at note 44 *et seq.*
33. 8 U.S.C. § 11357.
34. 8 U.S.C. § 11357(a).
35. 8 C.F.R. § 1287.1.
36. Immigration Reform And Control Act, Pub. L. No. 99-603, § 116, 100 Stat. 3359, 3384 (1986) (codified at 8 U.S.C. § 1357(d)).
37. *Navia-Duran v. INS*, 568 F.2d 803 (1st Cir. 1977).
38. *Caroll v. United States*, 267 U.S. 132, 154 (1925); *Almeida-Sanchez v. United States*, 413 U.S. 266 (1973).
39. *See U.S. v. Henry*, 604 F.2d 908, 915 (5th Cir. 1979).
40. The term "functional equivalent" of the border was first coined in *Almeida-Sanchez v. INS*, 413 U.S. 266, 272–73 (1973). *See U.S. v. Jackson*, 825 F.2d 853 (5th Cir. 1987) for a fuller discussion of what this term means. According to *Jackson*, in order to be the "functional equivalent" of a border, a checkpoint must be essentially "international" in character and thereby intercept no more than a negligible number of domestic travelers. 825 F.2d at 860.
41. *United States v. Martinez-Fuerte*, 428 U.S. 543, 563 (1976).
42. *Id.* at 552, 557–58.
43. *Id.* at 572.
44. *United States v. Brignoni-Ponce*, 422 U.S. 873, 882 (1975).
45. *Id.* at 881.
46. *Id.* at 884, 886–87.
47. *U.S. v. Cortez*, 449 U.S. 411 (1981).
48. *Id.* at 419. For other cases holding that roving patrol stops were justified under the *Brignoni-Ponce* standard, see *U.S. v. Hernandez-Gonzalez*, 608 F.2d 1240 (9th Cir. 1979) and *U.S. v. Magana*, 797 F.2d 777 (9th Cir. 1986). For cases holding that roving patrol stops were *not* justified, see *U.S. v. Lamas*, 608 F.2d 547 (5th Cir. 1979) and *Nicacio v. INS*, 768 F.2d 1133, 1137 (9th Cir. 1985) (Hispanic appearance and presence in an area where illegal aliens frequently travel not enough to justify roving patrol stop).
49. *United States v. Martinez-Fuerte*, 428 U.S. at 566 n.19.
50. *Ibid.* at 552.

51. *See U.S. v. Maxwell*, 565 F.2d 596 (9th Cir. 1977).
52. 8 U.S.C. § 11357(a)(1).
53. *U.S. v. Brignoni-Ponce*, 422 U.S. 873 (1975); *Wong Chung Che v. INS*, 565 F.2d 166 (1st Cir. 1977).
54. *U.S. v. Brignoni-Ponce*, 422 U.S. at 884 n.9. As already discussed, the Court held that suspicion of illegal alienage was necessary for a roving Border Patrol stop of a *vehicle* but reserved the question of what level of suspicion is required to stop and question *persons*, as the issue was not presented in the case before the Court. Given that there is generally *less* fourth amendment protection in a vehicle, particularly one near the border, it would *seem* that the same level of suspicion should be required to stop and question *persons* as is required to stop *vehicles*—illegal alienage. However, the Supreme Court has thus far avoided reaching this issue. *See infra* text at note 54 *et seq*.
55. *INS v. Delgado*, 466 U.S. at 221.
56. *Illinois Migrant Council v. Pilliod*, 548 F.2d 715 (7th Cir. 1977). A similar position is taken by the D.C. Circuit in *Cheung Tin Wong v. INS*, 468 F.2d 1123 (D.C. Cir. 1972) (INS officers allowed to stop and question persons solely on a belief that they are aliens, but "forcible detentions of a temporary nature for the purposes of interrogation" permitted only when there is a "reasonable suspicion" of illegal status). *See also Lau v. INS*, 445 F.2d 217 (D.C. Cir. 1971) (same).
57. *Marquez v. Kiley*, 436 F. Supp. 100 (S.D.N.Y. 1977). Given the Supreme Court's decision in *INS v. Delgado*, 466 U.S. 210 (1984), it is questionable whether this case remains good law. *See infra* text at note 59 *et seq*.
58. *Shan Gan Lee v. INS*, 590 F.2d 497 (3d Cir. 1979).
59. *INS v. Delgado*, 466 U.S. at 218–20.
60. *Id.* at 230 (Brennan, J., dissenting).
61. *Id.* at 221.
62. *Lau v. INS*, 445 F.2d at 223; *Cheung Tin Wong v. INS*, 468 F.2d at 1126.
63. *Terry v. Ohio*, 392 U.S. 1 (1968).
64. *Brown v. Texas*, 443 U.S. 47, 51 (1979); *Terry v. Ohio*, 392 U.S. 1, 30 (1968).
65. *Lau v. INS*, 445 F.2d 217 (D.C. Cir. 1971); *Cheung Tin Wong v. INS*, *supra* note 56.
66. *United States v. Salter*, 521 F.2d 1326 (2d Cir. 1975).
67. *Lee v. INS*, 590 F.2d 497, 502 (1st Cir. 1979).
68. *Babula v. INS*, 665 F.2d 293, 297 (3d Cir. 1981).
69. For fuller discussion of this point, *see Development in the Law:*

Immigration Policy and the Rights of Aliens, 96 Harv. L. Rev. 1286, 1374–75 (1983).

70. U.S. Const. amend. IV. In some cases, however, courts have held that circumstances did not constitute reasonable suspicion sufficient to justify interrogation or detention. *See Nicacio v. INS*, 768 F.2d 1133, 1136 (9th Cir. 1985) (reasonable suspicion must be based on objective standards; alien's Hispanic appearance, presence in an area where illegal aliens travel, and avoidance of eye contact with INS officers, insufficient).
71. *Lau v. INS*, 445 F.2d 217 (D.C. Cir. 1971); *United States v. Zubia-Sanchez*, 448 F.2d 1232 (9th Cir. 1971); *United States v. Saldana*, 453 F.2d 352 (10th Cir. 1972); *U.S. v. Hernandez-Lopez*, 538 F.2d 284 (9th Cir. 1976).
72. *Zepeda v. INS*, 753 F.2d 719 (9th Cir. 1983); *Ramirez v. Webb*, 599 F. Supp. 1278 (W.D. Mich. 1984). *See infra* text at note 74 *et seq.*
73. *U.S. v. Brignoni-Ponce*, 422 U.S. at 886–87; *Matter of Cachiguango*, 16 I. & N. 205 (1977); *Lee v. INS*, 590 F.2d 497, 502 (1st Cir. 1979); *Tejeda-Mata v. INS*, 626 F.2d 721, 724 (9th Cir. 1980). See also Deptartment of Justice Press Release of Dec. 3, 1976, with attached directive to service field officers, stating that street interrogations should only be conducted when there is a reasonable belief of alienage based on specific articulable facts, and setting forth the relevant factors.
74. *Brignoni-Ponce*, 422 U.S. at 886.
75. *Id.*
76 *U.S. v. Ortega-Serrano*, 788 F.2d 299 (5th Cir. 1986).
77. *U.S. Elder*, 425 F.2d 1002 (9th Cir. 1970). *See also U.S. v. Miranda*, 426 F.2d 283 (9th Cir. 1970) (search under vehicle hood upheld on grounds that INS agents previously discovered aliens under vehicle hoods); *U.S. v. Wright*, 476 F.2d 1027 (5th Cir. 1973) (search of spare tire well upheld, since often used to conceal aliens).
78. *Almeida-Sanchez v. INS*, 413 U.S. 266, 272 (1973).
79. *Ibid.*
80. *United States v. Ortiz*, 422 U.S. 891, 895–96 (1975).
81. *See supra* text at notes 41–43.
82. *U.S. v. Ortiz*, 422 U.S. at 897.
83. *U.S. v. Garcia*, 516 F.2d 318 (9th Cir. 1975).
84. *See, e.g., U.S. v. Oyarzum* 760 F.2d 570 (5th Cir. 1985). *See also* Comment, *Functional Equivalents of the Border, Sovereignty and the Fourth Amendment*, 52 U. Chi. L. Rev. 119 (1985).
85. *United States v. Jackson*, 825 F.2d 853 (5th Cir. 1987).
86. *Id.* at 860. *See also U.S. v. Browning*, 634 F. Supp. 1101 (W.D. Tex. 1986).

87. *Almeida-Sanchez v. U.S.*, 413 U.S. 266 at 283–84 (Powell, J., concurring); at 288 (White, J., dissenting) (1973). See also *U.S. v. Jackson*, 825 F.2d at 853, describing circumstances under which area warrants may be issued and emphasizing that the scope of the search thereby authorized must be limited to parts of the vehicle where a person could be hidden. See also *U.S. v. Martinez-Fuerte*, 514 F.2d 308 (1975), *rvsd.* 428 U.S. 543 (1976), rejecting an attempt by the INS to use "magistrate's area warrants" authority to search automobiles at checkpoints, since the warrants were not based upon probable cause and delegated "too much discretion to border patrol agents . . . [to] detain anyone driving north on the highway."
88. *U.S. v. Ortiz*, 422 U.S. at 897 n.3.
89. *Chimel v. California*, 395 U.S. 752 (1969); *Warden, Maryland Penitentiary v. Hayden*, 387 U.S. 294 (1967).
90. *Blackie's House of Beef, Inc. v. Castillo*, 659 F.2d 1211 (D.C. Cir. 1981), *cert. denied*, 455 U.S. 940 (1982); *Int'l Molders' and Allied Workers' Local Union v. Nelson*, 799 F.2d 547, 552 (9th Cir. 1986).
91. *Blackie's*, 659 F.2d at 1226; *Int'l Molders'*, 799 F.2d at 552.
92. *Int'l Molders' and Allied Workers' Local Union v. Nelson*, 799 F.2d 547, 552 (1986). *See also Int'l Molders' and Allied Workers' Local Union v. Nelson*, 674 F. Supp. 294 (N.D. Cal. 1987) (warrant-authorized seizure, must meet more rigorous probable cause standard).
93. *Blackie's*, 659 F.2d at 1218; *Int'l Molders'*, 799 F.2d at 552.
94. 8 U.S.C. § 11324a.
95. *INS v. Delgado*, 466 U.S. at 224 (Powell, J., concurring); *U.S. v. Martinez-Fuerte*, 428 U.S. 543 (1976); *LaDuke v. Nelson*, 762 F.2d 1318, 1329 (9th Cir. 1985).
96. *LaDuke v. Nelson*, 762 F.2d 1318 (9th Cir. 1985).
97. *Illinois Migrant Council v. Pilliod*, 531 F. Supp. 1011, 1022–23 (N.D. Ill. 1982).
98. *Ramirez v. Webb*, 835 F.2d 1153 (6th Cir. 1987). In this case INS officers used an administrative warrant to search for illegal aliens housed in a barn that was part of a commercial farm operation.
99. *Schneckloth v. Bustamonte*, 412 U.S. 218 (1973).
100. *Hon Keung Kung v. District Director, INS*, 356 F. Supp. 571 (E.D. Mo. 1973); *Cuevas-Ortega v. INS*, 588 F.2d 1274 (9th Cir. 1979).
101. *See U.S. v. Rodriguez*, 532 F.2d 834 (2d Cir. 1976) (consent to accompany arrested person to retrieve passport did not authorize INS agents to question at random all persons found in house). *But see Cordon de Ruano v. INS*, 554 F.2d 944 (9th Cir. 1977) (officers invited into a home can question persons found there).
102. *INS v. Lopez-Mendoza*, 468 U.S. 1032 (1984). In this decision the

Court endorsed the position already taken by the Board of Immigration Appeals in *In re Sandoval*, 17 I. & N. 70 (1979).

103. *INS v. Lopez Mendoza*, 468 U.S. at 1044–46.
104. *Id.* at 3490 n.5; *Matter of Toro*, 17 I. & N. 340 (BIA 1979).
105. For fuller discussion of this point *see generally* A. Fragomen, A. Del Rey, S. Bernsen, *Immigration Law & Business* § 18.4(b)(2), at 8–47, 48 (1988).
106. *Arguelles-Vasquez v. INS*, 786 F.2d 1433 (9th Cir. 1986).
107. *Matter of Garcia-Flores*, 17 I. & N. 325 (BIA 1979); *U.S. v. Calderon-Medina*, 591 F.2d 529 (9th Cir. 1979).
108. *Navia-Duran v. INS*, 568 F.2d 803 (1st Cir. 1977); *Cuevas-Ortega v. INS*, 588 F.2d 1274 (9th Cir. 1979); *Matter of Garcia*, 17 I. & N. 319 (BIA 1979). For fuller discussion, *see generally* A. Fragomen, A. Del Rey, S. Bernsen, *Immigration Law and Business* § 18.4(b)(1), at 8–44, 45, *see infra* text at notes 115–18.
109. 8 U.S.C. §11357(a)(3); *See also Almeida-Sanchez v. United States*, *supra* note 30.
110. *See Illinois Migrant Council v. Pilliod*, 540 F.2d 1062 (7th Cir. 1976), *modified en banc*, 548 F.2d 715 (1977).
111. Pub. L. No. 99–606, § 116, 100 Stat. 3359, 3384 (1986), codified at 8 U.S.C. § 1357(d).
112. 8 U.S.C. §§ 1357(a), 1225(a).
113. *See Harisiades v. Shaughnessy*, 342 U.S. 580 (1952); *Nai Cheng Chen v. INS*, 537 F.2d 566 (1st Cir. 1976); *Avila-Gallegos v. INS*, 525 F.2d 666 (2d Cir. 1975). However, *Miranda* warnings are necessary when INS questioning is likely to elicit responses that are incriminating, i.e., that will subject the individual to *criminal* as opposed to civil penalties. *United States v. Mata-Abundiz*, 717 F.2d 1277 (9th Cir. 1983).
114. 8 C.F.R. §§ 287.3; 242.2.
115. *Navia-Duran v. INS*, 568 F.2d 803 (1st Cir. 1977). *Cuevas-Ortega v. INS*, 588 F.2d 1274 (9th Cir. 1979); *Attoh v. INS*, 606 F.2d 1273 (D.C. Cir. 1979).
116. *Id. See also Matter of Garcia*, 17 I. & N. 319 (BIA 1979).
117. *See, e.g., Schneckloth v. Bustamonte*, 412 U.S. 218, 226 (1973).
118. *Navia-Duran v. INS*, 568 F.2d at 808. *See also Attoh v. INS*, *supra* note 115.
119. 8 U.S.C. §§ 1325, 1326.
120. *Matter of Sandoval*, 17 I. & N. 70, 72 (BIA 1979).
121. *See Estes v. Potter*, 183 F.2d 865 (5th Cir. 1950).
122. *Chavez-Raya v. INS*, 519 F.2d 397 (7th Cir. 1975); *U.S. v. Alderete-Deras*, 743 F.2d 645 (9th Cir. 1984).
123. *See Wong Kwok Sui v. Boyd*, 285 F.2d 572 (9th Cir. 1960).

124. 8 U.S.C. § 1361.
125. 8 C.F.R. § 287.4(a)(2).
126. 8 C.F.R. § 287.4(d).
127. 8 U.S.C. §§ 1357(a)2, 1252(a).
128. *Yam Sang Kwai v. INS*, 411 F.2d 683 (D.C. Cir. 1969); *La Franca v. INS*, 413 F.2d 686 (2d. Cir. 1969). *See also U.S. v. Perez-Castro*, 606 F.2d 251 (9th Cir. 1979).
129. *Cabral-Avila v. INS*, 589 F.2d 957 (9th Cir. 1978).
130. *See, e.g., Contreras v. U.S.*, 672 F.2d 307, 308 (3d Cir. 1982).
131. 8 U.S.C. § 1304(e). *Martinez v Nygaard*, 831 F.2d 822, 828 (9th Cir. 1987); *Benitez-Mendez v. INS*, 760 F.2d 907, 909 n.2 (9th Cir. 1985).
132. O.I. 242.6(c).
133. 8 C.F.R. § 242.1 (1988).
134. 8 C.F.R. § 242 (1988).
135. 8 U.S.C. § 1252(a) (1982).
136. *U.S. v. Witkovich*, 353 U.S. 194 (1957); *Barton v. Sentner*, 353 U.S. 963 (1957).
137. *Matter of Toscana-Rivas, et al.*, Int. Dec. 2257; *see* 8 C.F.R. § 1103.6(a)(2) (1988), *see INS v. National Center for Immigrants Rights*, 791 F.2d 1353 (remanded by U.S. Supreme Court in light of IRCA).
138. *Carlson v. Landon*, 342 U.S. 524 (1952).
139. *See id.* at 540.
140. O.I. 242.6(c).
141. *Carlson*, 342 U.S. at 544.
142. *Barbour v. District Director*, 491 F.2d 573, 578 (5th Cir. 1974) (citing 342 U.S. 524).
143. *Id.*
144. *Belfrage v. Shaughnessy*, 212 F.2d 128 (2d Cir. 1959); *Daniman v. Esperdy*, 113 F. Supp. 283 (S.D.N.Y.), *aff'd on other grounds*, 210 F.2d 564 (2d Cir. 1953).
145. *Japanese Immigrant Case*, 189 U.S. 86; 8 U.S.C. § 1252(b); 8 C.F.R. § 242.10–16.
146. 8 U.S.C. § 1362 (1982).
147. *Trench v. INS*, 783 F.2d 181, 183 (10th Cir. 1986) (quoting *Burquez v. INS*, 513 F.2d 751, 754 (10th Cir. 1975)).
148. *Gastelum-Quinones v. Kennedy*, 374 U.S. 469 (1963).
149. 8 U.S.C. § 1361 (1982).
150. *Woodby v. INS*, 385 U.S. 276 at 290 (1966) (citing the standard set by *Schneiderman v. United States*, 320 U.S. 118 (1943)).
151. *INS v. Lopez-Mandoza*, 468 U.S. 1032 (1984).
152. 8 U.S.C. § 11362.
153. *Aquilera-Enriquez v. INS*, 516 f.2d 565, 573 (6th Cir. 1975) (DeMascio, J., dissenting); *see Morrissey v. Brewer*, 408 U.S. 471 (1972).

154. *In re Gault*, 387 U.S. 1 (1967).
155. *Aquilera-Enriquez*, 516 F.2d at 573 (DeMascio, J., dissenting).
156. *Castro-Nuno v. INS*, 577 F.2d 577 (9th Cir. 1978).
157. *Rios-Berrios v. INS*, 776 F.2d 859 (9th Cir. 1985).
158. *Nunez v. Boldin*, 537 F. Supp. 578 (S.D. Tex. 1982).
159. 8 U.S.C. § 1282(b); *see also Japanese Immigrant Case*, 189 U.S. 86.
160. 8 U.S.C. § 1252(f).
161. 8 C.F.R. § 242.5.
162. 8 C.F.R. § 242.17.
163. 8 U.S.C. § 1254(e).
164. 8 U.S.C. § 1255(a); 8 C.F.R. § 242.17(a).
165. 8 U.S.C. § 1254(a)(3). This provision overrules *INS v. Phinpathya*, 464 U.S. 183 (1984) (holding that an alien's three-month absence from the country negated the seven-year continuous physical presence requirement).
166. *Matter of Anderson*, 16 I. & N. Dec. 506 (1978).
167. *INS v. Rios-Pineda*, 471 U.S. 444 (1985).
168. 8 U.S.C. § 1254.
169. 8 U.S.C. § 1259.
170. 8 U.S.C. § 1182(c).
171. *See Arias-Uribe v. INS*, 466 F.2d 1198 (9th Cir. 1972) (refusal to require a waiver for a narcotics offender because it would "render inoperative those provisions of the Act which make deportation mandatory for aliens who have been convicted of a narcotics offense").
172. 8 U.S.C. § 1182(i).
173. *Reid v. INS*, 420 U.S. 619 (1974); *INS v. Errico*, 385 U.S. 214 (1966).
174. 8 U.S.C. § 1253(h); INA §1243(h).
175. *INS v. Stevic*, 467 U.S. 407, 429/30 (1984).
176. 8 U.S.C. § 1158(a).
177. 8 U.S.C. § 1101(a)(42).
178. *INS v. Cardoza Fonesca*, 94 L. Ed. 2d 434 (1987).
179. *Vides-Vides v. INS*, 783 F.2d 1463 (9th Cir. 1986).
180. O.I. 242.1(a)(22).
181. 8 C.F.R. § 242.16.
182. 8 C.F.R. § 242.17.
183. *Jay v. Boyd*, 351 U.S. 345 (1956).
184. 8 C.F.R. § 242.17(a).
185. *Jay v. Boyd*, 351 U.S. 345.
186. *Matter of Arai*, 13 I. & N. Dec. 494.
187. *Matter of Tonga*, 12 I. & N. Dec. 212.
188. *Tomboc v. Rosenberg*, 427 F.2d 677 (9th Cir. 1970).
189. *Matter of Zavala*, 10 I. & N. Dec. 628.
190. *Matter of Lee*, 13 I. & N. Dec. 236.

191. *Matter of Tayeb*, 12 I. & N. Dec. 739.
192. *Matter of M.*, 3 I. & N. Dec. 490.
193. *Matter of S.*, 5 I. & N. Dec. 409.
194. 8 U.S.C. § 1253(a).
195. 8 U.S.C. § 2533(h); *see also* ch. III.
196. *Committee of Central American Refugees v. INS*, 795 F.2d 1434 (9th Cir. 1986), *modified*, 807 F.2d 769 (9th Cir. 1987).
197. 8 C.F.R. § 13.1(b).
198. 8 U.S.C. § 1105(a)(1); *Foti v. INS*, 375 U.S. 217 (1963).
199. U.S. Const., art. I, § 19, cl. 2; 8 U.S.C. § 1105(a)(9).
200. *Kessler v. Strecker*, 307 U.S. 22 (1939).
201. 8 U.S.C. § 11105a(a)(6).
202. 8 U.S.C. § 11105(a)(3).
203. *See ex parte Endo*, 323 U.S. 283 (1944).
204. *Foo v. Shaughnessy*, 234 F.2d 715 (2d Cir. 1955).
205. *Jiminez v. Barber*, 252 F.2d 550 (9th Cir. 1958), *stay denied*, 355 U.S. 943 (1958).
206. For a discussion of the congressional procedures involved in the enactment of private immigration bills, *see* Rules, House Judiciary Committee; Statement, Rep. Peter Rodino, 117 Cong. Rec. H-2635 (Apr. 17, 1971); and Note, *Private Bills and Immigration*, 68 Harv. L. Rev. 1083 (1956).

VII
Registration, Criminal Laws, and Extradition

Aliens in the United States are subject, of course, to the same laws that govern all people in this country. Aliens who commit crimes, no less than citizens, are accountable for their conduct. But apart from the general laws that apply to all persons in the United States, there are provisions of several statutes that apply only to aliens. These include, among others, laws that define illegal practices under the Immigration and Nationality Act.

Are aliens in the United States required to register with the police or with any government agency?

There is no requirement that aliens register with local police departments or other state authorities. Although on previous occasions cities and states have adopted laws requiring alien registration, the United States Supreme Court has held such laws unconstitutional because control over aliens is placed in the federal government, not in state and local governments.[1] However, aliens are required to register with the INS as a consequence of the Alien Registration Act of 1940.[2]

There are diverse registration forms for aliens, depending upon the category of the alien in the United States.[3] If any single document may be regarded as the basic element of the INS Identification System, it would be the Alien Registration Receipt Card, form I-151/551, which is issued to aliens who are lawful permanent residents in the United States. All nonimmigrants are generally given the I-94 form upon entry into the United States. The I-94 card reflects their status and length of stay. It is also given to parolees admitted to this country since they are admitted temporarily; however, form I-94 is not a document used for refugees.

If the nonimmigrant is permitted to work in the United States, his I-94 card will be stamped "employment authorized." However, such authorization is not needed for immigrants in the United States. The alien registration card itself is proof of their eligibility to be employed.

Aliens who have been granted permanent residence, those who have been placed under deportation proceedings, and those who have been questioned regarding their eligibility to enter the United States at the time of entry are given alien registration numbers. All INS files of these individual aliens begin with the letter *A* followed by an eight-digit number. The alien's *A* number is used on all documents from the INS and should be used by the individual when communicating with the INS. Nonimmigrants in the United States generally are not given these numbers. In these instances, the number that should be used in communicating with the INS depends upon the status that the alien has in this country and the type of proceeding in which he or she is involved. Access to information contained in the individual's file can be obtained pursuant to the Freedom of Information Act[4] or the Privacy Act.[5]

Which aliens are required to register under the Alien Registration Act?

All aliens who are in the United States for more than thirty days, except those specifically exempted by statute, are required to be fingerprinted and to register with the INS.[6]

Which aliens are exempt?

All aliens who obtain either immigrant or nonimmigrant visas meet the registration requirements when they apply for their visas. Fingerprinting, however, is not required of (1) a nonimmigrant alien whose country does not fingerprint American visitors to that country; (2) other nonimmigrants who remain in the United States and maintain their nonimmigrant status for no more than one year; (3) children under the age of fourteen; and (4) diplomats, members of international governmental organizations, and their families.[7]

Are citizens of Canada and Mexico treated differently?

Sometimes. Citizens of Canada and Mexico may obtain border-crossing cards, which allow them to enter the United States for up to seventy-two hours, but travel is restricted to within twenty-five miles of the border.

How does an alien show that he or she is lawfully in the United States?

An alien who has been admitted to the United States for permanent residence is issued an Alien Registration Receipt Card, commonly known as a "green card." An indication of permanent resident alien status is also noted in the individual's passport. An alien who has been admitted to the United States as a nonimmigrant is issued an Arrival-Departure Card.

Every alien over the age of eighteen is required to carry an Alien Registration Receipt Card or Arrival-Departure Card at all times.[8] It is this document that INS officers seek to examine when they question a person "believed to be an alien" concerning his right to be in the United States. (*See* ch. VI.)

It is illegal for an alien to make copies of either document. If the Alien Registration Receipt Card or the Arrival-Departure Card is lost, new cards will be issued by the INS upon application.[9]

Are aliens required to notify the INS of their address?

Yes. All aliens are required to furnish the INS their address within ten days of their entry to the United States. The information provided for the issuance of the Arrival-Departure Card, form I–94, and the Alien Registration Receipt Card, form I–151/551, serves this purpose. Aliens must also provide notice to INS within ten days of any change of address, using the form AR–11.[10]

Failure to comply with any of these requirements is a violation of criminal law and may subject the alien to imprisonment as well as to deportation.[11]

Is it a crime for an alien to enter the United States in violation of the immigration laws?

Yes. It is a criminal violation of the law for an alien to enter the United States at a time or place that has not been designated by the INS, to evade examination or inspection by immigration officers, or to obtain entry by making false statements or by concealing information regarding material facts.[12] It is also a crime for an alien who has previously been ordered deported to reenter the United States unless he or she has obtained consent in advance to reapply for admission.[13] Bringing aliens into the United States illegally, harboring or concealing them are also crimes. Knowingly hiring an unauthorized alien is not regarded as "harboring";[14] however, it is a violation of the "employer sanctions" provisions of the immigration law. (*See* ch. II.)

Other offenses relating to the illegal entry of aliens that are punishable by imprisonment or fine include coming to the United States as a stowaway,[15] assisting subversives,[16] and entering this country as a prostitute.[17]

Is it a crime for an alien to be in the United States in violation of the immigration laws?

Simply *being* in the United States is not a crime. There must be an additional act by the alien, and it must be willful and deliberate before the conduct can be regarded as criminal. In addition to the crimes relating to illegal entry of aliens to the United States, there are two offenses that are crimes for which aliens may be sent to jail or fined under the immigration laws.

An alien who has been previously deported and has reentered the United States without securing permission in advance from the Attorney General to reapply for admission is punishable for entering or being "found" in the United States.[18] Although a constitutional challenge has been made to the provision that being "found" in this country is a crime, the Supreme Court has never ruled on the question. The only lower court to decide the issue has upheld the law.[19]

It is also a crime for an alien crewman to remain in the United States willfully beyond the time permitted on his landing permit.[20]

Certain aliens who have been ordered deported may be convicted and imprisoned if they fail or refuse to depart within six months after the entry of a final order of deportation. These include aliens who have been ordered deported on political or criminal grounds, who have been involved in prostitution or conduct relating to narcotics, or who have violated the registration requirements imposed upon aliens.[21] Although the constitutionality of this statute has been upheld,[22] it has become generally unenforceable. A conviction requires a showing that the deportable alien has willfully failed to apply for travel documents to be received in another country, that his or her failure to apply for such documents is unjustified, and that there is a country willing to accept the deportable alien from the United States.[23]

The INS is also authorized to apprehend aliens and deport

them as criminal aliens if they have been (1) convicted of a crime of moral turpitude committed within five years of entry and imprisoned for a year or more or (2) convicted of two or more crimes involving moral turpitude (not arising from a single action) at any time after entry. Crimes of moral turpitude include murder, manslaughter, rape and sodomy. (*See* ch. IV.)

Other aliens who may be in the United States illegally because they have violated the conditions under which they were admitted, or because they have stayed in this country beyond the time authorized by the INS are subject to deportation but are guilty of no violation of criminal law.

Do state and local police officers have the power to arrest and detain aliens for violating the immigration laws?

Usually no. The enforcement of immigration laws is generally left to the INS. But some state laws grant local police the authority to arrest persons who violate federal criminal laws, including criminal immigration statutes.[24] In addition, the Anti-Drug Abuse Act of 1986 includes a requirement that state law enforcement officials notify INS when they arrest any individual suspected of being an undocumented alien on drug charges.

May an alien be arrested without a warrant by an immigration officer?

An immigration officer is authorized to make an arrest without a warrant in two circumstances: (1) when the alien is attempting to enter the United States illegally in plain view of the officer; and (2) when an alien is believed to be in the United States illegally and the officer has "reason to believe" that the alien is likely to escape before a warrant can be obtained for his arrest.[25] Failure to meet these requirements may render the arrest illegal.[26]

May aliens be extradited for crimes committed in other countries?

Yes, but only if there is an extradition treaty between the United States and the country that seeks his or her extradition.[27] The offense must be identified in the treaty as "extraditable"[28] and must usually have been committed in the territory of the requesting country.[29] The offenses typically include major crimes such as murder, kidnapping, robbery, larceny (including embezzlement and obtaining property by false pretenses), counterfeiting, and in recent treaties, aircraft hijacking and violations of narcotics laws.[30] They do not include "political offenses"[31] or violations of military obligations, such as desertion.[32] In addition, extradition is barred if the statute of limitations has run out[33] and the alien can no longer be prosecuted. Extradition may also be barred if the offense is not a crime in both the United States and the requesting country.[34]

Is an alien entitled to a hearing before he or she can be extradited?

Yes. Hearings are required and are usually held before a United States magistrate acting for a federal district court. The requesting country must show the person to be extradited is the person sought, a factual statement of the offense and the law violated, and evidence that the accused has committed the crime. Although a formal trial is not conducted to determine guilt, the requesting state must produce evidence sufficient to establish a reasonable ground to believe that the person to be extradited is guilty.[35]

NOTES

1. *Hines v. Davidowitz*, 312 U.S. 52 (1941).
2. 26 Stat. 670.
3. See 8 C.F.R. § 264.1 for the listing of the various types of registration categories of aliens.
4. 8 C.F.R. § 103.10.
5. 8 C.F.R. § 103.20.
6. 8 U.S.C. § 1302.
7. I U.S.C. § 1201(b); 8 C.F.R. § 264.1.
8. 8 U.S.C. § 1304(e).
9. 8 C.F.R. § 264(h).
10. 8 U.S.C. § 1305.
11. 8 U.S.C. § 1305.
12. 8 U.S.C. § 1325.
13. 8 U.S.C. § 1326.
14. 8 U.S.C. § 1324.
15. 18 U.S.C. § 2199.
16. 8 U.S.C. § 1327.

17. 8 U.S.C. § 1328 and 18 U.S.C. § 2424(a).
18. U.S.C. § 1326.
19. *United States v. Alvarado-Soto*, 120 F. Supp. 848 (S.D. Calif. 1954).
20. 8 U.S.C. § 1282(c); *U.S. v. Cores*, 356 U.S. 405 (1958).
21. 8 U.S.C. § 1252(d).
22. *U.S. v. Spector*, 343 U.S. 169 (1952); *Wiczynski v. Shaughnessy*, 185 F.2d 347 (2d Cir. 1950).
23. *U.S. v. Heikkinen*, 355 U.S. 273 (1958).
24. In 1979 INS adopted guidelines governing the enforcement of immigration laws by local police. The guidelines stated that "whether local or state law enforcement officers have the legal authority to enforce the criminal provisions of the immigration laws is a question of state law, since nothing in the Constitution or federal law prohibits such enforcement." *INS Guidelines* M-69, at 40–41 (rev. June 1979). In 1983 the INS revised these guidelines to encourage an even more active state and local police role in enforcing the criminal immigration statutes. *See Revised INS Guidelines*, 60 Interpreter Releases 172–73 (1983). *See generally*, *United States v. Salinas-Calderon*, 728 F.2d 1298 (10th Cir. 1984).
25. *Diozo v. Holland*, 243 F.2d 571 (3rd Cir. 1957); *U.S. v. Meza-Campos*, 500 F.2d 33 (9th Cir. 1974).
26. *U.S. v. Perez-Castro*, 606 F.2d 251 (9th Cir. 1979).
27. *Factor v. Laubenheimer*, 290 U.S. 276 (1934). Approximately 100 countries have entered into extradition treaties with the United States.
28. *Wing's Case*, 6 Op. Atty. Gen. 85.
29. See Evans, *The New Extradition Treaties of the United States*, 59 Am. J. Int. Law 351–62 (Apr. 1965).
30. See Evans, *The New Extradition Treaties of the United States*, 59 Am. J. Int. Law 351–62 (Apr. 1965).
31. *Karadzole v. Artukovic*, 247 F.2d 198 (9th Cir. 1957), *vacated on other grounds*, 355 U.S. 393 (1958), *surrender denied on remand sub nom United States v. Artukovic*, 170 F. Supp 383 (S.D. Cal 1959); Deere, *Political Offenses in the Law and Practice of Extradition*, 27 Am. J. Int. Law 247–70 (1933); Evans, *Reflections upon the Political Offense in International Practice*, 57 Am. J. Int. Law 1–24 (1963).
32. VI Hackworth, *Digest of International Law*, sec. 758 (1943).
33. *Caputo v. Kelly*, 96 F.2d 787 (2d Cir. 1938).
34. *Collins v. Loisel*, 259 U.S. 309 (1922).
35. *See* 18 U.S.C. § 651; *Neely v. Henkel*, 180 U.S. 109 (1901).

VIII
The Rights of Alien Students

There are approximately 350,000 foreign students enrolled in colleges and universities in the United States.[1] These individuals, as distinguished from those who are permanent residents or aliens who have been admitted as nonimmigrants for other purposes, are admitted to the United States as nonimmigrant students and are officially under the supervision of the Immigration and Naturalization Service. To be allowed to enter and remain in the United States, prospective foreign students must be accepted by an INS-approved educational institution, demonstrate that they have adequate financial support, maintain a full course of study as bona fide students, and, if employment is needed, request permission in advance to work in the United States.

The INS sets general regulations and guidelines governing the rights of foreign students, but INS district offices are given some latitude to interpret these provisions for themselves. As a result, there can be considerable variation in INS decisions affecting individual foreign students. If a serious problem with the INS should arise, a student is urged to consult with the foreign student adviser or other designated school official[2] at his or her educational institution, the educational attaché of the embassy, or any one of several organizations that address the needs and rights of foreign students.

How does a foreign student who wants to study in the United States obtain a visa?

A foreign student who wants to study in the United States must first be issued a nonimmigrant student visa before he or she can legally enter the country. A visa, which is an official document, stamped on a page of a passport, authorizes admission into a particular country and may be obtained from any American consulate issuing nonimmigrant visas. It is recommended that a student applying for a visa does so through the nearest American consulate in his or her country of legal residence in order to avoid delay. A consulate outside of an applicant's home country may require additional justification for considering the application and will usually contact the student's home consulate to obtain a background report before making a decision. This procedure is followed to prevent an applicant who has been denied a student visa at one consulate from obtaining a visa at another consulate.[3]

What are the requirements for obtaining a visa to study in the United States?

The visa applicable for most foreign students is known as an F-1 nonimmigrant student visa. This type of visa is open to all students enrolled in an academic or language program (undergraduate, postgraduate or postdoctoral study, and/or research) that has government approval for that purpose.[4] The school in which the student plans to enroll will issue an eligibility form—the I-20AB (also called Certificate of Eligibility)—which is necessary to obtain the F-1 visa. This form should be given to the American consul to obtain a visa and to the immigration officer when the student arrives in the United States.

In addition, foreign students must have proof that they will be able to support themselves in the United States as full-time students with a scholarship, personal funds, or the assistance of close relatives including any who may be living in the United States. Foreign students must also present evidence that they have the educational background to pursue their intended course of study, and that they intend to leave the United States upon completion of their studies. Other qualifications that foreign students must meet include proving that they have a residence to which they will return and are proficient in English or will receive sufficient training once in the United States.[5]

What other type of visa is available for foreign students?

Besides the F-1 there are two other visa categories whereby foreign students may enter the United States to study. The J-1 category is open to students enrolled in an exchange visitor program for advanced academic study and research at an institution accredited by the United States Information Agency.[6] The sponsoring institution will issue a form IAP-66, which will be required both to obtain a visa and then to enter the United States. It should be noted that in some cases students or their academic institutions may have some leeway in determining whether to apply for an F-1 or a J-1 visa. Since there is a significant difference between the two visa categories, students who may be eligible for either should consult with their academic institution regarding the appropriate visa. For example, aliens in J-1 status may be required to fulfill a two-year foreign residence requirement before changing to permanant residence status under certain circumstances.

The M-1 category is open to students accepted by vocational or other recognized nonacademic institutions approved by the Attorney General and usually involves only limited periods of stay. M-1 visa holders may be allowed to work in the United States for practical training. Again, students should consult their academic institution regarding their specific eligibility for an M-1 visa.[7]

What documents must a foreign student or exchange visitor present to the INS in order to enter the United States?

To enter the United States a foreign student must present a student visa that has been issued by an American consulate abroad, a "certificate of eligibility" granted him or her from the academic institution the student has been enrolled to enter, and a passport. A passport is a travel document usually issued by one's country of citizenship that shows the bearer's origin, identity, nationality, and other vital facts that are necessary to enter a foreign country. It is especially important to be sure that all documents are valid through the time that the student intends to remain in the United States.[8]

Can a student change schools and lawfully remain in the United States?

Yes. But a student is required initially to attend the school that issued the certificate of eligibility presented to the American consulate as the basis for his or her visa. Failure to attend the educational institution for which permission was granted to come to the United States to study is a ground for terminating student status and can result in deportation.[9]

A foreign student can transfer schools without prior INS approval, provided that proper procedure of notifying the INS is followed.[10]

The student must obtain the proper government form (form I-20AB) from the school where he or she intends to transfer, complete it, and then give it to the designated school official (usually the foreign student adviser) at the new institution within fifteen days after the start of classes. The official must then complete his or her portion of the form and submit it to the INS within thirty days of receipt of the completed form I-20AB from the student. The school official must also verify the standing of the student at the last institution attended, as well as determine that the student is currently attending classes at the new school.

Little participation is required from the designated official at the previous school, with the exception that he or she must be notified by the student of the student's intention to transfer, and that verification be supplied to the INS that the student had been enrolled in a full course of study during his or her last term at the former school.

If the student has not pursued a "full course of study" at his or her previous school, the student has technically fallen out of status and must then apply for, and be granted, reinstatement by the INS before requesting a transfer to another school. Problems can arise if the notification process is not followed properly and in a timely manner by both the student and the designated official at the new school.

Can a foreign student change his or her field of study?

Yes, but shifts to unrelated fields are treated with suspicion that the student is not "bona fide." The student must show that he or she has an "educational program" and that the change in his or her field of study is not intended merely to extend the student's stay in the United States.[11]

Can foreign students work in the United States while they are going to school?

Questions regarding foreign student employment fall into two broad categories: on-campus employment and off-campus employment.

On-campus employment is generally related to a student's academic program and, as such, would not require prior INS authorization. Such employment is usually part of a scholarship, fellowship, work-study program, or is otherwise pursuant to academic study. Foreign students may engage in this type of employment or any other type of on-campus employment that does not displace a citizen or permanent resident worker, provided that it is performed on the school's premises and is authorized by the educational institution. Students are not allowed to exceed twenty hours of work per week while school is in session, although students may work full-time when their school is out of session, provided that the job is on-campus. After students have completed their courses of study, they are no longer eligible for on-campus employment, except as it relates to practical training, which will be explained later. The foreign student adviser should be consulted before accepting on-campus employment.

Off-campus employment requires the explicit permission of the INS and is prohibited for students during their first year of study in the United States or for students who are enrolled in an academic program for less than one year. To be authorized for off-campus employment, the foreign student adviser or designated school official must certify to the INS that the student is in good academic standing and is carrying a full course of study; has demonstrated economic necessity because of unforseen circumstances (devaluation of currency in the student's home country, unexpected cutoff of financial support from his or her family, sudden increases in tuition or the cost of living, etc.); has shown that working will not interfere with his or her studies; and that the student has agreed not to work more than twenty hours per week when school is in session. Full-time employment is permitted when school is not in session. Completion of the course of study or changing schools ends the authorization.

Foreign students who engage in off-campus employment without INS approval are in violation of their student status and risk deportation.[12]

What other opportunities are there for foreign students to work in the United States?

Foreign students may work in a "practical training" program that is related to their course of study, the purpose of which is to give them the opportunity to implement what they have learned in school if it is shown that comparable training is not available in the students' home countries.[13] Foreign students who are eligible may obtain a maximum of twelve-months practical training in two six-month increments after the completion of their courses of study, although practical training can also be authorized before the completion of studies under certain circumstances and for work-study programs.[14]

It is very important for foreign students to get the exact details concerning employment and practical training from their foreign student advisers or designated school officials. INS requirements for practical training are time-limited and subject to specific conditions for different types of studies and training. INS decisions relating to employment for students vary significantly with both circumstances and the individual INS district office involved.

Do foreign students have the right to engage in extracurricular activities?

Yes. Although INS officers and FBI agents have on occasion investigated and harassed foreign students who have participated in demonstrations and engaged in other activities, foreign students, including nonimmigrant aliens, have the same first amendment rights, with the exception of being an anarchist or a Communist (*see* ch. IV), as other students.[15]

Does an arrest or a conviction for a criminal offense affect a foreign student's status?

An arrest does not; however, a conviction for an offense involving moral turpitude is a ground for deportation (*see* ch. IV). A conviction for any other type of offense will not affect a foreign student's status unless he or she is imprisoned for a period so prolonged that it "meaningfully interrupts his studies."[16]

Can the spouse and children of a nonimmigrant student or an exchange visitor come to the United States as visitors?

Yes. The family of a nonimmigrant student must show that they have sufficient resources to live in the United States without working. The spouse of an exchange visitor is permitted to be employed but not for the purpose of supporting the exchange visitor.[17]

How long may aliens remain in the United States as students?

Generally, foreign students may remain as long as is reasonably necessary to complete their schooling. Foreign students must apply for an "extension of stay" with the INS only if they have taken too long to complete any one academic program,[18] or if they have remained in student status for eight consecutive years.[19] The time frames that are necessary to complete a given academic program will be made known to the student by the foreign student adviser or designated school official.

INS regulations concerning the specific timing for filing applications for extensions are complex. It is advised that if the students are considering changing their academic programs, they consult with their adviser about potential filing deadlines. Students who need an extension of time and who miss the deadlines for filing will be out of status and may not be granted reinstatement to student status without showing good cause.

Can an alien who has entered the United States as a tourist, as a business visitor, or in another nonimmigrant category change his or her status in this country to that of a student?

Yes. However, a change of status will not be approved for nonimmigrants who have committed fraud to obtain their visa by withholding information from or giving false information to a consul.[20]

As a general rule, aliens who intend to study in the United States are required to obtain a nonimmigrant student visa or, where applicable, an exchange visitor's visa. They are not permitted to use another type of visa to gain entrance to the United States and, after their admission to this country, to change to student status. An exception is made for students who have established their eligibility for a student visa but have not selected their school. In that case, a B-2 visa may be issued with the notation "prospective student—school not yet selected."

Must a nonimmigrant alien have a student or an exchange visitor's status in order to attend school in the United States?

No. Such status is required only for aliens who are in the United States for the sole purpose of studying. Tourists and other visitors are not prevented from attending school or taking courses of study in this country provided that they maintain their nonimmigrant status. They are not required to obtain certificates of eligibility from the educational institution they attend, nor are they required to apply for student or exchange visitor status.

Can foreign students who have failed to attend school, changed schools, or worked without permission maintain or be restored to nonimmigrant student status?

Yes, but not routinely. The decision to overlook violations of a student's status is made "at the discretion" of the INS district director. It will usually be granted only if the violation was not "intentional," or when a student has worked without permission if the need to work arose because of emergency circumstances. The treatment of students who have failed to comply with immigration requirements varies at each INS office.

Depending upon the INS officer making the decision, students in identical circumstances may be restored to student status, placed under deportation proceedings, and promptly ordered to leave the United States. Alternatively, without restoration to student status, a student may be permitted to remain in the country long enough to complete the school term and, in some cases, the student's course of study until graduation.

NOTES

1. In 1986, there were approximately 343,000 foreign students enrolled in INS-approved institutions. (63 Interpreter Releases 1005 (Nov. 3, 1986).

   The admission of foreign students to study in the United States was first codified in the Immigration Act of 1924, which established their admission as "non-quota immigrants." The Immigration and Nationality Act of 1952 extended this policy to the present day.
2. *See* 8 C.F.R. § 214.3. The term "designated school official" is particularly important. Only designated school officials are authorized to sign relevant INS forms governing the enrollment, transfer, and employment of foreign students. While the designated school official may include the foreign student adviser, not all schools have such advisers or limit their designation accordingly. Check with the school in which you are enrolled or the INS for more information.
3. 22 C.F.R. § 41.110.
4. *See* 8 C.F.R. § 214.2(f). Enrollment in a full-time course of study is necessary for the maintenance of lawful F–1 status. A full-time course

of study is generally defined for undergraduates as twelve semester or quarter hours of instruction per academic term, when the course load requires payment of full tuition or is for administrative purposes considered full-time.

5. 22 C.F.R. § 41.45.
6. 8 C.F.R. § 214.2(j).
7. 8 C.F.R. 214.2(m).
8. 22 C.F.R. § 41.111–12.
9. 8 C.F.R. § 214.2(f)(2).
10. 8 C.F.R. § 214.2(f)(8).
11. 8 C.F.R. § 214.4(f)(7).
12. 8 C.F.R. § 214(f)(6).
13. 8 C.F.R. § 214.2(f)(10).
14. 8 C.F.R. § 214.2(f)(10)(i)(A).
15. *Bridges v. California*, 314 U.S. 252 (1941).
16. *In re Murat-Kahn*, Int. Dec. 2237.
17. 22 C.F.R. § 41.65; 63.5.
18. 8 C.F.R. §§ 214.2(f)(7)(ii)(A)(B)&(C).
19. 8 C.F.R. § 214.2(f)(7)(i).
20. 8 U.S.C. § 1258; 8 C.F.R. § 248.

IX

The Right of Aliens to Work

To the economist, the flow of people to settle America has been a source of wealth that has helped to develop the nation's economy. The rapid growth of industry in this country has been due, in part, "to the fact that the United States was spared the cost of producing a considerable fraction of its population," to the economic value of the labor of migrants, and to their demand for goods and services.[1]

To many of the people who had already settled in the United States, the incoming migrant has at various times been regarded as a threat. Apart from ethnic, racial, and religious prejudices, each wave of immigrants to America has been met with resistance because of the belief that the "cheap labor" of the incoming alien undermines the living standards of those already here.[2]

The result has been a mix of federal and state laws designed partly to reduce overall immigration as a solution to the "competition of alien labor," partly to exclude aliens from coming to work in the United States except in occupations where there are shortages, and partly to restrict certain occupations to citizens.

While the laws have had considerable impact upon the number of aliens coming to the United States, the specific countries from which they come, and the way in which they enter, as well as upon the ability of aliens in this country to pursue various occupations, there is widespread belief that the economic and social factors that have drawn people to the United States have been a stronger force than the laws that have sought to exclude them. Between 1869 and 1974, approximately 1.8 million immigrants entered the United States in what is called the "migratory stream" from Mexico.[3] Legal permanent admissions to the United States peaked at approximately 800,000 persons. At the present time, net immigration—legal plus undocumented persons—probably exceeds 750,000 per year.

The Immigration Reform and Control Act of 1986 (IRCA), which is a set of amendments to the Immigration and Nationality Act, is the most recent response to this flow of illegal entrants to the United States. IRCA has made it unlawful, for the first time in history, to hire or to recruit or refer for a fee an individual who is not authorized to work in the United States.[4] Employers who violate this provision by knowingly hiring, recruiting, or referring an unauthorized alien are subject to civil penalties, ranging from $250 to $2,000 for a first offense and up to $10,000 for subsequent violations. IRCA even imposes criminal penalties on employers who engage in a "pattern or practice" of hiring violations.[5] However, it is especially important to remember that employers can easily comply with the employer sanctions requirement if they follow the relatively straightforward procedure designed to verify an individual's work authorization.

The impact of employer sanctions on the entry of undocumented immigrants has yet to be determined, but it is certain that Spanish-speaking and foreign-born citizens as well as lawful aliens will have to overcome an additional hurdle in getting a job.[6]

The laws that impose citizenship as a requirement for employment in specific occupations are generally unenforceable in view of a series of Supreme Court decisions upholding the right of aliens to work. But for certain employment, including the right to work for the federal government, citizenship remains a requirement.[7]

Are aliens permitted to work in the United States?

Yes, but aliens' right to work and the type of work they may perform depend in part upon their status under the immigration laws and to some extent upon state and federal laws that impose conditions upon the employment of aliens.

What general restrictions on employment are imposed by the immigration laws?

Aliens who are permanent residents are entitled to reside in the United States indefinitely and are not subject to any general employment restrictions. However, if they become permanent residents upon the basis of an Alien Employment Certification to work for a specific employer or upon the basis of a petition to give them a preference because of their occupation, they must have the bona fide intention to perform the work upon which their permanent residence is based. Although permanent resident aliens who obtained their status in this manner may change their employment, if they fail to work for the employer who sponsored them or in the occupation for which they were approved, they risk deportation if they were inadmissible at the time of entry on grounds of fraud.[8]

Permanent resident aliens are generally entitled to equal treatment under state law absent a compelling reason to justify distinctions between aliens and citizens. However, the states can restrict even a permanent resident alien's access to employment in areas involving "important governmental functions," such as schoolteachers or police officers.[9]

Various categories of aliens who are admitted to the United States as nonimmigrant visitors are not permitted to work. These include visitors for pleasure, aliens who are passing through the United States as transit visitors, and with limited exceptions, the spouses and children of nonimmigrant aliens.[10]

Which nonimmigrant aliens may work?

Generally nonimmigrant aliens may work only if specifically authorized under the terms of their immigration status. In fact, the overwhelming majority of aliens who enter the United States lawfully each year do so as nonimmigrant visitors in the B visa category (e.g., tourists, visiting family, business, etc.), which precludes activities in this country that will result in the alien's employment here. Nonimmigrant aliens who may work in this country include:

1. Employees of foreign governments and their personal servants
2. Business visitors who are employed by a foreign business to perform temporary services in the United States, such as selling, negotiating contracts, engaging in business consultations, training personnel to maintain foreign-manufactured equipment, and accompanying as a personal servant a visitor performing functions for a foreign business
3. Crewmen who perform services on board vessels or aircraft
4. Aliens who are promoting international trade, or who have made or are making substantial investments in the United States
5. Representatives of foreign governments to interna-

tional governmental organizations and the employees of such organizations

6. Aliens who perform temporary services of an "exceptional nature," as persons of "distinguished merit and ability," aliens who perform temporary services in occupations in which there is a shortage in the United States, or aliens who are trainees
7. Representatives of foreign newspapers, periodicals, radio, television, and other information media
8. Fiancé(e)s of American citizens who have come to the United States to be married
9. Aliens who have been admitted to the United States under exchange programs to teach, conduct research, demonstrate special skills, or receive training, if employment has been approved as part of the program

In addition, students may be permitted to work with the permission of the INS. (*See* ch.VIII.)

Do any of these nonimmigrant aliens need the approval of the U.S. Department of Labor to work in the United States?

Yes. Aliens who are admitted as temporary workers to perform temporary services in occupations in which there is a shortage of qualified workers in the United States need the approval of the Department of Labor. Qualified workers for this purpose include U.S. citizens, permanent resident aliens, and refugees, but not other nonimmigrant aliens. Special procedures are provided for the recruitment of foreign agricultural labor and for other types of temporary workers in the United States. In each case, the DOL must certify that qualified persons are not available in the United States to perform the work and that the employment of aliens will not adversely affect the wages and working conditions of U.S. workers.[11]

Which aliens qualify as persons of "distinguished merit and ability"?

The H-1 nonimmigrant visa category is used by companies and other organizations to employ temporarily aliens who qualify as persons of "distinguished merit and ability" in professional positions that require the particular individual's special capabilities.

The categories of persons considered to be of "distinguished merit and ability" include aliens who have professional occupations in medicine, science, engineering, the arts and humanities, and similar fields, as well as athletes and entertainers who have achieved public recognition, and who show that the services they will be performing in the United States are for a temporary period. Approval is usually granted in increments of one to three years, with a possible maximum in exceptional cases of five years.

What penalties are imposed on non-immigrant aliens who work without obtaining permission from INS?

Generally, such aliens are subject to deportation for violating their status in the United States. However, their treatment will vary depending upon their status. Tourist and transit visitors will usually be required to leave the United States or be placed under deportation proceedings. The spouses and children of nonimmigrants, depending upon the policy of various INS district offices, will usually be permitted to remain in the United States until the purpose of the principal nonimmigrant's stay in this country has been fulfilled. Students who work without permission can be treated harshly and have been ordered deported both for working without permission and, when authorized to work, for working more hours than permitted.

Are criminal penalties imposed upon an alien who works without securing permission from the INS?

No. There is no law that makes it a crime for an alien to be employed without the approval of the INS.

Are there any controls over alien employment?

Yes. As discussed previously, the Immigration Reform and Control Act (IRCA) of 1986 introduced sanctions for those employers who knowingly hire persons not authorized to work. IRCA also established procedures for employers to accept documentation from prospective employees to show employment authorization and to keep that documentation on file.[12]

Are aliens who are illegally in the United States forbidden to work?

No. There is no federal law that makes it unlawful for an

"undocumented alien" to work. But an alien who is illegally in the United States can be deported for having entered or for being in this country unlawfully. Employment by such an alien in itself does not result in any additional penalty or make the alien more deportable. Only those aliens who have been lawfully admitted to the United States upon the condition that they not be employed become deportable by working.

Judicial decisions have limited INS authority to detain an alien in custody to effect deportation unless the alien has a serious criminal record, is a threat to public safety or security, or, as an alien charged with being a Communist, is likely to continue to "carry out the objectives of the world communist movement."[13]

Despite the regulation, the restriction on the employment of deportable aliens has not been widely invoked by INS. In some circumstances, INS district directors will give deportable aliens written permission to be employed by stamping on their passports or immigration forms the phrase "Employment Authorized." These aliens include those who cannot be deported because no country will accept them, those who have applications pending to become lawful permanent residents or who have been permitted to remain in the United States while their applications for immigrant visas are being processed abroad, and others who have been granted permission to remain in the United States temporarily.

Are aliens able to obtain Social Security cards to work?

Yes, but there are restrictions. In 1972, Congress adopted legislation restricting the availability of Social Security account numbers to aliens lawfully in the United States.

The Social Security Administration will issue unrestricted Social Security cards to United States citizens, permanent resident aliens, and aliens authorized by the INS to work.[14] Other aliens who are lawfully in the United States as nonimmigrants may obtain a Social Security number for nonwork purposes, such as for school, bank accounts, and tax payments. However, if an alien obtains a Social Security number that is not valid for employment, his record is coded and the INS will be notified if employment returns are found using that number.

Can aliens employed in the United States but present in this country illegally bring lawsuits to recover minimum wages and other employee benefits?

Yes. The fact that an alien may be in the United States illegally cannot be used by an employer to cheat him out of any rights he may have for minimum wages, workmen's compensation, or other employee benefits. In fact, the Supreme Court has held[15] that undocumented workers were "employees" with the scope of protections offered by the National Labor Relations Act. Since one of the purposes of the immigration statute is to protect U.S. workers from competition by aliens, courts generally have not allowed an employer to escape liability for wages and other employee rights by claiming that his or her employee is in the United States illegally.[16]

What are the state laws that restrict an alien's right to work?

Most states have laws that limit employment in various professions and occupations to citizens or to aliens who have declared their intention to become citizens. These statutes are unconstitutional, but they may continue to be enforced in some states. The proscribed occupations include accountants, architects, attorneys, barbers, chiropractors, cosmetologists, dentists, dental hygienists, embalmers, engineers, manicurists, midwives, nurses, opticians, optometrists, pharmacists, physical therapists, physicians, practical nurses, podiatrists, psychologists, teachers, and veterinarians.

Why are these state laws unconstitutional?

Both the fifth amendment, which applies to the federal government, and the fourteenth amendment, which applies to the state governments, provide that "no person shall be deprived of life, liberty or property without due process of law." The fourteenth amendment also provides that "no state shall deny to any person within its jurisdiction the equal protection of the laws." The significant term in these clauses, as they relate to aliens, is the word "person." This word, of course, includes aliens. The protection of these amendments is therefore not limited to United States citizens.

In 1886, the Supreme Court held that a municipal ordinance that in effect discriminated against Chinese laundry operators was a violation of the Equal Protection Clause.[17] In 1915, the Supreme Court invalidated an Arizona statute that required that 80 percent of the employees of businesses having more than five employees be "qualified electors or native-born citizens of the United States."[18] The Court affirmed the "right to work for a living in the common occupations of the community" as being of the "very essence of personal freedom and opportunity that it was the purpose of the [fourteenth amendment] to secure."

The not-so-common occupations, however, were left unprotected. In the same year, 1915, a statute limiting employment of persons on "public works" to citizens of the United States and requiring a preference for citizens of the state was sustained on the theory that the "property and resources of a state are for the benefit of its citizens."[19] In 1926, the Supreme Court held that aliens could be denied licenses to operate pool and billiard rooms on the ground that it was "not shown to be irrational" to exclude aliens from the "conduct of a dubious business."[20]

By 1948, the Supreme Court found racial classifications "suspect" in holding unconstitutional a statute that barred the issuance of commercial fishing licenses to persons who were "ineligible to citizenship."[21] In this case, the racial classification had been purposely designed to exclude one particular group of aliens—Asians who under the immigration laws in force at the time were not eligible for citizenship. In 1971, in a case dealing with the eligibility of aliens for welfare benefits, the Supreme Court repeated that classifications based upon alienage are "inherently suspect and subject to close judicial scrutiny." Such suspect classifications can be justified only where the state shows a "compelling need" for the classification.[22] Two years later, in 1973, the Supreme Court held that no such compelling need had been established by a state to justify the determination to bar an attorney who was not a citizen of the United States from practicing law.[23] It also invalidated a state civil service statute in New York that limited positions in the competitive civil service to citizens.[24]

Despite the clear trend of the Supreme Court's rulings, state laws barring aliens from certain kinds of employment are still on the books and continue to be enforced until individually challenged in the courts.

Does the federal government deny employment to aliens?

Yes, for most positions. In September 1976, following a Supreme Court decision that struck down a Civil Service Commission regulation that, with limited exceptions, barred aliens from federal employment, President Ford issued an Executive Order prohibiting any employment in the competitive service (which includes most federal employees) for persons who are not citizens or nationals of the United States.[25]

The Supreme Court had held by a 5–4 decision in 1976 that the only concern of the Civil Service Commission "is the promotion of an efficient federal service," and that it could not justify its prohibition of employment to aliens upon the grounds of foreign policy, immigration control or economic considerations, nor could it impose "wholesale deprivation of employment opportunities" to "millions of lawfully admitted resident aliens" for the sake of "administrative convenience."[26]

In his Executive Order, President Ford declared that it is "in the national interest to preserve the long-standing policy of generally prohibiting the employment of aliens in the competitive service," except where "specific cases or circumstances" warrant such employment.[27]

Whether the Executive Order is valid remains an open question. The Supreme Court "assum[ed] without deciding that (various) national interests would adequately support an explicit determination by Congress or the President to exclude all noncitizens from the federal service," but it expressly stated that its opinion "intimate[d] no view as to whether (certain statutory) federal citizenship requirements are or are not susceptible to constitutional challenge."[28]

Aliens are eligible to work for various governmental agencies under special exceptions granted by specific statutes or under other authority. The Postal Service, a governmental corporation, originally denied aliens employment but during the course of the litigation in the Supreme Court abandoned the citizenship requirement except for employees in sensitive and policy-making positions.[29]

In addition, the Department of Defense, the Atomic Energy Commission, the National Aeronautics and Space Administration, and the Foreign Claims Settlement Commission are authorized to employ aliens generally. The Department of Agriculture, the Department of State, and certain other agencies may employ aliens for specific positions.[30]

Apart from these exceptions, citizens of countries linked to the United States in mutual defense agreements, the Philippines, and aliens from Poland and the Baltic countries who are permanent residents are also eligible for federal employment.[31]

Can aliens obtain state licenses?

Usually, but not always. State laws that deny certain kinds of licenses to aliens are probably unconstitutional. If a license is required in order to work or to engage in a business, the decisions of the Supreme Court relating to the right of aliens to work indicate that such licenses may not be denied to permanent resident aliens in the United States. However, the Supreme Court has not yet invalidated discriminatory laws against aliens on the ground that such discrimination is in itself unconstitutional. Its approach has been to require the government to show that there is a "compelling," "overriding," "important," or "substantial" need for such discrimination. It has described the burden of proof the government must meet to show such need as "heavy."

Can aliens obtain federal licenses?

Federal statutes now deny licenses to aliens to register and operate aircraft, vessels, radio stations, and atomic energy facilities.

There have been no court challenges of the requirement for citizenship for such licenses. It is doubtful whether the Supreme Court would invalidate laws by Congress that restrict the issuance of licenses in occupations that could be regarded as related to national security. In 1975,[32] the Supreme Court indicated that citizenship may be a proper requirement for "sensitive" positions and "assumed" that "national interests" could support an "explicit determination by Congress or the President to exclude all noncitizens from the federal service." It would follow from this approach that congressional statutes that deny licenses to aliens in such sensitive activities as piloting aircraft or seagoing vessels, radio and television communications, and atomic energy functions would not be regarded as improper.

NOTES

1. Spengler, *Some Economic Aspects of Immigration into the United States*, 21 Law & Contemp. Prob. 235–55, at 241 (Spring 1956).
2. O. Handlin, *The Uprooted* (1951); J. Higham, *Strangers in the Land* (2d ed. 1965).
3. Frisbie, *Illegal Migration from Mexico to the United States*, 9 Int. Migration Rev. 3–13 (Spring 1975); Cardenas, *United States Immigration Policy Toward Mexico*, 2 Chicano L. Rev. 66–91, 90–91 (Summer 1975).
4. 8 U.S.C. § 1324a. However, the employer sanctions provision does not apply to union hiring halls that refer or recruit for a fee workers who are union members or pay union dues. *See* 8 C.F.R § 274a.1(h),(j).
5. 8 U.S.C. § 1324a(f).
6. *See* H.R. Rep. No. 682, 99th Cong. 2d Sess., pt. 2 (1986).
7. *See Hampton v. Wong*, 426 U.S. 88 (1976); *In re Griffiths*, 413 U.S. 717 (1973); *Takahashi v. Fish and Game Commission*, 334 U.S. 410 (1948).
8. 8 U.S.C. §§ 1182(a)(19) and 1251(a)(1).
9. *See Ambach v. Norwich*, 441 U.S. 61 (1979) (schoolteachers); *Foley v. Connelie*, 435 U.S. 291 (1978) (police officers).
10. 8 C.F.R. § 214.
11. 8 C.F.R. § 214.2(6)(h)(3)(i).
12. *See supra*.
13. *U.S. v. Witkovich*, 353 U.S. 194 (1959); *Carlson v. Landon*, 342 U.S. 524 (1952); *Rubinstein v. Brownell*, 206 F.2d 449 (D.C. Cir. 1953), *aff'd.*, 346 U.S. 929 (1954) (per curium, by equally divided court).
14. 20 C.F.R. § 422.103.
15. *Sure-Tan Inc. v. NLRB*, 467 U.S. 883 (1984).
16. The House Judiciary Report on IRCA says that it is not the intention of the committee that the employer-sanctions provisions diminish in any way the powers of labor relations or labor standards agencies to remedy unfair practices committed against undocumented employees, *supra*, at 58. Whether the NLRB will comply with the legislative history is yet to be seen.
17. *Yick Wo v. Hopkins*, 118 U.S. 356 (1886).
18. *Truax v. Raich*, 239 U.S. 33 (1915).
19. *Heim v. McCall*, 239 U.S. 175 (1915).
20. *Clarke v. Deckebach*, 274 U.S. 392 (1927).
21. *Takahashi v. Fish and Game Commission*, 334 U.S. 410 (1948).
22. *Graham v. Richardson*, 403 U.S. 365 (1971).
23. *In re Griffiths*, 413 U.S. 717 (1973); a recent change in the Rules of the New York Court of Appeals permits not only aliens, but foreign

lawyers to be licensed as "legal consultants" to provide with specified exceptions, various counseling services. The legal consultant must reside in New York. See Rules for the Licensing of Legal Consultants, pt. 521, Rules of the New York Court of Appeals for the Admission of Attorneys and Counsellors-at-Law.

24. *Sugarman v. Dougall*, 413 U.S. 634 (1973).
25. 41 Fed Reg. 37, 301 (Sept. 2, 1976).
26. *Hampton v. Mow Sung Wong*, 426 U.S. 88 (1975).
27. *See* note 29.
28. *Hampton v. Mow Sung Wong, supra* note 30.
29. Postal Service Personnel Handbook, § 317.3, *as amended by* Postal Bulletin, May 2, 1974, § 317.31, p. 2, 5 C.F.R. § 338.101; Public Works Appropriation Act, 1970, 83.
30. 10 U.S.C. 7473 (Department of the Navy—scientific and technical positions); 20 U.S.C. 46a (Smithsonian Institution—scientific and technical positions); 22 U.S.C. 1044(e) Department of State—Foreign Service Institute); 42 U.S.C. 2473(b)(10) (National Aeronautics and Space Administration—all employment); 84 Stat. 1489 (Department of Agriculture—Foreign Agriculture Service); 84 Stat. 2029 Department of Defense—all employment); 84 Stat. 890 Atomic Energy Commission—all employment); 84 Stat. 1059 Foreign Claims Settlement Commission—all employment; 84 Stat. 1061 (United States Information Agency—translators); 84 Stat. 823 (Library of Congress—up to ten positions).
31. 56 Stat. 422 (1942); 57 Stat. 196 (1943); 67 Stat. 435 (1953).
32. *Supra* note 30.

X

The Right of Aliens to Own Property

The concept of private property is so fundamental in the American economic and social fabric that the Bill of Rights places it on an equal footing with life and liberty. Essentially, the right of all persons to own property is afforded protection by due process of the law. But this general rule has only applied, at least from a historical perspective, to United States citizens and not aliens.

The acquisition and ownership of property by aliens has been the subject of different policies in the history of this country. Generally, aliens have always been permitted to acquire and own personal property. In the early history of the United States, the ownership of real property was limited to citizens and to aliens who declared their intention to become citizens. In later years, beginning in the 1850s, incitement first against the Chinese and later the Japanese led to enactment of laws in the western states that barred or restricted the ownership of land by aliens who were "ineligible to citizenship." Congress had provided that natives of Asian countries could not be naturalized as United States citizens. The consequence of these statutes was therefore to prevent these nationals from owning land. As recently as 1923, the United States Supreme Court upheld restrictions prescribed by West Coast states against land ownership by Orientals, finding such restrictions justified by considerations of safety and sovereignty.[1]

Today most of the laws that prohibited ownership of land by aliens have been repealed or are not enforceable. Chinese, Filipinos, East Indians, and then all other Asians became eligible for naturalization by a series of Acts of Congress between 1943 and 1952. (*See* ch. XV) The passage of these Acts ended the prohibition against the ownership of land by natives of Asian countries. In 1948 the Supreme Court ruled that a California law that barred the ownership of land for agricultural purposes by aliens "ineligible to citizenship," while permitting it for other aliens, was a denial of the equal protection of the laws.[2] It should be noted, however, that the Court's decision outlawed discrimination against citizens only when it is based on racial ancestry. Nonetheless, opinions by the Supreme Court in other cases involving the rights of aliens suggest that the remaining discriminatory ownership laws are no longer valid.

Do aliens have the right to own property?

Generally, yes. An alien who lives in the United States now has essentially the same right as a citizen to own property. Two clauses in the fourteenth amendment protect this right. One clause forbids a state to "deprive any person of life, liberty or property without due process of law." The other forbids a state to "deny any person within its jurisdiction the equal protection of the laws." Those guarantees apply to "persons" and not merely "citizens." They therefore protect aliens as well as citizens.[3] Nevertheless, distinctions have been made between the right of aliens and citizens to own real and personal property.

There are also differences in the right to own property by aliens who do not live in the United States. These aliens are not protected by the fourteenth amendment. Their right to own land in the United States is based primarily on laws adopted by each state but may be subject to treaties between the United States and foreign countries. Treaty provisions with many countries assure the right of their nationals to purchase and inherit real property, and any inconsistent or conflicting state statutes are superseded by the superior authority of the treaty.[4]

Aliens now can also inherit land, except there are still certain operative restrictions against inheritance of land by nonresident or enemy aliens.[5] But to the extent that such state restrictions have been keyed to reciprocal treatment of American nationals, they have generally been invalidated as an impermissible intrusion into the conduct of foreign affairs, which is exclusively the concern of the federal—and not state—government.[6]

What is the difference between personal and real property?

Personal property is anything that is movable. It includes clothing, furniture, automobiles, tools, equipment—in a word, any goods. It also includes property that is "intangible"—money, checks, promissory notes, all types of negotiable instruments, stocks, bonds, contracts, business interests, licenses, copyrights, trademarks, patents, as well as agreements permitting the use of real property including leases, mortgages, and trusts.

Real property encompasses land and permanent improvements to land, such as buildings, fixtures, etc.

Are there restrictions on the right of aliens in the United States to own personal property?

Almost all types of personal property can be owned and used by aliens in the United States, with the exceptions of guns and other firearms and some businesses that are licensed by the local, state, or federal government.

A federal statute adopted in 1968 makes it illegal for an alien unlawfully in the United States "to receive, possess, or transport" any firearm or to employ another person for that purpose.[7] Various state laws have forbidden aliens to own firearms for the purpose of killing wild game[8] or to own for any purpose revolvers or other weapons.[9] The former statute was upheld by the Supreme Court in 1914 against a claim that it denied aliens equal protection of the laws. More recent Supreme Court decisions suggest that such a restriction would be invalid.[10]

Aliens are also frequently denied a license to sell alcoholic beverages[11] and licenses to own radio stations;[12] atomic energy facilities,[13] including atomic energy licenses for medical therapy;[14] aircraft;[15] vessels engaged in coastal fishing or shipping;[16] or mineral rights.[17] The statutes that deny alcoholic beverage licenses to aliens seem clearly to be unconstitutional in view of the Supreme Court's decisions relating to commercial fishing licenses and the practice of law. Whether the denial of licenses to aliens for defense-related business and activities would be held unconstitutional is open to question.

Are there any restrictions on the right of aliens to obtain copyrights?

Yes. Aliens must be "domiciled" in the United States at the time their work is first published in order to obtain a copyright or to be eligible under treaties giving copyright protection to foreign nationals.[18]

When are aliens "domiciled" in the United States? Aliens become domiciliaries of the United States if they are living in this country with the intention of residing here permanently, even if they are not permanent residents under the immigration laws, or if they are permanent resident aliens who are out of the United States temporarily.[19]

Other classes of aliens—including those living in the United States temporarily, those living abroad, and those who have moved to this country after their work has been published—are entitled to obtain copyrights only if there is an agreement between the United States and the alien's home country that provides reciprocal rights. The Universal Copyright Convention and bilateral agreements that are in force between the United States and more than seventy-five countries afford copyright protection to writers whose work has been published in those countries, as well as to their citizens.[20]

Are there restrictions on the right of aliens to obtain patents?

Except for a specific prohibition in the Trading with the Enemy Act,[21] any alien inventor may obtain a patent. The sole requirement with regard to nationality is that the applicant must state the country of which he is a citizen.[22]

The Trading with the Enemy Act prohibits an application for a patent for an invention "made" in a territory or state hostile to the United States by "nationals" of that country, unless permitted by the Attorney General.[23]

Are there restrictions on the right of aliens to register a trademark?

No. Any alien, whether in the United States or in a foreign country, may register a trademark for business use in the United States.[24]

Are there restrictions on the right of nonresident aliens to own personal property?

Yes. The property rights of nonresident aliens are controlled by both federal and state laws.

Federal law includes treaties as well as Acts of Congress. For the most part, treaties dealing with questions of property are intended to assure the right of aliens to own personal property in the United States reciprocally with the right of American citizens to own personal property in foreign countries. When and where such treaties are in effect, they are superior to any state law denying rights of ownership to aliens.[25]

The Trading with the Enemy Act, another federal law, permits the Secretary of the Treasury to seize without compensation any property in the United States belonging to "enemy aliens," whether they live in this country or elsewhere. The Secretary of the Treasury may also freeze the assets of any foreign national and block the transfer of those assets without a license. These powers can only be invoked during the time of war, but their continued exercise may be prolonged in periods of "national emergency," which the President is empowered to proclaim.[26]

Apart from federal laws, state laws that are not inconsistent with national authority can regulate the right of ownership. Most states do not prohibit nonresident aliens from owning personal property in the United States. However, some states have laws permitting such ownership by inheritance only if American citizens have the same right in the alien's country. Laws in other states provide that if a nonresident does not appear to demand inherited personal property within a certain time, whether personally or through a representative, the property can be taken by other relatives or the state.[27]

May aliens own land?

Generally, yes. As noted earlier, most of the laws restricting the right of aliens to own land have been repealed. At one time, a number of states forbade the ownership of land by aliens "ineligible to citizenship." These laws were intended to bar ownership of land by Asians, who, under prior naturalization laws, could not become citizens of the United States. The bar to naturalization against aliens from Asian countries was repealed by the Immigration and Naturalization Act of 1952, which, in removing nationality restrictions in the naturalization laws, rendered inoperative state laws forbidding ownership of land by such aliens.[28]

Early decisions of the courts upheld the power of a state to deny ownership of land within its borders to both resident and nonresident aliens. In 1923, the Supreme Court held that the power to confine ownership of land to citizens was properly related to the welfare and safety of a state.[29] However, there seems little doubt that these decisions are no longer valid.

In 1948, the Supreme Court avoided a direct ruling on the constitutionality of a statute forbidding ownership of land by "aliens ineligible to citizenship," but the effect of the decision, which was cast in terms of the rights of citizens to acquire land regardless of their racial or national origins, was to throw doubt upon continuing bars against land ownership by aliens.[30] Subsequent decisions of the Supreme Court, as noted in an earlier chapter, indicate that at least a "compelling need" must be shown by the state to bar ownership of land by aliens.

But serious restrictions do exist on the opportunity for aliens to own land. The Supreme Court decisions cited above do not tell the whole story. For example, restrictions on alien ownership are imposed by a number of federal laws relating to mineral assets, energy, alien enemies, the District of Columbia, and U.S. territorial possessions.[31] In addition, a remarkable variety of restrictions on alien ownership of land have survived in state statutes.[32] Moreover, concern over increased foreign purchases of agricultural land in the United States led to the enactment of the Agricultural Foreign Investment Disclosure Act of 1978.[33] This statute requires any foreign person who acquires or transfers any interest, other than a security interest, in agricultural land to submit a report to the Secretary of Agriculture within ninety days, identifying such person and the property involved, the purchase price, the intended use of the property, and any other information required by the regulation.[34] Failure to submit such reports, or submission of incomplete or false reports incurs a civil penalty not exceeding 25 percent of the value of the property, recoverable by civil suit.[35] Such legislation places an extra burden on aliens who transact in agricultural lands.

Finally, apart from the rights that may derive from the Constitution, treaties between the United States and other countries frequently assure the rights of the nationals of each country to own and inherit land in the other. Such treaties override any state statutes barring land ownership to aliens.[36] However, land, like personal property, can be seized by the federal government under the Trading with the Enemy Act.

Do states still restrict the ownership of land by aliens?

Yes. Seven states place limitations on the period of time an alien may own land, on the amount of land that may be owned, and occasionally on the type of land: Illinois, Indiana, Kentucky, Minnesota, Nebraska, Pennsylvania, and South Carolina.[37]

In addition, only aliens who have declared their intention to become citizens of the United States may own land in U.S. territories and the District of Columbia.[38] The prohibition does not apply only where treaty provisions permit aliens of foreign countries to own land in the United States. Nondeclarant aliens may also hold land acquired through inheritance or foreclosure for the collection of debts, but only for a period of ten years.[39]

May aliens bring lawsuits in courts in the United States to enforce property, personal or other rights?

Yes. Aliens, as persons in the United States, have the same rights as citizens to seek judicial relief for any claims or to redress any wrongs. This right applies to all aliens regardless of whether their status is that of lawful permanent residents, of nonimmigrants or of being in the United States either illegally or under "color of law." However, any other state or federal requirement for residence within the jurisdiction of the court must be met.[40]

NOTES

1. *Terrace v. Thompson*, 263 U.S. 197, 44 S. Ct. 15, 68 L. Ed. 255 (1923); *Webb v. O'Brien*, 263 U.S. 313, 44 S. Ct. 112, 68 L. Ed. 318 (1923); *See also Frick v. Webb*, 263 U.S. 326, 44 S. Ct. 115, 68 L. Ed 323 (1923); *Porterfield v. Webb*, 263 U.S. 225, 44 S. Ct. 21, 68 L. Ed. 278 (1923); *Coacrill v. California*, 268 U.S. 258, 45 S. Ct. 490, 69 L. Ed. 944 (1924).
2. *Oyama v. California*, 332 U.S. 633, 68 S. Ct. 269, 92 L. Ed. 249 (1948); *see also* Sullivan, *Alien Land Laws*, 36 Temp. L.Q. 15 (1962).
3. U.S. Const., amend. XIV. In addition, Congress in 1987 amended Section 214 of the Housing and Community Development Act of 1980, which prohibited federal housing assistance to anyone who is not a United States citizen or a legal resident of the United States. Consequently, aliens may now benefit from public or subsidized housing.
4. *Hauenstein v. Lynham*, 100 U.S. 483 (1880); *see Aliens and Citizens* 3 Am. J. Juris. 2d. § 2006, at 889; *see also Techt v. Hughes*, 229 N.Y.

222 (1920), *cert. denied*, 254 U.S. 643 (1921), in which Judge Cardozo pointed out that the basis of the common law preclusion of inheritance was a fear that land inheritance by aliens could tend to the destruction of the realm, and characterized this rationale as "artificial and far-fetched."

5. *See Techt v. Hughes*, *supra* note 4.
6. *Zschernig v. Miller*, 389 U.S. 429, 88 S. Ct. 664, 19 L. Ed. 2d 683, *reh'g denied*, 390 U.S. 974 (1968).
7. Omnibus Crime Control and Safe Streets Act, 18 U.S.C. app. §§ 1201–1202.
8. *Patsone v. Pennsylvania*, 232 U.S. 138 (1914).
9. The provisions of State and Local Firearms Laws have been published by the Bureau of Alcohol, Tobacco, and Firearms, Department of the Treasury. *See* 41 Fed. Reg. 25,651–887 (June 22, 1976).
10. *Graham v. Richardson*, 403 U.S. 365 (1971); *Takahashi v. Fish and Game Commission*, 334 U.S. 410 (1948).
11. Fourteen states and the District of Columbia permit aliens to hold alcoholic beverage control licenses: Alaska, California, Connecticut, Delaware, Florida, Georgia, Hawaii, Indiana, Nevada, New Jersey, New York (but the alien must pursue an application for citizenship), South Dakota, Virginia, and West Virginia.
12. 47 U.S.C. § 303.
13. 42 U.S.C. § 2133.
14. 42 U.S.C. § 2134.
15. 49 U.S.C. § 1401.
16. 46 U.S.C. § 11,672(a).
17. 30 U.S.C. § 22. Aliens, however, are permitted to declare their intention to become citizens to explore and purchase mineral deposits.
18. 17 U.S.C. §§ 9(a)–(c); *see also* Pub. L. No. 94–553 for expanded copyright protection for stateless persons and others for works created after Jan. 1, 1978.
19. *Alves v. Alves*, 262 A.2d 111 (D.C.C.A. 1970).
20. Copyright protection in the United States is provided for the nationals of the following countries through the Universal Copyright Convention, the Buenos-Aires Copyright Convention, or by bilateral agreement: Algeria, Andorra, Argentina, Australia, Austria, Bangladesh, Belgium, Bolivia, Brazil, Bulgaria, Cambodia (Khmer Republic), Cameroon, Canada, Chile, China, Colombia, Costa Rica, Cuba, Czechoslovakia, Denmark, Dominican Republic, Ecuador, El Salvador, Fiji, Finland, France, Germany, Ghana, Greece, Guatemala, Haiti, Honduras, Hungary, Iceland, India, Ireland, Israel, Italy, Japan, Kenya, Laos, Lebanon, Liberia, Liechtenstein, Luxembourg, Malawi, Malta, Mauritius, Mexico, Monaco, Morocco, Netherlands, New Zealand,

Nicaragua, Nigeria, Norway, Pakistan, Panama, Paraguay, Peru, Philippines, Poland, Portugal, Romania, Senegal, South Africa, Soviet Union, Spain, Sweden, Switzerland, Thailand, Tunisia, United Kingdom, Uruguay, Vatican City, Venezuela, Yugoslavia, Zambia. Formal agreements have not been entered into with the governments of other countries, but those countries that have become independent since 1941 may be recognizing the treaties ratified during their colonial status. On Oct. 31, 1988, President Reagan signed the treaty making the United States a party to the Berne Convention for the Protection of Literary and Artistic Works. Certain amendments of the Copyright Act of 1976, known as the Berne Convention Implementation Act of 1988, will go into effect on Mar. 1, 1989. These amendments will enable the United States to comply with the Berne Convention. The major changes set forth in the Berne Convention Implementation Act of 1988 may be summarized as follows: the use of a copyright notice is permissive; there is a two-tier system of regulation, whereby works originating in a foreign Berne Convention country need not be registered as a prerequisite to bringing an infringement action; statutory damages have been doubled; moral rights have not been substantially addressed in the Implementation Act; and provisions of the Implementation Act are effective only as to any cause of action arising on or after the effective date of the Implementation Act.

21. 50 U.S.C. app. § 5.
22. 35 U.S.C. § 115; *Shaw v. Cooper*, 7 Pet. (32 U.S.) 292 (1833).
23. 8 C.F.R. §§ 507–542(d).
24. 15 U.S.C. § 1126.
25. 3 Am. J. Juris 2d, *supra*, at 889; *see Hauenstein v. Lynham, supra*; *Kolorrat v. Oregon* 366 U.S. 187 (1961).
26. 50 U.S.C. app. § 1, *et seq*.
27. *See supra* note 25.
28. 8 U.S.C. § 1422.
29. *Terrace v. Thompson*, 263 U.S. 197 (1923); *Webb v. O'Brien, supra*.
30. *Oyama v. California, supra*. In 1952, the California Supreme Court subsequently described the California Land Law barring ownership of land by aliens ineligible to become citizens as an "instrument for effectuating racial discrimination" and held that it was a violation of the fourteenth amendment. *See Fujii v. California*, 38 Cal. 718, 242 P.2d 617 (1952).
31. *See* 48 U.S.C. §§ 1501–1502, and additional federal statutes cited in *Foreign Investments in U.S. Real Estate, report printed in* 14 Real Property, Probate and Trust Journal (American Bar Association) 1, 4 (1979) (hereafter ABA Report).

32. A detailed summary of the current restrictions in each state and the District of Columbia appears in ABA Report 18 *et seq*. (*see* note 31).
33. Act of Oct. 14, 1978, Pub. L. No. 95–460, 92 Stat. 1263, codified at 7 U.S.C. § 3501 *et seq*. The legislative reports are H.R. Rep. No. 1570, S. Rep. No. 1072, 95th Cong.
34. § 2, 7 U.S.C. § 3501(a).
35. § 3, 7 U.S.C. § 3502.
36. *Hauenstein v. Lynham*, *supra* note 4.
37. Illinois permits aliens to hold realty for a period of six years, after which the state may compel sale. 6 Ill. Ann. Stat. § 1-2. Ind. authorizes escheat to the state of land in excess of 320 acres owned by aliens for a period of five years. 32 Ind. Stat. Ann. § 1-8-12. Kentucky provides for escheat of land owned by aliens for eight years. Ky. Rev. Stat. §§1331-290, 300. But resident aliens may hold land for twenty-one years if used for residence or occupation. Ky. Rev. Stat. §§ 1381, 320. Minnesota limits ownership of land to aliens who have not declared intent to become citizens to 90,000 square feet, unless acquired by inheritance or is a farm of no more than 160 acres or the alien's right to ownership of land is assured by treaty. Minn. Ann. Stat. § 500.22 *et seq*. Nebraska forbids the ownership of land by aliens for more than five years, except for land within a three-mile zone of cities and villages, land used for manufacturing or industrial purposes, including railroads, common carriers, and public utilities, Neb. Rev. Stat. §§ 76-402, 412-414. New Jersey permits ownership of land by aliens who are domiciled and resident within the United States, provided that they have not been arrested or interned as enemy aliens. N.J. Stat. §§146.3-18. Pennsylvania permits all aliens except enemy aliens to inherit property (Purdon's Pa. Stat. Ann. §§ 68-22, 20-2518, 68-24) but allows purchase only by aliens who declare intention to become citizens and limits ownership to 5,000 acres. *Id.* §§ 68-25, 30, 32. South Carolina limits the ownership of land by aliens to 500,000 acres. Code of Laws, §§157-101, 103.
38. 48 U.S.C. §§ 1501, 1503, 1508.
39. 45 D.C. Code § 1501.
40. In the State Courts, *see Catalanatto v. Palazoo*, 259 N.Y.S. 2d 473, 475–76 (New York, 1965); *Janusis v. Long*, 188 N.E. 288 or (Mass. 1933); in the federal courts *see Williams v. Williams*, 328 F. Supp. 1380 (D.V.I. 1971); *Martinez v. Fox Valley Bus Line*, 17 F. Supp. 576 (N.D. Ill. 1936).

XI
Aliens and Taxes

A person's immigration status is the basic criterion that determines whether, and at what rates, he or she will be subject to U.S. taxes. But the correlation between immigration status and taxes is not always a perfect one. Generally, aliens who live in the United States must usually pay taxes on the same basis as citizens, although there are differences.[1] The laws imposing income, estate, and other taxes are complex. There are also treaties between the United States and various foreign countries that permit different treatment for nationals of such treaty countries. An alien who has tax questions or problems should consult an attorney who practices tax law.

Are aliens in the United States required to pay taxes?

Yes. They must pay sales, property, income, social security, estate, and other taxes on the same basis as citizens. But the federal income and estate tax laws distinguish between "resident" and "nonresident" aliens, and exemptions from certain taxes are provided for limited categories of aliens.[2] State income tax laws vary with regard to the determination of residence but generally do not distinguish between the residence requirements for citizens and for aliens.

Who are resident aliens under the federal income tax law?

It is important to note that the income tax regime imposed on aliens depends upon their residence. The threshold question, then, is how to determine residence. Congress has enacted legislation that profoundly affects the taxation of aliens who maintain certain ties with the United States. Two federal laws provide a statutory definition of "resident alien" for tax purposes and contain a series of mechanical tests based upon immigration status and presence in the United States.[3] If an alien meets these definitions of residency, he or she is taxed to the same extent as a U.S. citizen. Conversely, if the alien does not fall within these mechanical tests, then he or she is treated as a nonresident alien subject to a lesser rate of taxation. In addition, any other alien who has been present in the United States for one year is *presumed* to be a resident under tax laws, regardless of the alien's status under the immigration laws.[4] Resident alien status is not removed by temporary absences from the United States until the alien actually abandons residence in this country.[5] Nonimmigrants as well as aliens illegally present in the United States are covered by this definition of a "resident alien," but the presumption can be overcome by proof that the alien is in this country only on a brief visit.[6]

Who are regarded as nonresident aliens?

It should be recalled that the intention to make a home in the United States is the controlling criterion in determining the tax status of the alien. The nonresident alien is defined as a transient or sojourner, and all aliens are deemed nonresidents unless it is proved that they have become residents.[7] Thus, under both tax and immigration laws, an alien lawfully admitted for permanent residence as an immigrant will ordinarily be deemed a resident alien, and an alien admitted as a nonimmigrant for a short and definite period will ordinarily be deemed a nonresident alien.[8] Since 1986, an alien not admitted for permanent residence has been regarded as a resident only if he or she meets the "substantial presence" test. The "substantial presence" test for a calendar year generally means presence in the United States for at least thirty-one days during the current year and a total of at least 183 days during that year and the two preceding calendar years.[9]

More specifically, nonresident aliens include any alien who does not have a residence in the United States; an alien who has diplomatic status or is employed by an international governmental organization or foreign government; an alien who has been admitted to the United States as a nonimmigrant for a limited time, such as a tourist who remains for six months; a student who is remaining for the school year; and an alien crewman who has been admitted to the United States on a landing permit.[10]

What is the difference in income tax liability between resident and nonresident aliens?

Resident aliens, like citizens, must pay taxes on all of their income, even if the source is outside the United States. In other words, alien residents are taxed on their worldwide income. The rate of tax is scaled according to taxable income.[11] The tax rate levied on the alien, unless he or she is engaged in trade or business in the United States, is a flat 30 percent of taxable income, and a lower rate may be operative under the terms of a tax treaty or convention with the alien's home country.[12]

Certain classes of nonresident aliens are exempt from taxes on earnings in the United States, including employees of foreign sovereigns or of international organizations, diplomatic representatives, consular officers, and employees of consulates.[13] Note that if any such aliens are also lawful permanent residents of the United States, they could forfeit such permanent resident privileges unless they forego certain privileges and immunities, including exemption from income tax liability.[14] Aliens admitted as students or exchange visitors, if such aliens are employed by foreign governments or organizations, may be exempt from taxation.[15] Moreover, scholarship and fellowship grants received by some nonresident alien students or exchange visitors usually are exempt from tax, while in other cases such scholarships and fellowships may only be subject to a reduced tax rate.[16]

What are the differences in tax treatment given to citizens and to resident aliens?

A resident alien cannot claim an exemption for tax purposes for any dependent, except a spouse, who does not live in the United States, Canada, Mexico, Panama, or the Canal Zone. A citizen may claim dependents regardless of where they live.[17]

As noted elsewhere, the United States is one of the few nations that taxes its citizens on their worldwide income. The United States basically imposes the same system on resident aliens. Resident aliens are taxed on their worldwide income, whether or not that income is remitted to the United States and irrespective of its geographic source. Accordingly, proceeds from the sale of property located outside the United States, for example, foreign real estate, will be subjected fully to U.S. tax liability. But the foreign tax credit system allows some relief.[18] Under this approach, the resident alien generally can credit his foreign income taxes against his United States income taxes. It should be borne in mind, though, that the foreign tax credit is subject to certain limitations, which may defer or prevent the crediting of his or her foreign income taxes. Unused foreign tax credits can also be carried back two years and forward five years and be applied against U.S. taxes before they expire.

Under certain circumstances, citizens are not taxable on income earned from services performed outside the United States, in United States possessions, or derived from sources protected under a treaty. Resident aliens do not have these benefits unless covered by a tax treaty between the United States and the alien's home country.[19]

As a general matter, no alien—whether deemed a resident or a nonresident for tax purposes—is permitted to leave the United States unless that alien first obtains a tax clearance certificate, known as a "sailing permit" or "certificate of compliance," from the Internal Revenue Service.[20] The only aliens exempt from this requirement are certain persons with diplomatic or quasi-diplomatic status; certain other nonimmigrants who have no taxable United States income, including F-1 students, H-3 trainees, B-1 or B-2 visitors, aliens who enter with border-crossing cards or who do not require documents; and alien commuters from Canada or Mexico.[21] Citizens are treated differently in that there is no requirement to obtain such a certificate.

How do departing aliens obtain a certificate of compliance?

By applying to the local Internal Revenue Service office in the area where they have lived in the United States or in the city from which they intend to depart. The application cannot be made earlier than thirty days prior to the scheduled date for the alien's departure. Unless aliens can show that they have paid all income taxes due for the preceding three years, or that taxes will be paid regardless of their departure from the United States, they will be required to file a tax return and to pay all income taxes before a permit will be issued.[22]

Aliens who are deported or are leaving the United States under enforced voluntary departure, that is, at their own expense but under the supervision of INS deportation officers, are not usually required to show payment of taxes. However, immigration judges have required aliens to show proof of payment of taxes before permission to leave the United States voluntarily has been granted. Where aliens have large amounts of money or other assets in their possession at the time of their departure, INS officers will notify the Internal Revenue Service to facilitate the collection of any taxes due.[23]

What is the income tax liability of permanent resident aliens who leave the United States?

If aliens are leaving the United States for only a temporary visit abroad, those aliens maintain their status as permanent resident aliens and are taxed as though they were living in the United States.[24] Those aliens who intend to abandon their status as permanent residents may file an income tax return as a nonresident alien. If they have not lived in the United States during the taxable year, they will be treated as nonresident aliens.[25] The filing of a nonresident alien income tax return will be regarded by the Department of State and by the INS as an abandonment of the alien's status as a permanent resident.[26] In those circumstances, the alien may not return to the United States as a permanent resident but must obtain a new immigrant or nonimmigrant visa.

Who are resident aliens under the federal estate tax laws?

It is crucial to understand that the definition of a resident alien for purposes of the income tax laws is inapplicable to estate and gift taxes. On the one hand, aliens are regarded as residents for income tax purposes if they have the intention of remaining in the United States permanently, if their intention is indefinite, or if they intend to leave the country only after having resided here for a prolonged period.[27] On the other hand, aliens are regarded as residents for the purposes of federal estate tax purposes only if they are "domiciled" in the United States. "Domicile" in this instance means residence coupled with an intention to remain here indefinitely, i.e., it is one's home. And since a person can only have one domicile, the concept of being "domiciled" in the United States for federal estate and gift taxes is more restrictive than that of income tax residence, since the latter is premised on mechanical tests, e.g., possession of a "green card" or "substantially being present" in the United States. Therefore, aliens may find themselves residents for income tax purposes but nonresidents for federal and estate tax purposes. A plausible example is a merchant who remains in the United States for 183 days during the year (he would be a resident for income taxes) but intends to return to his foreign domicile where he has social and economic ties (he would be a nonresident for federal estate and gift taxes). An alien who is in the United States as a "nonimmigrant" under the Immigration and Nationality Act has been held to be a nonresident for estate tax purposes, since that alien does not have domicile in this country.[28]

Is there a difference in estate tax treatment for citizens and for resident aliens?

Yes, where there are treaties between the United States and the country of the alien's citizenship. Resident aliens who own property outside the United States could be subject to the payment of estate taxes to both the United States and their home country unless they are given a foreign tax credit by one of the countries.[29]

Do estate taxes cover nonresident aliens?

Yes, but only for property in the United States, including stocks and bonds in American firms, at the time of the alien's death. The tax treatment for nonresident aliens differs from that provided both for resident aliens and citizens and also varies depending upon tax treaties. The estates of citizens and resident aliens are exempt from taxes if the net value of the estate is below $192,800.[30] The exemption for the estates of nonresident aliens is $60,000.[31] The rate of taxation is also different. For resident aliens and citizens, the rate ranges from 18 percent on the first $10,000 of the taxable estate to 50 percent of the amount over $2.5 million.[32] For nonresident aliens, the rate is 6 percent on the first $100,000, increasing to 30 percent on the taxable estate above $2 million.[33] Aliens who are citizens of countries that have tax treaties with the United States should refer to those treaties, since they may modify the tax treatment provided under the Internal Revenue Code. In addition, for gift tax purposes, gifts to an alien spouse exceeding $100,000 a year are taxable. This provision takes effect for gifts made on or after July 14, 1988, and for persons dying after the date of enactment.[34]

Additionally, amendments to the tax law in 1988 introduced provisions antagonistic to aliens, including a provision that takes away from a surviving spouse who is not a United States citizen.[35] This means that surviving spouses must pay estate tax on the entire estate of the deceased spouse within nine months of his or her death.

How do customs laws apply to aliens?

Aliens who are returning permanent residents of the United States are subject to the same requirements as citizens. They must pay a duty on all purchases above a total value of $400 and on alcoholic beverages in excess of one quart.[36]

Aliens entering the United States either as immigrants or as nonimmigrant visitors are not subject to these limitations. All their personal effects intended for their own use may be brought in duty free. Household effects intended for personal use may also be imported without duty over a period of ten years from the date of the alien's last arrival in the United States, provided that the alien has previously used them for a period of one year. Automobiles and other vehicles may similarly be imported without duty, provided that they are not sold within the following year.[37]

NOTES

1. *See United States Tax Guide for Aliens,* Pub. L. No. 519, Internal Revenue Service (1975) (hereinafter cited as *Tax Guide*); *see also Foreign Scholars and Educational and Cultural Exchange Visitors,* Pub. L. No. 514, Internal Revenue Service. *Cook v. Tait,* 265 U.S. 47 (1924); 26 C.F.R. §§ 1.1–1(b), 1.871-1.
2. *Tax Guide,* chs. 1 and 2, 1–4; 26 C.F.R. § 1.871-2(b).
3. *See* the Deficit Reduction Act (DRA) of 1984, § 138, Pub. L. No. 98-369; Internal Revenue Code (IRC) § 17701(b).
4. Rev. Rul. 69–611, 1969–2 Cum. Bull. 150; 26 C.F.R. §§ 1.871, 1.871-2.
5. 26 C.F.R. § 1.871-13; *Tax Guide,* at 5–6.
6. *Tax Guide,* at 2.
7. 26 C.F.R. §§ 1.871-2, 1.871-4; *Tax Guide,* at 1; *Hecravarria v. U.S.,* 374 F. Supp. 128 (S.D. Ga. 1974) (obtained lawful admission for permanent residence and reentry permits, presumption of nonresidence overcome).
8. *See Moorhead v. U.S.,* 774 F.2d 936 (9th Cir. 1985) (alien commuter subject to Social Security tax).

9. *See Portanora v. U.S.*, 690 F.2d 169 (Ct. Cl. 1982) (30 percent rate applicable because nonresident having interest in gas and oil leases was not engaged in trade or business.
10. *Tax Guide*, at 1, 2.
11. See *supra* note 1.
12. *Tax Guide*, at 3–4, 18–20; 26 U.S.C. § 871; 26 C.F.R. § 1.871-7; *see* list of Countries with Tax Treaties. Included are most European countries, some African countries, only two countries in Asia (Pakistan and Japan), and, apart from former territories of the United Kingdom, no countries in the Western Hemisphere.
13. 26 U.S.C. §§ 892, 893; 26 C.F.R. §§ 1.892-1, 1.893.1; *Tax Guide*, at 1, 18.
14. *See also* 26 C.F.R. § 1.893-1; *Tax Guide*, at 19.
15. An information guide, titled "Tax Advice for Foreign Scholars and visitors on Official Educational and Cultural Exchange Programs," may be obtained from the Internal Revenue Service.
16. *Id.* at 14; 26 U.S.C. § 872(b), as amended; 26 C.F.R. § 1.872-2(b).
17. *Tax Guide*, at 4; 26 U.S.C. §§ 151(b), 152(b).
18. I.R.C. §§ 901–908.
19. *Tax Guide*, at 4; 26 U.S.C. §§ 894, 911, 931. Rev. Rul. 72-330 permits exemption from income tax for resident aliens who spend seventeen out of eighteen months abroad on the portion of salary earned abroad up to a limited amount for citizens of countries that have nondiscrimination treaties with the United States. These countries include Austria, Belgium, Canada, Denmark, Finland, France, Germany, Ireland, Luxembourg, Norway, Pakistan, Sweden, Switzerland, Trinidad, Tobago, South Africa, and the United Kingdom. *See also* Rev. Rul. 72–598. The effect of invoking the benefit provided by the treaty for IRS purposes upon the alien's status as a permanent resident under the Immigration and Nationality Act has not been the subject of any published decision, but the alien's status would appear to be protected if the "nondiscrimination" clauses of the tax treaties have any force.
20. *Tax Guide*, at 21–23; 26 U.S.C. § 6851(d); 26 C.F.R. § 1.6851-2.
21. Id.
22. Id.
23. Hearings, Subcommittee of the Committee on the Judiciary, House of Representatives, 92d Cong. 2d Sess. "Illegal Aliens," pt. 5, at 1316-14.
24. 26 C.F.R. § 1.871.5; Rev. Rul. 70-461, 1970 Cum. Bull. 149.
25. *Tax Guide, at* 2.
26. Airgram, Department of State, Feb. 11, 1972, Ref. App. D, Services for INS, 22 C.F.R. § 42.23 note 2.
27. 26 C.F.R. § 1.871-2(b).

28. Rev. Rul. 74-364.
29. Estate tax conventions are in effect between the United States and Australia, Canada, Finland, France, Greece, Ireland, Japan, Norway, South Africa, Switzerland, and the United Kingdom.
30. I.R.C. § 2010(a).
31. 134 Cong. Rec. 11,034 (daily ed. Oct. 21, 1988).
32. I.R.C. § 2001(c).
33. I.R.C. § 2101(d).
34. I.R.C. § 2503(b).
35. Technical and Miscellaneous Revenue Act of 1988 at § 2056.
36. Customs Hints for Returning Residents, Bureau of Customs, U.S. Department of Treasury.
37. Customs Hints for Visitors (Nonresidents), Bureau of Customs, U.S. Department of Treasury.

XII
Aliens and Military Service

The obligation to bear arms in defense of the United States is recognized primarily as an obligation of citizenship.[1] But Congress has imposed varying obligations on resident aliens to perform military service since the first World War.

In the past, all aliens—immigrant and nonimmigrant—were required to perform military service during both war and peace when conscription laws were in force. At the present time, there is no compulsory service in the armed forces, and the requirements for registration with Selective Service Boards have been suspended.

Previous laws requiring military service have had an impact upon aliens that continues to affect their rights, particularly their eligibility to become citizens and their ability to return to the United States after a trip abroad. These problems affect persons who claimed exemption from military service because they were either aliens or citizens of neutral countries, or because they departed or remained out of the United States in order to avoid military service, including persons who expatriated themselves as U.S. citizens.

Are aliens subject to the Selective Service laws?

Yes. Every male alien between the ages of eighteen and twenty-six years, except one who has been lawfully admitted to the United States as a nonimmigrant and who has maintained that status, was required to register at a local Selective Service Board for training and service in the armed forces of the United States. Aliens required to register included those admitted as permanent residents; aliens who entered the United States illegally; and those who entered lawfully as nonimmigrants, but who have violated the conditions of their status by remaining longer than permitted or otherwise.[2] The procedures for registration were terminated in March 1975, when it was announced that new procedures for "periodic registration" would be adopted.[3] Currently, an annual registration system is in effect.

Are aliens subject to induction?

Not now. The Selective Service System is on a "standby

basis" at the present time. The draft ended on June 30, 1973. Only volunteers now enter the armed forces.

Can aliens join the armed forces?

Yes. Aliens who are lawful permanent residents may enlist in every branch of the armed forces—the Air Force, the Army, the Marine Corps, and the Navy. To enlist in the Coast Guard, the alien must file a declaration of intention to become a United States citizen. However, aliens are not eligible to serve as officers in any of the armed forces.[4]

Do aliens obtain any special benefit through their service in the armed forces?

Yes. The usual requirement that a citizenship applicant must be a lawful permanent resident for five years (three years for a spouse of a citizen) is waived for aliens who have had honorable service during wartime, including the Vietnam War.[5]

Were any aliens exempt from liability to serve in the armed forces?

Yes. An alien who was a citizen of a country allied with the United States in a mutual defense treaty, including the NATO and SEATO countries, and who completed at least twelve months of active military duty in the armed forces of that country was regarded as having completed his military service in the United States, provided that reciprocal treatment is given by the alien's country to United States citizens. Forty-five allied countries have such reciprocal arrangements with the United States.[6]

Aliens who are citizens of countries that have treaties permitting the exemption of their nationals from military service in the United States could claim exemption on this ground.[7] Fifteen countries have treaties of this kind with the United States.[8] However, any "treaty alien" who claimed exemption upon this basis is permanently barred from becoming a naturalized citizen of the United States.[9] Since any alien who is ineligible to become a citizen is also barred from becoming a permanent resident of the United States,[10] aliens who have claimed military exemption as "treaty aliens" are unable either to obtain immigrant visas for permanent residence or, if already present in the United States, to change their status to become permanent residents. This prohibition applies to all such aliens even if they are married to citizens or permanent residents or are parents of children born in the United States.

Is there any relief from this barrier to permanent residence?

Yes. But only for an alien who has been in the United States for at least seven years, and who can show that his deportation would result in extreme hardship to himself or to a spouse or children who are citizens or permanent residents.[11]

In addition, a permanent resident alien who has claimed military exemption as a "treaty alien," and who thereafter leaves the United States on a temporary visit may be permitted to return as a permanent resident if he has previously lived in the United States for seven consecutive years.[12]

Does the bar apply to aliens who seek to enter the United States as nonimmigrants?

No.[13]

Are there any provisions for amnesty or clemency for an alien who either left the United States in order to avoid military service, or who, without leaving the country, obtained relief from military service as a foreign national?

No. The Presidential Proclamation establishing a clemency program for persons who avoided military service during the Vietnam War specifically excludes aliens from its benefits.[14] The immigration law provides that "persons" who have left or remained outside the United States to avoid wartime military service and aliens who are "ineligible to citizenship" cannot be admitted as permanent residents. This provision affects not only persons who were aliens when they left this country but also citizens who surrendered their American citizenship or who become citizens of another country.[15]

An alien who was relieved from military service on the ground of his alienage is permanently ineligible to become an American citizen. If such an alien has left the United States, even for reasons not related to military service, he is barred from returning as a permanent resident, unless his departure was temporary, and he has had seven years of consecutive residence in this country.

Is clemency available for aliens who have been convicted of violations of the Selective Service laws?

Yes. A violation of the Selective Service laws subjects an alien to deportation only if the Attorney General finds that the alien is an "undesirable resident."[16] Clemency for such an alien is available if the Attorney General vacates the finding. An alien who has been convicted of a Selective Service law violation remains under the threat of deportation, however, so long as the Attorney General, acting through the INS, can find that he is an "undesirable resident."

NOTES

1. *See* Borchard, *Diplomatic Protection of Citizens Abroad*, at 11; *Hines v. Davidowitz*, 312 U.S. 52, 61 S. Ct. 399, 85 L. Ed. 581 (1941); *Kennedy v. Mendoza-Martinez*, 372 U.S. 144, 83 S. Ct. 554, 92 L. Ed. 2d 644 (1963); *United States v. Schwimmer*, 279 U.S. 644, 49 S. Ct. 448, 73 L. Ed. 889 (1929).
2. 50 U.S.C. app. § 455(a) (13).
3. Proclamation 4360, 40 Fed. Reg. § 14567 (Apr. 1, 1975).
4. Air Force Training Manual, 33-2; 601 Army Reg. 210: Marine Corps Order, at 1100.61; Navy Recruiting Manual, paras. 4/9(b); *see also* 10 U.S.C. § 3253, *as amended*.
5. 8 U.S.C. § 1440(a).
6. 42 Op. Att'y. Gen. 28 (Apr. 1, 1968).
7. *Id.*
8. *Id.* The countries with current treaties providing for exemption are Argentina, Austria, China, Costa Rica, Estonia, Honduras, Ireland, Italy, Latvia, Liberia, Norway, Paraguay, Spain, Switzerland, and Yugoslavia.
9. 8 U.S.C. § 1426(a).
10. 8 U.S.C. § 1182(a)(22).
11. 8 U.S.C. § 1254(a)(1).
12. 8 U.S.C. § 1182(c).
13. 8 U.S.C. § 1182(a)(22).
14. Proclamation No. 4313, 1974 U.S. Code Cong. & Adm. News 4335, 39 Fed. Reg. 33,293.
15. 8 U.S.C. § 1182(a)(22).
16. 8 U.S.C. § 1251(a)(17).

XIII
The Right of Aliens to Receive Government Benefits

In order to determine whether government benefits are available to an alien, it is necessary to take into account the immigration status of the alien and the eligibility requirements of the particular benefits program. Aliens in certain categories of status are generally eligible for benefits, assuming they meet income and other program requirements, including those granted permanent residence status,[1] those admitted from abroad as refugees,[2] those granted asylum,[3] and those permitted to come into the United States in immigration "parole" status.[4] Aliens in other categories of status are almost never eligible for public benefits, including those who are admitted temporarily into the United States as nonimmigrants, and those who overstayed their permitted stay or who come without valid travel documents (passports or visas).

Aliens in certain categories of status are restricted by the terms of their immigration status from receipt of certain forms of public assistance, including aliens who receive temporary residence status under the general legalization provisions of the Immigration Reform and Control Act of 1986 (IRCA),[5] who were barred for five years from receiving certain forms of federal assistance, and those who receive status under the Seasonal Agricultural Workers provisions of the 1986 law,[6] who are disqualified from receiving aid for dependent children or certain Medicaid payments for a five-year period. Other categories of aliens are eligible to receive benefits if it is determined that they are "permanently residing in the United States under color of law" (PRUCOL).[7] This particular standard is the subject of different judicial interpretations and continuing controversy.[8]

Is it possible for an alien to jeopardize his or her immigration status through the receipt of government benefits?

Yes. Aliens who are considered by the authorities to be "likely at any time to become public charges"[9] are inadmissible to the United States and may be barred from entry. This exclusion applies to both immigrants and nonimmigrant visitors, as well as to returning resident aliens. The standard applied by the authorities involves an analysis of the totality of the alien's circumstances.[10] Factors that may be considered include age, health, past and current income, education, and job skills. The federal poverty income guidelines are used by the authorities in the determination, and past receipt of public benefits is an important, but not a controlling, factor. Aliens with income below the poverty guidelines may still avoid exclusion on public charge grounds by submitting affidavits of support from persons who undertake a moral obligation to support the alien. Also, bonds may be posted by aliens seeking to enter the United States to ensure that they will not take public benefits.[11] Such bonds are considered a condition for admission, have a minimum amount of $1,000, and are subject to review and cancellation five years after admission.[12] A special and more liberal public charge standard applies to aliens who receive temporary residence under the Immigration Reform and Control Act of 1986.

Additionally, aliens who have entered the United States as, for example, permanent residents, who have within five years after such entry become public charges "from causes not affirmatively shown to have arisen after entry,"[13] may be expelled from the United States. Deportations under this provision are relatively few, and the standards applied by the courts are narrow and generally interpreted in favor of the alien.[14] However, the receipt of public benefits presents a risk of expulsion from the United States if such receipt is not caused by factors arising after an alien acquires permanent residence status.

What government benefits are available to aliens?

AFDC

Aid to Families with Dependent Children[15] provides financial assistance as well as other services to eligible children who live with either a parent, certain specified relatives, or who are under foster care. As with other benefits programs, each recipient must generally possess a Social Security number in order to receive benefits under AFDC.[16] Those aliens who have received employment authorization, or whose status permits employment, are able to receive Social Security cards and would be able to apply for AFDC benefits if otherwise eligible. In the case of an eligible child of an undocumented alien parent, a federal court has ruled that a policy of denying day-care benefits to eligible children who are United States citizens or aliens lawfully present in the United States, but whose parents cannot supply a Social Security number or other proof of their lawful status, violates federal and state law.

In New York, for example, the standards for aliens' eligibility are relatively liberal. In a leading case, a federal court of appeals adopted an expansive interpretation of the term "permanently residing in the United States under color of law" in which the term was deemed to mean "lasting" or "enduring" rather than "forever."[17] On the other hand, in California, another court of appeals concluded that an asylum applicant was present "under color of law" but that his status was not necessarily "permanent."[18] Such individuals, therefore, were considered to fail to meet the permanency of residence required for program benefits and are thus ineligible for such benefits.

SSI

Supplemental Security Income[19] provides a minimum income level to eligible individuals who are blind, disabled, or who have attained age sixty-five. A consent judgment in a federal court class action, adopted in regulations, lists categories of aliens that are included under the PRUCOL concept, such as "any other alien residing in the United States with the knowledge and permission of the INS and whose departure . . . the INS does not contemplate enforcing."[20] An expanded concept of eligibility is thus used in the program. Moreover, the granting of immigration status need not be official. It is sufficient if it appears from the facts in the case that the INS does not intend to enforce the individual's departure in the forseeable future.

MEDICAID

This federal program enables states to provide "(1) medical assistance on behalf of families with dependent children and aged, blind or disabled individuals whose income and resources are insufficient to meet the cost necessary in medical services, (2) rehabilitation and other services to help such families and individuals retain capacity for independence or self care."[21] Aid is in the form of reimbursement for services rendered on behalf of the Medicaid recipient.

In most cases, aliens who are eligible for SSI are also eligible for Medicaid. However, where AFDC recipients are involved, eligibility is somewhat more restrictive. In 1986, Medicaid was made available to all aliens seeking emergency services regardless of their immigration status. A court in New York has also ordered the state not to deny Medicaid coverage for prenatal care to alien women, regardless of their immigration status, if a child would be a U.S. citizen when born.[22]

MEDICARE

Medicare is a program that provides health insurance for the elderly. Generally, there is no bar to aliens receiving reimbursement for hospital and other health-related expenses under the general Medicare provisions. For those who are not eligible under these provisions, however, and instead must rely on special transitional provisions or voluntary election, there is a five-year permanent and continuous residency restriction that has been upheld by the Supreme Court as not violating an alien's right to due process of law.[23]

SOCIAL SECURITY

Old-age, survivors, and disability insurance (OASDI)[24] furnishes benefits to the elderly, physically or mentally disabled, and, in some instances, to the spouse, child, or parent of the beneficiary. Immigration status is generally not a bar to such entitlement. However, to meet employment qualifications, a valid Social Security number must be presented. This requirement may impede an undocumented alien from collecting benefits, since such numbers are issued only to United States citizens, permanent residents, or aliens who are in a status that permits employment or who have received employment authorization from the INS. (Social Security numbers without work authorization can be issued to aliens in lawful nonimmigrant status for various nonwork related reasons, including opening bank accounts or enrolling in school.)

Once eligibility has been established, two more restrictions may bar access to benefits. First, no benefits are payable to an individual for any month in which the Social Security Administration has been notified by the Attorney General that an alien has been deported under the Immigration and Nationality Act.[25] Second, no benefits will be paid before the month in which the alien is thereafter lawfully readmitted into the United States for permanent residence. A federal court upheld this last restriction as not in violation of an alien's due process rights.

FOOD STAMPS

The food stamps program is the most restrictive in terms of eligibility of aliens. Undocumented aliens cannot qualify under "color of law" or any other standard. Only the following specific categories of aliens are eligible: permanent residents, refugees, those granted asylum, those granted withholding of deportation or exclusion, parolees, and conditional entrants. The Food Stamp Application (form 385) has been amended to include a statement signed by each household member attesting to his or her citizenship or alien status.[26]

Aliens who receive status under the IRCA legalization program[27] are ineligible for food stamps unless they are qualified for SSI due to age, disability, or blindness.[28] Seasonal Agricultural Workers (SAWs) are eligible for food stamps. Aliens who receive adjustment status through the Cuban/Haitian program are eligible for any programs of assistance to which they were previously entitled.

HOUSING

Generally, there are no alien restrictions on the use of funds for homeless shelters.

Legislation in 1980[29] and 1987[30] provides restrictions on the entitlement of aliens to HUD-financed programs. However, because an April 1, 1986, final rule was never made effective, the legislation has not been implemented. Until a new final rule is published and made effective, aliens are not restricted against using assisted housing.[31] The Department of Housing and Urban Development (HUD) has most recently proposed changing the availability of financial assistance for housing for aliens.[32] The proposed rule specifies that only permanent residents, refugees or asylees, persons granted withholding of deportation, and persons legalized under the Immigration Reform and Control Act of 1986 (IRCA) would be eligible for housing assistance.

EDUCATION

In 1982, the Supreme Court held that constitutional equal protection requires that undocumented school-aged alien children be entitled to the same free public school education as is provided to children who are United States citizens or lawful permanent residents.[33] In that same year, the Court also held that a state university's policy that categorically denied instate status to domiciled nonimmigrant aliens in G–4 status violated the Supremacy Cause as federal law granted them special benefits.[34]

Postsecondary education grants may be made available to U.S. citizens, lawful permanent resident aliens, and aliens in the United States for other than a temporary purpose who are residents of the Northern Mariana Islands or the Trust Territory of the Pacific Islands.[35] Similarly, federal loan programs are available to such aliens, as are work-study program benefits.

UNEMPLOYMENT INSURANCE

The unemployment compensation program is a federal-state effort to provide financial assistance for unemployed workers who are out of work through no fault of their own.[36] Aliens who meet the PRUCOL standard qualify. Even undocumented aliens may be eligible for unemployment compensation under this category; however, no clear definition has emerged from the case law. Some courts have interpreted the standard broadly to include situations where the INS has knowledge of an alien's presence and has acquiesced in that presence by not enforcing departure.[37] On the other hand, the same category has been interpreted narrowly, making eligible only those aliens who, after having their particular cases reviewed, have been granted an immigration status that allows them to remain in the United States for a definite period.[38]

The 1986 immigration law effectively requires that an alien applying for unemployment compensation have work authorization. Since federal law now requires that all aliens be authorized to work in order for an employer to be free from sanction, applicants for unemployment insurance benefits, who must be ready, able, and willing to take new employment, will need to show employment authorization subsequent to November 6, 1986, in order to qualify for benefits.[39]

AGRICULTURE AND LAND RIGHTS

Farm owners, landlords, tenants, and sharecroppers, regardless of citizenship or alien status, are eligible to obtain crop insurance and indemnities for losses for cotton, grains, sugar, milk, and various other agricultural products. Loans made by the Farmers Home Administration (FHA) for business and industrial uses are restricted to citizens and permanent residents.[40] FHA Loans for ownership and operation of farm or ranches are restricted to U.S. citizens or resident aliens.[41]

Guaranteed loans for rural housing on either farm or nonfarm land are available for permanent resident aliens and for those admitted on indefinite parole, including persons residing in the island possessions and Trust Territories.[42] Loans for rural electrification and telephone service are available without regard to citizenship or alienage.[43]

Direct loans to purchasers of single-family rural residences are available for permanent resident aliens and for those admitted on indefinite parole. Such loans are also available to persons residing in the island possessions and trust territories.[44] Loans for rural rental housing are made available to developers for housing. Regulations directed to developers receiving rural rental housing loans expressly permit permanent resident aliens to occupy such housing.[45] In addition, rural rental housing bars expressly forbid discriminating against tenants on the basis of race, religion, sex, mental status, or handicap.[46]

The Agricultural Foreign Investment Disclosure Act of 1978[47] requires any foreign person who acquires or transfers any interest, other than a security interest, in agricultural land to submit a report to the Secretary of Agriculture within ninety days, identifying such person and the property involved, the purchase price, the intended use of the property, and any other information required by the regulation.[48] Failure to submit such reports, or submission of incomplete or false reports, incurs a civil penalty not exceeding 25 percent of the value of the property, recoverable by civil suit.[49]

Eligibility to acquire public lands is restricted to U.S. citizens. The Federal Land Policy and Management Act of 1976 discontinued all homestead grants to U.S. citizens and permanent resident aliens.

LEGAL SERVICES

Aliens who are indigent, like U.S. citizens, have a right to appointed counsel in criminal cases. However, legal assistance in civil cases, including deportation or exclusion proceedings, is less certain.

Free legal assistance in noncriminal proceedings is ordinarily provided through the Legal Services Corporation (LSC),[50] which provides federal funding for local legal services programs. However, because LSC funds may be used only to provide services "for or on behalf of U.S. citizens and specific eligible aliens,"[51] most classifications of aliens, aside from permanent residents, are unable to obtain legal assistance.

In an emergency situation, assistance can be provided, even if the alien is not physically present or cannot obtain representation, but only for the duration of the emergency.[52] In addition, no verification is required respecting citizenship or eligible alien status for consultations by phone and when only brief advice is provided.[53] The restrictions apply solely to the utilization of funds granted by the Legal Services Corporation, and aliens not eligible for assistance under the terms of such funds may be represented free of charge when funds from other sources are used.

Proposed rules would further restrict the current policy of providing legal services to aliens.[54] The proposals would prohibit LSC-funded attorneys from representing newly legalized aliens for five years—and U.S. citizens and otherwise eligible aliens—if an ineligible alien would receive more than an incidental benefit from the representation.[55] The proposed ban is unclear in scope. Concern has been expressed that the ban could even "bar LSC attorneys from assisting U.S. citizen children in obtaining public benefits, such as those available under the Aid to Families with Dependent Children program, if one of the parents is an ineligible alien, on the theory that the parent would benefit more than incidentally from the child's receipt of financial assistance."[56]

NOTES

1. 45 C.F.R. § 1233.50(b) (1987).
2. 8 U.S.C. § 1157.
3. 8 U.S. § 1158.
4. 8 U.S.C. § 1181(d)(5).
5. Pub. L. No. 99-603 (1986).
6. 8 U.S.C § 1160(g).
7. *See Holly v. Lavine*, 553 F.2d 845 (2d Cir. 1977), *cert. denied*, 435 U.S. 947 (1978); *Berger v. Secretary of HEW*, Civ. Action No. 76-1420 (E.D.N.Y. 1978), *aff'd sub. nom Berger v. Heckler*, 771 F.2d 1556 (2d Cir. 1985).
8. *St. Francis Hospital v. D'Elia*, 71 A.D.2d 110, 422 N.Y.S.2d 110 (1979), *aff'd sub. nom. South Nassau Communities Hosp. v. D'Elia*, 53 N.Y.2d 827, 440 N.Y.S.2d 185, 422 N.E.2d 830 (1981). *Papadopoulos v. Shang*, 414 N.Y.S.2d 152, 67 A.D.2d 84 (1st Dept. 1979); *Cruz v. Commissioner of Public Welfare*, 395 Mass. 107, 478 N.E.2d 1262 (1985).
9. 8 U.S.C. § 11182 (a)(15); *see* Board of Immigration Appeals decision in *Atanacio* reported in 56 Interpreter Releases 515a (Nov. 7, 1979).
10. *See* C. Gordon and H. Rosenfield, *Immigration Law and Procedure* § 2.39 (1988).
11. 8 C.F.R. § 1213.
12. 8 C.F.R. § 103.6(c).
13. 8 U.S.C. § 1251(2)(8).
14. *See Matter of B.*, 3 I. & N. Dec. 323 (B.I.A. 1948); *Matter of M.*, 2 I. & N. Dec. 694 (B.I.A. 1946).
15. 42 U.S.C. § 601 *et seq.*
16. 42 U.S.C. § 602 (2)(25); 45 C.F.R. § 232.10.
17. *Ruiz v. Blum*, 549 F. Supp. 871 (S.D.N.Y. 1982).

18. *See Darces v. Woods*, 35 Cal. 3d 871, 201 Cal. Rptr. 507, 679 P.2d 458 (1984).
19. 42 U.S.C. § 1381, *et seq.*; 20 C.F.R. § 1416.101 *et seq.*
20. 8 U.S.C. § 1158(b).
21. 42 U.S.C. § 1369 *et seq.*
22. No. CY–79–1740 (E.D.N.Y.).
23. *Mathews v. Diaz*, 426 U.S. 67 (1976).
24. 42 U.S.C. 401 *et seq.*; 20 C.F.R. § 422, *et seq.* (1987).
25. 8 U.S.C. § 1251(a) (1982).
26. 53 Fed. Reg. 39,433 (Oct. 7, 1988).
27. 8 U.S.C. § 1255 a (H).
28. 8 U.S.C. § 1255(a)(II)(2).
29. Pub. L. No. 96–399; 42 U.S.C. § 1436a.
30. Pub. L. No. 100 242.
31. *See* 65 Interpreter Releases 1049 (Oct. 24, 1988).
32. 53 Fed. Reg. 41,038–41,081 (Oct. 19, 1988).
33. *Plyler v. Doe*, 475 U.S. 202 (1982), *See Pena v. Board of Education in the City of Atlanta*, 620 F. Supp. 293 (1985).
34. *Toll v. Moreno*, 458 U.S. 1. (1982).
35. 34 C.F.R. § 690.4.
36. 42 U.S.C. § 501, *et seq.*; 26 C.F.R. §131; 26 U.S.C. § 3301 *et seq.*; 20 C.F.R. §1640 *et seq.*
37. *See Vasquez v. Review Board of Indiana Employment Secretary Division*, 489 N.E.2d 171 (Ind. App. 1985); *Arteaga v. Industrial Commission*, 703 P.3d 654 (Colo. 1985); *Rubio v. Employment Division*, 66 Or. App. 525, 674 P.2d 1201 (Or. 1984); *Antillon v. Department of Employment Security*, 688 P.2d 455 1984); *Gillar v. Employment Division*, 704 P.2d 533 (Or. 1985).
38. *Esparaza v. Valdez*, 612 F. Supp. 241 (D. Colo. 1985).
39. 8 U.S.C. § 1324(b)(II)(c).
40. 7 U.S.C. §§ 1100, 1331–1340, 1341–1350, 1421; 41 U.S.C. §§ 1781–1787; 7 C.F.R. §§ 271.1(e), 1842.3.
41. 7 C.F.R. §§ 1980.175 (a)(1)(i); telephone interview with Mr. Jeffrey O'Neill, Farm Home Administration, U.S. Department of Agriculture, on Oct. 27, 1988.
42. 42 U.S.C. §§ 1472, 1490; 7 C.F.R. § 1822.4.
43. 7 U.S.C. §§ 901–915, 922–940.
44. 7 C.F.R. § 1944.9(c).
45. 7 C.F.R. § 1944.211(a)(1).
46. 7 C.F.R. § 1944.215(h).
47. Act of Oct. 14, 1978, Pub. L. No. 95-640, 92 Stat. 1263 (codified at 7 U.S.C. § 3501 *et seq*). *See* H.R. Rep. No. 1570, S. Rep. No. 1072, 95th Cong.

48. § 2, 7 U.S.C. § 3501(a).
49. § 3, 7 U.S.C. § 3502.
50. Pub. L. No. 93-355, *as amended*, Pub. L. No. 95-222; 42 U.S.C. § 2996–2996(K).
51. 45 C.F.R. § 1626(c).
52. 45 C.F.R. § 1626.5(e).
53. 45 C.F.R. § 1626.5(f).
54. 53 Fed. Reg. 40,914–17 (Oct. 19, 1988).
55. *Id.*
56. *See* 65 Interpreter Releases 1094 (Oct. 24, 1988).

XIV

The Right of Aliens to Become Citizens

Congress is mandated under the Constitution to establish a "uniform rule of naturalization."[1] It is therefore charged with the responsibility of determining the conditions upon which an alien may become a United States citizen. The first Congress implemented this authority in 1790.[2] The Immigration and Nationality Act of 1952[3] substantially codified existing law and is the statutory foundation of the current provisions relating to immigration, citizenship, and naturalization. To date, the Act of 1952 has undergone three major changes: the 1965,[4] 1976,[5] and 1986[6] amendments. The courts have so far held that naturalization is a "privilege," and that Congress can impose any requirement it chooses as a condition for naturalization.[7]

For much of American history, immigration and nationality laws have been racist. The very first Congress provided that only "free white persons" could be naturalized.[8] After the Civil War and the passage of constitutional amendments abolishing slavery, assuring citizenship to all persons born in the United States, and requiring the states to give equal protection of the laws to all persons, Congress modified the racial barrier to citizenship only for persons of African descent.[9] Indigenous nonwhite races in North and South America did not become eligible for naturalization until 1940;[10] Chinese until 1943;[11] natives of India and the Philippines until 1946;[12] and Japanese, Koreans, Polynesians, Thais, and other persons of Asian ancestry until 1952.[13]

Today, all legal bars based on race, color, or national origin, as well as prohibitions against women married to aliens, have been removed. But there are requirements remaining that pose problems for aliens. These arise from their economic, political, and religious beliefs, their social conduct, and their private behavior. To a limited extent, these issues have been examined by the courts in defining "good moral character," "attachment to the principles of the Constitution," and the oath regarding their military obligation to the United States required of aliens when they are naturalized.

Other requirements affecting eligibility for naturalization involve residence and physical presence in the United States, age, family relationships, knowledge of English, and an understanding of the form of government in the United States.

Which aliens in the United States are eligible to become citizens?

Generally, only lawful permanent residents who have been admitted for residence for five years immediately prior to their petition for naturalization are eligible to become United States citizens.

Are there exceptions to the general rule concerning eligibility for citizenship?

Yes. There are exceptions to this statutory class of aliens, including spouses of United States citizens;[14] and spouses of United States citizens who enter into qualified overseas occupations (employment abroad with the government of the United States; American institutions of research; American enterprises engaged in trade and commerce abroad; international organizations of which the United States is a party; or organizations established in the United States, which direct them to go abroad as ministers of religion, priests or missionaries).[15] Included also are aliens who serve honorably in the armed forces continuously for at least three years, who file for naturalization while still in the service, or within six months thereafter, and who may be naturalized without regard to residence;[16] alien widow[er]s of active duty military personnel, provided the petitioner is living in marital union with the deceased United States citizen at the time of his or her demise and while he or she was serving honorably in the Armed Forces;[17] aliens who have assisted United States national security interests, i.e., persons who have contributed significantly to United States intelligence activities;[18] and alien children who are adopted while under sixteen years of age by United States citizens.[19] Other aliens who are in the United States under nonimmigrant status, or who are in the country illegally, are not eligible to apply for naturalization.[20]

What about citizenship under 1986 amendments to the immigration law?

The Immigration Reform and Control Act of 1986[21] established a program to legalize the status of certain aliens who had been residing unlawfully in the United States since January 1, 1982; Haitians and Cubans who had been present since January 1, 1982, and known to the immigration authorities; and certain agricultural workers.[22] Such aliens will be entitled to apply for "permanent resident" status, thereby rendering them eligible ultimately for United States citizenship.

What requirements must be met by a lawful permanent resident to become a naturalized citizen?

A prescribed period of residence and physical presence in the United States,[23] knowledge of the English language,[24] a demonstrable knowledge of the American form of government,[25] good moral character,[26] and an attachment to the principles of the Constitution.[27]

Is there an age requirement?

Yes. An applicant for citizenship must be eighteen to file a petition for naturalization. However, in most circumstances, alien children under eighteen may become citizens, if otherwise eligible, through the actions of their parents. A parent who is a U.S. citizen may file a petition for naturalization on behalf of an alien child under eighteen.[28] The alien child of one citizen and one alien parent becomes a citizen automatically upon the naturalization of his or her alien parent, if he or she is under sixteen and is living in, or comes to, the United States as a permanent resident before he or she is sixteen.[29] Citizenship is acquired similarly for a child of alien parents.[30] A gap exists between ages sixteen and eighteen for the children of alien parents. They are too young to file petitions for naturalization on their own behalf but too old to become citizens automatically upon the naturalization of their alien parents. Although these children may meet all other requirements for citizenship, they must wait until they are eighteen before they can apply for citizenship.

How long must a permanent resident alien reside in the United States before he or she is eligible to become a citizen?

Five years from the date he or she became a permanent resident but three years for a person who is married to a U.S.

citizen spouse at the time of application. Six months' residence is also required in the state where the applicant files a petition for naturalization.[31]

Does the requirement of residence mean that the applicant must be physically present in the United States throughout the prescribed period?

No. However, absences from the United States can affect eligibility to become a citizen. The time requirements are computed exactly. There are frequent cases in which applicants for naturalization have been delayed in their ability to become citizens because they were not present in the United States for the required periods. The applicant must be physically present in the United States at least half of the time required for residence—eighteen months for spouses of citizens, thirty months for all others. One year's absence from the United States breaks the continuity of an applicant's prior residence in the United States and requires the commencement of a new period of residence. Absences of more than six months but less than one year require proof that the applicant did not intend to abandon his residence in the United States. Absences of less than six months require no explanation.[32]

Are there exceptions to the requirements for physical presence and residence in the United States?

Yes. Various exceptions are provided for aliens and the alien spouses and children of citizens who are employed in activities abroad that are government supported or that promote the public interest. Such employment includes working abroad for the U.S. government, approved research institutions, or agencies such as Radio Free Europe, American-owned businesses engaged in foreign trade, international governmental organizations, or a U.S. religious organization as a cleric or missionary. Aliens employed in these fields are permitted to be absent from the United States for more than a year without breaking the continuity of their residence but are generally required to have resided in this country for one year before going abroad and must establish the purpose of the employment outside the United States in advance. Employees of the U.S. government and Radio Free Europe are also relieved of the requirement that they be physically present in the United States for one-half of the period of prescribed residence.[33]

Residence and physical presence requirements are also waived for alien children of U.S. citizens, veterans and members of the armed forces, and certain former U.S. citizens.[34]

How well must an applicant know English and understand the American form of government to become a citizen?

Applicants are required to know "simple words and phrases" in English. They must be able to understand the questions given to them in "ordinary English" by a naturalization examiner regarding their eligibility to become a citizen and must be able to read and write a short sentence in everyday usage at the level of elementary school literacy. The materials used are taken from picture textbooks on English and the U.S. government, published by the Government Printing Office and available to the public.[35]

The questions relating to the American government and U.S. history are based upon the applicant's education, background, age, and length of residence in the United States. They generally deal with the structure and functions of the three branches of government, the identity of leading figures in American history, and major provisions in the Constitution and Bill of Rights.

An applicant for citizenship is given at least three opportunities during a one-year period to meet the literacy and understanding requirements. Aliens who are illiterate because of physical incapacity and aliens over fifty years of age who have lived in the United States for twenty years are excused from the literacy requirement.[36]

Is the requirement constitutional that a citizenship applicant know the English language?

Spanish-speaking applicants for naturalization have challenged the requirement as a denial of equal protection of the laws on the basis that many native-born citizens, especially of Spanish-speaking origin, do not speak, read, or write English. The Supreme Court has never ruled on the question, but the lower courts have upheld the requirement.[37]

What is meant by "good moral character"?

The requirement that an applicant for citizenship must be a person of good moral character has been a part of the naturalization laws since 1790. The only certainty regarding its definition is that it is determined on a case-by-case basis. Although it has been said that because it is a federal statute affecting citizenship, "good moral character" must be determined uniformly throughout the entire country, most judicial decisions hold that it is based upon the "standards of the average citizen of the community in which the alien resides." It does not require the "highest degree of moral excellence," nor does it refer to a person's reputation.[38]

Applicants for naturalization must establish that they have been of good moral character during the prescribed period (five or three years) immediately preceding the filing of their petition, but the court may nonetheless take into consideration conduct prior to the required period as a matter of discretion.[39]

The naturalization law specifies that aliens shall not be found to be of good moral character if during the required period they were habitual drunkards; committed adultery; practiced polygamy; were involved in prostitution; helped for profit an alien to enter the United States illegally; committed and were convicted of a crime involving moral turpitude or of two offenses resulting in five years' imprisonment; were convicted of any narcotics violation, including marijuana;[40] obtained their income mainly from illegal gambling or have had two gambling convictions; gave false testimony to obtain a benefit under the immigration and nationality laws; served six months in a penal institution for a conviction of any offense; and have at any time been convicted of murder.[41] In addition to the conduct specified by the statute, the courts, with the recommendation of the INS, have barred citizenship to aliens who have willfully failed to support their families,[42] committed incest,[43] engaged in sexually perverse activities,[44] or practiced homosexual conduct.[45]

Does a finding that an alien has engaged in any of the conduct described above mean that the person is automatically barred from becoming a citizen?

No. Courts have disagreed in their definitions of certain

conduct as well as in the determination of whether it prevents an alien from obtaining citizenship. The difference in views has been especially marked in the area of sexual behavior.

Adultery, for example, has been held not to be a bar to a finding of good moral character unless it was a violation of a criminal law;[46] unless it "tends to destroy an existing, viable marriage" and is a "threat to public morality"; when it is an isolated act by a person separated from his or her spouse;[47] when it has been committed in the belief that the other person is unmarried or without knowledge that the sexual partner has an undissolved marriage.[48]

A federal district court in New York granted citizenship to a homosexual in a decision that held that the private consensual behavior of an alien is not relevant in determining good moral character. Since the ground of the court's ruling is that naturalization can be conditioned only upon conduct that is public or adversely affects others, it suggests that the naturalization statute may be subject to constitutional limitations.[49] This view corresponds to the generally accepted doctrine that Congress cannot require the surrender of a constitutional right to obtain a government benefit.[50]

But while homosexuality may not be invoked to deny a petitioner's good moral character, it has been held that addiction to drugs may demonstrate the lack of good moral character and hence may act as a bar to naturalization.[51]

A more recent decision by a federal court in Oregon dealt directly with the question of whether homosexual conduct prevents a finding that a person is of good moral character. Noting the changing attitude of the community, the court found that it "regards homosexual behavior between consenting adults with tolerance, if not indifference," and that such conduct does not "so offend that the 'ordinary person' . . . would think it immoral."[52]

The bar against the naturalization of aliens who have been convicted of criminal offenses similarly has not been absolute. A conviction of one petty offense, which would not be a ground for excluding an alien from the United States, is not a basis for denying citizenship.[53] A pardon and expungement of a murder conviction may render the convicted alien eligible for citizenship.[54]

What is meant by the requirement that an applicant for citizenship be "attached to the principles of the Constitution," and that the applicant be "well disposed to the good order and happiness of the United States?"

The quoted phrases do not have a hard-and-fast definition. Apart from specific naturalization provisions affecting anarchists and Communists and requirements dealing with military obligations, the language has been interpreted to mean that a citizenship applicant must have a commitment to the basic form of government in the United States, although advocacy of peaceful and constitutional change of government is not a bar to citizenship.[55] Anarchists, Communists, and persons who advocate the overthrow of the United States government by force or violence or by "other unconstitutional means" are barred from citizenship. The naturalization statute provides that membership in Communist organizations during the preceding ten years is a sufficient basis for denying naturalization, without proof of personal advocacy of communist ideas, unless the applicants show that their membership was involuntary, occurred when they were under the age of sixteen, or was required in order for them to obtain the essentials of living.[56]

Under these exceptions, aliens who have belonged to foreign Communist organizations during the prescribed period have been naturalized when it was shown that membership was automatic with enrollment in a school or required in order to get or keep a job, but not merely to improve economic status or to obtain higher education.[57]

Are the political conditions upon naturalization subject to challenge for being in violation of the Constitution?

Although a 1931 decision by the Supreme Court held that naturalization is a "privilege, to be given, qualified, or withheld as Congress may determine,"[58] recent decisions by both the Supreme Court and lower courts suggest that congressional power over naturalization may be limited by the first and fifth amendments.[59] It is uncertain that a Supreme Court that has tended to uphold the power of Congress to provide for the deportation of permanent resident aliens who are members of the Communist party would rule that they are eligible for citizenship. However, the Court might hold that there must be personal advocacy of forbidden beliefs in order to meet the requirement of due process, that the prohibition against the advocacy of the "economic, international, and governmental doctrines of world communism" is too vague or, without supporting action or advocacy of violence, is protected by the first amendment's assurance of free speech.[60]

How do military obligations affect an alien's eligibility to be naturalized?

In three ways. First, any person who has deserted the military service during wartime or has left the United States to avoid induction into the armed forces is permanently ineligible to become a citizen. Conviction by a court-martial or other court is required for the bar to become effective.[61]

Second, an alien who has applied for, and been granted, relief from military service upon the ground that he is an alien is also barred from citizenship.[62] However, this bar does not apply to an alien who was not liable for military service[63] or to one whose application for relief was induced by mistaken information provided by responsible officials.[64] Third, all applicants for citizenship are required to take an oath that they will "bear arms on behalf of the United States when required by law." Excepted is a conscientious objector, who may be permitted to take an oath to perform either noncombatant service in the armed forces or "work of national importance under civilian direction."[65]

What evidence is required for a citizenship applicant to establish that he is a conscientious objector?

The naturalization law, which followed the original language in the Selective Service statute, requires that opposition to military service must be based upon "religious training and belief," which has been defined to mean a "belief in a relation to a Supreme Being involving duties superior to those arising from any human relation." It does not include beliefs that are primarily "political, sociological, or philosophical or a merely personal moral code."[66]

Subsequent Supreme Court decisions have held that a person could qualify as a conscientious objector if his or her beliefs are deeply held, moral, ethical, or religious in nature even though he or she does not believe in a Supreme Being.[67] Neither is it necessary for a conscientious objector to belong to a religious denomination in which opposition to war and killing is a central tenet of the faith.[68]

Conscientious objection, however, must be to all wars and to war in all forms. Persons who are opposed only to "unjust wars" have been held by the Supreme Court not eligible to be treated as conscientious objectors for the purpose of the Selective Service laws. This view applies also to eligibility for citizenship.[69]

What procedures are required for an alien to become a citizen?

The first step is to file an application, known as an Application to File a Petition for Naturalization (N-400), with the local office of the INS where the applicant lives, together with photographs, a fingerprint card, and a biographical information form. After preliminary processing and investigation, the applicant is required to appear, with two supporting witnesses, before an examiner of the INS to be questioned regarding his or her eligibility for citizenship.[70]

If no adverse information has been elicited either by the questioning of the applicant or from other sources, further investigation is waived. If the applicant is eligible for citizenship, he or she thereafter files a formal petition for naturalization in either the federal or the state court that has jurisdiction over the applicant's place of residence and appears, when notified, before the court to be naturalized in a formal ceremony.[71]

If information is obtained that indicates the applicant may not be eligible for naturalization, he or she is subjected to a thorough personal investigation, which includes the right to subpoena witnesses before a naturalization examiner. In proceedings before that examiner, the applicant is entitled to be represented by counsel, to be informed of adverse evidence, to introduce evidence on his or her behalf, and to examine witnesses. Upon completion of the proceeding, a recommendation that the applicant be naturalized may be presented to the court, either with or without a summary of the evidence. In cases where there is adverse evidence, it is usual for the examiner, although recommending naturalization, to submit proposed findings to the court. A recommendation that the applicant be denied naturalization must be accompanied by a summary of the evidence, findings of fact, and conclusions of law.[72]

Where questions are raised regarding the applicant's eligibility for naturalization, the applicant may withdraw the application only with the consent of the INS or at the discretion of the court. Consent is normally given. If the INS examiner recommends citizenship, the court usually accepts the recommendation and grants naturalization. Where a denial of naturalization is recommended, the petitioner is entitled to a full hearing before the court with the right to produce witnesses in support of his or her application.[73]

A decision by the court is like other judicial decisions and may be appealed to an appellate court.[74]

May an alien change his or her name in a naturalization proceeding?

Yes. If an alien wishes to change his or her name, the naturalization statute authorizes the court to issue the Certificate of Citizenship in the name selected by the applicant.[75]

May citizenship be taken away from naturalized citizens?

Yes. But only if the citizenship has been obtained illegally by concealment of a material fact or by willful misrepresentation.[76]

Generally, the INS discourages revocation proceedings if many years have elapsed since the judgment of naturalization and the party has since conducted himself or herself as a good citizen and possesses the necessary qualifications for citizenship.[77] Revocation proceedings will not be undertaken if, as an alien, the denaturalized citizen would not be deportable and would be able to reacquire citizenship.[78]

Where proceedings have been instituted, citizenship has been revoked upon the basis of illegality for failure to comply with statutory requirements for naturalization, such as omitting documents when submitting the petition for naturalization,[79] lacking the prescribed period of residence,[80] failing to take the oath of allegiance,[81] as well as absence of good moral character and lack of attachment to the Constitution.[82]

Revocations based upon concealment of a material fact or a willful misrepresentation require proof that if the true facts had been known, citizenship would not have been granted or that an ensuing investigation might have led to the discovery of information that would justify its denial.[83] A 1988 Supreme Court decision has substantially revised the standard to be applied in denaturalization proceedings, in determining the materiality of a fact concealed or willfully misrepresented in the naturalization proceedings.[84] The revised standard, while it makes it easier for the government to prevail in denaturalization proceedings grounded on illegal procurement, requires therefore a greater showing on the part of the government on the issue of materiality and will make it more difficult to prove fraud.

Thus, citizenship was revoked thirty-five years after naturalization because the applicant claimed to be in the real estate business, when the evidence showed that he was a bootlegger.[85] Communists and Nazis have been denaturalized for concealing their associations and complicity in concentration camp killings, in some instances because the fact was regarded as material, and in others because it was regarded as cutting off inquiry that might have led to a denial of citizenship.[86]

The grounds for revoking citizenship must be proved by "clear, unequivocal, and convincing evidence which does not leave the issue in doubt."[87]

Are there grounds for revoking citizenship for conduct after naturalization?

Yes. A naturalized citizen who during a ten-year period following naturalization refuses to testify before a congressional committee regarding his or her "subversive activities," and is convicted of contempt, can be denaturalized for obtaining citizenship fraudulently.[88] This provision has never been tested in court, and it is doubtful that it is constitutional.

The statute provides that membership within five years following naturalization in an organization that would have been a basis for denying citizenship is *prima facie* evidence of lack of attachment to the Constitution, which in the absence of rebuttal evidence, is a ground for denaturalization.[89] Although the Supreme Court has sustained a revocation of citizenship where a pattern of personal conduct before and after naturalization established allegiance to a foreign government,[90] no decision has turned on mere membership in a proscribed organization. In view of the government's burden of proof required to justify denaturalization, it is doubtful also that this provision is constitutional.

A third ground for revocation arises if a naturalized citizen takes up permanent residence in a foreign country within five years of naturalization.[91] Since admission to the United States for permanent residence is an essential requirement for naturalization, the intent to abandon such residence has been held to be a basis for denaturalization.[92] Departure from the United States following naturalization and becoming a permanent resident of a foreign country is said to create a presumption of a fraudulent intent.[93] However, it can be rebutted by contrary evidence.

Apart from these grounds for revocation, there is no other power to deprive a naturalized citizen of citizenship. A statute which provided that naturalized citizens are expatriated by living in a foreign country for a period of years was held unconstitutional by the Supreme Court on the ground that Congress could not make distinctions between the rights of native-born and naturalized citizens.[94]

NOTES

1. U.S. Const., art. I, § 8, cl. 4.
2. Act of Mar. 26, 1790, 1 Stat. 103.
3. Act of June 27, 1952, 66 Stat. 163.
4. Act of Oct. 3, 1965, 79 Stat. 911.
5. Act of Oct. 20, 1976, Pub. L. No. 94-571, 90 Stat. 2703.
6. Consular Efficiency Act, Pub. L. No. 99-653, 100 Stat. 3655 (1986).
7. *United States v. McIntosh*, 283 U.S. 605 (1931); *United States v. Schwimmer*, 279 U.S. 644 (1929); *United States v. Ginsberg*, 243 U.S. 473 (1917).
8. Act of Mar. 26, 1790, 1 Stat. 103.
9. Act of July 14, 1870, 16 Stat. 256.
10. Nationality Act of 1940, 54 Stat. 1137, 1140.
11. Act of July 17, 1943, 57 Stat. 601.
12. Act of July 2, 1946, 60 Stat. 416.
13. 8 U.S.C. § 1422.
14. 8 U.S.C. § 1430(a).
15. 8 U.S.C. § 1430(b).
16. 8 U.S.C. § 1439(a).
17. 8 U.S.C. § 1430(d).

18. 8 U.S.C. § 1426(g).
19. Sec. 341(b) of the Immigration and Nationality Act.
20. 8 U.S.C. §§ 1427(a), 1439(a), 1440(a).
21. Pub. L. No. 99–603, 100 Stat. at 3359 (1986).
22. *See* 100 Stat. at 3359 *et seq.*
23. 8 U.S.C. §§ 1427(a), 1430(a).
24. 8 U.S.C. § 1423(1).
25. 8 U.S.C. § 1432(2).
26. U.S.C. § 1427(a)(3).
27. *Id.*
28. 8 U.S.C. § 1433.
29. 8 U.S.C. § 1431.
30. 8 U.S.C. § 1432.
31. 8 U.S.C. §§ 1427(a), 1430.
32. 8 U.S.C. § 1427(b).
33. *Id.*, 8 U.S.C. §§ 1428, 1430; 8 C.F.R. § 316, 319, List of Approved Institutions.
34. 8 U.S.C. §§ 1433, 1434, 1439, 1435.
35. 8 U.S.C. §§ 1423; 8 C.F.R. § 312.
36. *Id.*
37. *Trujillo-Hernandez v. Farrell*, Civil Action 72-B-806, (S.D. Tex. 1972).
38. *See* Note, Naturalization and the Adjudication of Good Moral Character: An exercise in Judicial Uncertainty, 41 N.Y.U. L. Rev. 545-83 (1972); *Repouille v. U.S.*, 165 F.2d 152 (2d Cir. 1947).
39. 8 U.S.C. § 1427(e).
40. 8 U.S.C. § 1101(f). Except for "a single offense of simple possession of 30 grams or less of marijuana."
41. *Id.*
42. *Re Petition of Malaszenko* 204 F. Supp. 744 (D.C.N.J. 1962).
43. *U.S. v. Vander Jagt* 135 F. Supp. 676 (D.C. Mich. 1955).
44. *Re Markiewicz* 90 F. Supp. 191 (D.C. Pa. 1950).
45. At least one state court has held that private consensual acts of homosexuality between consenting adults demonstrate a lack of good moral character. *Re Petition of Schmidt* 56 Misc. 2d 456, 289 N.Y.S.2d 89 (1968).
46. *Waldman v. INS*, 329 F.2d [illegible]2 (9th Cir. 1964). *But see Brea-Garcia v. INS*, 531 F.2d 693 (3d Cir. 1976), which holds that adultery is to be defined under state, civil law.
47. *Id. See Kim v. INS*, 514 F.2d 179 (D.C. Cir. 1975).
48. *In re Johnson*, 292 F. Supp. 381 (E.D.N.Y. 1968); *Dickhoff v. Shaughnessy*, 142 F. Supp. 535 (S.D.N.Y. 1956).
49. *In re Labady*, 326 F. Supp. 924 (S.D.N.Y. 1971).
50. *Speiser v. Randall*, 357 U.S. 513 (1958); *see* Van Alystine, *The Demise*

of the Right-Privilege Distinction in Constitutional Law, 81 Harv. L. Rev. 1439 (1968). *See also* Note, *Constitutional Limitations on the Naturalization Power*, 80 Yale L.J. 769–810 (1976).

51. *Petition of Suey Chin* 173 F. Supp. 510 (D.C.N.Y 1959).
52. *Petition of Brodie*, 394 F. Supp. 1208, (D. Ore. 1975).
53. Interim Decision 2066 (BIA 1970).
54. *Re Petition of De Angelis* 139 F. Supp. 779 (D.C.NY. 1956); *see also* 8 U.S.C. § 1101(f)(8).
55. *Schneiderman v. U.S.*, 320 U.S. 118 (1943).
56. 8 U.S.C. § 1424. *See also Berenyi v. District Director*, 385 U.S. 630 (1967), in which naturalization was denied for a false statement that petitioner was not a member of the Communist party.
57. 8 U.S.C. § 1424(d); *Rowoldt v. Perfetto*, 355 U.S. 155 (1957); *Galvan v. Press*, 347 U.S. 522 (1954); *Grymala Siedlecki v. U.S.* 285 F.2d 836 (5th Cir. 1961).
58. *United States v. McIntosh, supra.*
59. *Rogers v. Bellei*, 401 U.S. 815 (1971); *In re Weitzman*, 426 F.2d 439 (8th Cir. 1970). *In re Pasciattano*, 308 F. Supp. 818 (Conn. 1970); *Villaneuva-Jurado v. INS*, 482 F.2d 886 (5th Cir. 1973).
60. *Cf. Rowoldt v. Perfetto, supra*; *Schneiderman v. U.S., supra.*
61. 8 U.S.C. § 1425.
62. 8 U.S.C. § 1426.
63. *McGrath v. Kristensen*, 340 U.S. 162 (1950).
64. *Moser v. U.S.* 341 U.S. 41 (1951).
65. 8 U.S.C. 1448. The oath is set forth in 8 C.F.R. § 337.1(a).
66. *Id.*
67. *U.S. v. Seeger*, 380 U.S. 163 (1965); *Welsh v. U.S.* 333 (1970); *In re Weitzman, supra.*
68. *Rafferty v. U.S.*, 477 F.2d 531 (5th Cir. 1973).
69. *Gillette v. U.S.*, 401 U.S. 437 (1971).
70. 8 U.S.C. §§ 1445–1446; 8 C.F.R. §§ 334–335.
71. 8 C.F.R. § 335.12; 8 U.S.C. § 1447.
72. 8 C.F.R. § 335.11–13.
73. 8 U.S.C. § 1447.
74. *Tutun v. U.S.* 270 U.S. 568 (1926).
75. 8 U.S.C. § 1447(F).
76. 8 U.S.C. § 1451.
77. 340.1 INS Interpretation.
78. *Id.*
79. *U.S. v. Ness*, 245 U.S. 319 (1917).
80. *U.S. v. Beda*, 118 F.2d 458 (2d Cir. 1971).
81. *U.S. v. Siemzuch*, 312 F. Supp. 928 (E.D. Wisc. 1970).
82. *U.S. v. Title*, 132 F. Supp. 185, *aff'd.*, 363 F.2d 28 (2d Cir. 1959).

83. *Chaunt v. United States*, 364 U.S. 350 (1960); *United States v. Montabalno*, 236 F.2d 757 (3d Cir. 1956).
84. *Kungys v. United States*, 485 U.S. ___, 108 S. Ct. 1537 (1988).
85. *Id.*; *Fedorenko v. U.S.*, 449 U.S. 490 (1981). *Costello v. U.S.*, 365 U.S. 265 (1961).
86. *U.S. v. Genovese*, 236 F.2d 757 (2d Cir. 1959).
87. *Schneiderman v. U.S.*, 320 U.S. 118 (1943).
88. 8 U.S.C. § 1451(a).
89. 8 U.S.C. § 1451(c).
90. *Baumgartner v. U.S.*, 322 U.S. 665 (1944).
91. 8 U.S.C. § 1451(d).
92. *Luria v. U.S.*, 231 U.S. 9 (1913).
93. *Perrone v. U.S.* 26 F.2d 231 (1928).
94. *Schneider v. Rusk*, 377 U.S. 163 (1964).